Student Solutions Manual

SECOND EDITION

Calculus and Analytic Geometry

C. H. Edwards, Jr.
David E. Penney

The University of Georgia, Athens

PRENTICE-HALL, ENGLEWOOD CLIFFS, NEW JERSEY 07632

© 1986, 1982 by Prentice-Hall
A Division of Simon & Schuster, Inc.
Englewood Cliffs, NJ 07632

Previously published as *Student Manual, Calculus and Analytic Geometry*

Library of Congress Catalog Card Number: 85-63192

Printed in the United States of America

10 9 8 7 6 5 4 3

ISBN 0-13-111691-6 01

Prentice-Hall International (UK) Limited, *London*
Prentice-Hall of Australia Pty. Limited, *Sydney*
Prentice-Hall Canada Inc., *Toronto*
Prentice-Hall Hispanoamericana, S.A., *Mexico*
Prentice-Hall of India Private Limited, *New Delhi*
Prentice-Hall of Japan, Inc., *Tokyo*
Prentice-Hall of Southeast Asia Pte. Ltd., *Singapore*
Editora Prentice-Hall do Brasil, Ltda., *Rio de Janeiro*
Whitehall Books Limited, *Wellington, New Zealand*

Preface

This manual contains solutions to about every third problem in
<u>Calculus</u> <u>and</u> <u>Analytic</u> <u>Geometry</u>, second edition (1986), by C. H. Edwards,
Jr. and David E. Penney. Because the answers to most odd-numbered
problems are given in the Answer section of the text, corresponding
solutions are omitted here whenever the answer alone should suffice.
For similar reasons, whenever the answer alone to an even-numbered
problem is sufficient, we give only the answer. Sometimes only an
outline of the solution appears. When the solution consists of a
routine verification of a formula, we normally omit it. When a mere
suggestion should be enough for the solver, that's frequently all that
appears. Most important, when a solution would spoil the problem for
the solver, we omit the solution.

Many calculus problems can be solved by a variety of methods. We
have tried to use the most natural method wherever possible, and only in
rare instances have we put a "clever" method in its place, and then
only when its educational value justifies such substitution. In
particular, we used in working end-of-section problems only those
techniques already developed in preceding material.

We took care with accuracy, but errors are inevitable. We hope
that most are merely missing symbols that the reader can easily supply
or are typographical errors that can be corrected by considering the
proximity of keys on a typewriter keyboard. Nevertheless, we would very
much appreciate any corrections you can supply, no matter how trivial.

Please note the unconventional usage of three symbols: Because we
have no Greek lower case "theta" on this printwheel, we have chosen to
use the Greek letter ξ in its place, usually without further comment.
We have used the symbol $\sim$ for "approximately equal" and braces where
square brackets would be more appropriate for the same reason. In order
to be sure that fraction bars are not accidentally omitted, we have also
chosen to forego the aesthetic pleasure of right justification that you
may recall from the previous edition of this manual.

Finally, we must gratefully acknowledge the encouragement, advice,
and assistance of our colleagues and students in helping us correct
errors in the first edition of this manual. Faculty members of the
Department of Mathematics of the University of Georgia have been
especially helpful, and we offer them our thanks herewith. Any new
errors in this edition are, of course, entirely our responsibility.

C. H. E., Jr.

D. E. P.

June 1985

Contents

To Get The Most Out Of This Manual:

1. First try to work each problem on your own.

2. Then examine the solution to a _similar_ _but_ _different_ problem in this manual.

3. Using only the first line of the solution to the problem in question, try to complete the solution on your own.

4. If necessary, use the second line, then the third line, and so on.

5. Hone your skills by working _extra_ problems whose solutions appear here, even if they were not assigned. This will give you a stunning advantage over those calculus students who choose to do just enough to "get by."

Section 1.2

1. $|3 - 17| = |-14| = 14.$

4. $|5| - |-7| = 5 - 7 = -2.$

7. $|(-3)^3| = |-27| = 27.$

10. $-|7 - 4| = -|3| = -3.$

13. $2x - 7 < -3$: $2x < 4$; $x < 2$; Answer: $(-\infty, 2)$.

16. $2x + 5 \leq 9$: $2x \leq 4$, $x \leq 2$. Answer: $(-\infty, 2]$.

19. $-3 < 2x + 5 < 7$:
$$-8 < 2x < 2;$$
$$-4 < x < 1. \quad \text{Answer:} \quad (-4,1).$$

22. $3 < 1 - 5x < 7$: $2 < -5x < 6$, $-6 < 5x < -2$,
$-6/5 < x < -2/5$. Answer: $(-6/5, -2/5)$.

25. The <u>non</u>-solutions of $|1 - 3x| > 2$ satisfy $|1 - 3x| \leq 2$:
$-2 \leq 3x - 1 \leq 2$, $-1 \leq 3x \leq 3$, $-1/3 \leq x \leq 1$.
Answer: $(-\infty, -1/3) \cup (1, +\infty)$.

28. $2x + 1 > 0$ because $\dfrac{1}{2x + 1} > 3$. Then
$$2x > -1 \quad \text{and} \quad 1 > 3(2x + 1);$$
$$x > -1/2 \quad \text{and} \quad 2x + 1 > 1/3;$$
$$x > -1/2 \quad \text{and} \quad 2x > -2/3;$$
$$x > -1/2 \quad \text{and} \quad x < -1/3.$$

Answer: $(-1/2, -1/3)$.

31. $|1 - 5x| > 0$, so $\dfrac{1}{|1 - 5x|} > 0 > -1/3$

for all x <u>unless</u> $|1 - 5x| = 0$; that is, unless
$x = 1/5$. Answer: $(-\infty, 1/5) \cup (1/5, +\infty)$.

34. $(x - 2)(x - 2) < 0$: $x - 1$ and $x - 2$ are of opposite sign.
So $x < 1$ and $x > 2$ (which leads to <u>no</u> values of x), or else
$x > 1$ and $x < 2$. Answer: $(1, 2)$.

1

37. From $v = 800/p$ it follows that $100 \leqq \dfrac{800}{p} \leqq 200$.

But $p > 0$, so $\dfrac{1}{200} \leqq \dfrac{p}{800} \leqq \dfrac{1}{100}$;

therefore $4 \leqq p \leqq 8$.

40. $T/(2\pi) = \sqrt{L/32}$; $L/32 = T^2/(4\pi^2)$.
   But $3 < L < 4$, so $3/32 < L < 1/8$:

$$\frac{3}{32} < \frac{T^2}{4\pi^2} < \frac{4}{32};$$

$$\frac{12\pi^2}{32} < T^2 < \frac{16\pi^2}{32};$$

$$T > 0, \quad \text{so} \quad \frac{P}{4}\sqrt{6} < T < \frac{P}{2}\sqrt{2}.$$

46. $|a| = |(a - b) + b| \leqq |a - b| + |b|$, and therefore
   $|a| - |b| \leqq |a - b|$.

Section 1.3

4. $\sqrt{a + a^2 + a^4}$; $\sqrt{1 + (1/a)^2 + (1/a)^4}$;

   $\sqrt{1 + a + a^2}$; $\sqrt{1 + a^4 + a^8}$

7. $\sqrt{a^2 + 16} = 5$: $a^2 + 16 = 25$; $a^2 = 9$; $a = 3, -3$.

10. $2a^2 - a + 4 = 5$: $2a^2 - a - 1 = 0$;
   $(2a + 1)(a - 1) = 0$; $a = 1, -1/2$.

13. $(a + h)^2 - a^2 = 2ah + h^2$.

16. $\dfrac{2}{a + h + 1} - \dfrac{2}{a + 1} = \dfrac{2(a + 1) - 2(a + h + 1)}{(a + h + 1)(a + 1)}$

   $= -\dfrac{2h}{(a + h + 1)(a + 1)}$.

19. The exponent takes on all integral values (odd _and_ even) and no
   others. So $f(x)$ takes on the two values 1 and -1 but no
   others.

22. $(-\infty, +\infty)$.

25. Domain: Where $3x - 5 \geq 0$; that is, $x \geq 5/3$.

28. Only when the denominator $(x + 2)^2$ is zero is $g(x)$ undefined,
     so its domain is the set of all real numbers other than -2.

31. Because $x^2 + 9 > 0$ for all real x, $f(x)$ is defined
     for all real x.

34. Here the fraction $\dfrac{x + 1}{x - 1}$ must be nonnegative and its denominator
     nonzero. So $x + 1$ and $x - 1$ have the same sign, and $x \neq 1$
     as well. If $x + 1 > 0$ and $x - 1 > 0$, this implies $x - 1 > 0$,
     so $x > 1$. If $x + 1 < 0$ and $x - 1 < 0$, it follows that
     $x + 1 < 0$, so that $x < -1$.   It is also permissible for the
     numerator of the fraction to be zero, so $x = -1$ is also in the
     domain. Answer: $(-\infty, -1] \cup (1, +\infty)$.

37. A circle of area A, circumference C, and radius r satisfies
     the equations $A = \pi r^2$ and $C = 2\pi r$. Thus $r = \sqrt{A/\pi}$, and
     hence $C = 2\pi\sqrt{A/\pi}$, $0 < A < +\infty$.

40. If the box has height h, then its volume is $x^2 h$. Because it
     is given that $x^2 h = 125$, $h = 125/x^2$. The top and bottom of
     the box each have area x^2, and the four sides each have area
     xh, so the total area of the box is $A = 2x^2 + 4xh$. Answer:
     $A(x) = 2x^2 + (4x)(125/x^2) = 2x^2 + (500/x)$, $0 < x < +\infty$.

43. If the rectangle has height y, then its area is xy, which is
     known to equal 100. So $y = 100/x$. Its perimeter P is
     $2x + 2y$, so $P = P(x) = 2x + \dfrac{200}{x}$, $0 < x < +\infty$.

46. Let y denote the height of the box. Its total surface area is
     then $2x^2 + 4xy = 600$, so that

$$y = \frac{600 - 2x^2}{4x}.$$

     Hence its volume $V = x^2 y$ may be expressed in the form

$$V(x) = \frac{1}{4}(600x - 2x^3), \quad 0 < x < \sqrt{300}.$$

3

1. The line containing A and B has slope $\dfrac{1 - (-2)}{2 - (-1)}$ = 1,
    as does the line containing B and C.   Therefore the three
    points <u>do</u> lie on a single straight line.

4. m(AB) = 1 $\neq$ 8/7 = m(BC).   Not on one line.

7. m(AB) = 2,   m(BC) = -11/2,   and   m(AC) = -1/2.   Thus the
    points are not collinear and ABC is a right angle. The
    desired result follows.

10. y = -x + 1,   so   m = -1   and   b = 1.

13. $y = -\dfrac{2}{5}x + \dfrac{3}{5}$,   so   m = -2/5   and   b = 3/5.

16. Because L passes through (2,0) and (0,-3), it has
     slope 3/2 and y-intercept -3.   So the slope-intercept
     equation of L is

$$y = \frac{3}{2}x - 3.$$

     If you dislike fractions and minus signs, the equation of L
     may be written in the form 3x = 2y + 6.

19. Because L has angle of inclination 135°, it has slope
     -1, and thus point-slope equation y - 2 = -(x - 4);
     that is, x + y = 6.

22. The <u>other</u> line has equation $y = -\dfrac{1}{2}x + \dfrac{17}{2}$, and
     thus slope -1/2.   Because L is perpendicular, L has
     slope 2.   So its point-slope equation is y - 4 = 2(x + 2);
     alternatively, y = 2x + 8.

25. The parallel lines have slope 5, so a common perpendicular
     has slope -1/5.   One common perpendicular thus has equation
     $y = -\dfrac{1}{5}x.$ This line meets y = 5x + 1 in the point
     (-5/26, 1/26) and the line y = 5x + 9 in the point
     (-45/26, 9/26).   The answer is the perpendicular distance

4

between these two points, which is $\frac{4}{13}\sqrt{26}$.

28. Show that AB is parallel to CD, that BC is parallel to AD, that AB and CD have the same length, and that BC and AD have the same length. Finally show that the slopes m_1 of AC and m_2 of BD satisfy $m_1 m_2 = -1$.

34. Begin with the fact that $L = mC + b$ for some constants m and b; use the data in the problem to solve for m and b:

$$124.942 = 20m + b,$$
$$125.134 = 110m + b;$$

$m = \dfrac{192}{9000}$ and $b = \dfrac{186,773}{1500}$. Thus we have the approximation $L = (0.0213)C + (124.515)$.

Section 1.5

4. Parabola, opening upward, vertex at $(0,1)$, symmetric about the y-axis.

10. The graph has a discontinuity at $x = 1$. It is close to but below the x-axis for x large positive, close to but above the x-axis for x large negative. For $x < 1$ but close to 1, the graph is close to the vertical line $x = 1$, almost vertical, and large positive. For $x > 1$ but close to 1, the graph is close to the line $x = 1$, almost vertical, and large negative.

16. The graph is almost the same as the one of Problem 12, except that the discontinuity is located at $x = -3/2$.

22. The graph is similar to the one of Problem 20, though with the point of the V at $(3,0)$.

28. $x^2 - 2x + 1 + y^2 + 2y + 1 = 0$;
$(x - 1)^2 + (y + 1)^2 = 0.$
Only the single point $(1,-1)$ satisfies this equation.

34. This parabola opens downward with its vertex at $(1/2, 1/4)$.

36. There is a discontinuity at each integral value of x.

40. If x is not an integer, write x = n + p where n is an integer and 0 < p < 1. Then $f(x) = n + (-n - 1) + 1$, so $f(x) = 1$ if x is an integer and $f(x) = 0$ otherwise. So the graph is the same as the one of Problem 36.

Section 1.6

4. $f'(x) = -4x$.

10. $f(x) = 15x - 3x^2$, so $f'(x) = 15 - 6x$.

16. $\dfrac{dy}{dx} = 10 - 2x$; horizontal tangent at $(5,25)$.

22. $\dfrac{f(x + h) - f(x)}{h} = \dfrac{(x + h)^2 - (x + h) - 2 - (x^2 - x - 2)}{h}$

$= \dfrac{x^2 + 2xh + h^2 - x - h - 2 - x^2 + x + 2}{h}$

$= \dfrac{2xh + h^2 - h}{h} = 2x + h - 1 \;\rightarrow\; 2x - 1$ as $h \rightarrow 0$.

Thus $f'(x) = 2x - 1$. The slope at $(2, f(2))$ is $f'(2) = 3$, so an equation for the tangent line there is $y = 3(x - 2)$.

25. $f'(x) = \lim\limits_{h \to 0} \dfrac{f(x + h) - f(x)}{h}$

$= \lim\limits_{h \to 0} \dfrac{(x + h - 1)^2 - (x - 1)^2}{h}$

$= \lim\limits_{h \to 0} \dfrac{x^2 + 2xh + h^2 - 2x - 2h + 1 - x^2 + 2x - 1}{h}$

$= \lim\limits_{h \to 0} \dfrac{2xh + h^2 - 2h}{h}$

$= \lim\limits_{h \to 0} (2x + h - 2) = 2x - 2.$

Now $f'(2) = 2$ and $f(2) = 1$, so an equation for the tangent line at $(2, f(2))$ is $y - 1 = 2(x - 2)$.

28. $f'(x) = \lim\limits_{h \to 0} \dfrac{f(x + h) - f(x)}{h}$

$= \lim\limits_{h \to 0} \dfrac{(x + h)^4 - x^4}{h}$

$= \lim\limits_{h \to 0} \dfrac{x^4 + 4x^3h + 6x^2h^2 + 4xh^3 + h^4 - x^4}{h}$

$= \lim\limits_{h \to 0} (4x^3 + 6x^2h + 4xh^2 + h^3) = 4x^3.$

The tangent line at $(2,16)$ has slope 32, and thus equation $y - 16 = 32(x - 2)$.

31. You should find that $f'(x) = -\dfrac{2}{(x - 1)^2}.$

34. $\dfrac{dy}{dx} = -1 - 4x$; the slope at P is 3, so an equation for the tangent line there is $y - 4 = 3(x + 1)$, and an equation for the normal line there is $y - 4 = -\dfrac{1}{3}(x + 1)$.

37. Production: $f(x) = (20 + x)(200 - 5x) = 4000 + 100x - 5x^2$, $0 \leq x \leq 40$. $f'(x) = 100 - 10x$, and $f'(x) = 0$ when $x = 10$. The graph of f is a parabola opening downward, so its highest point is $(10, f(10)) = (10, 4500)$. Thus the maximum possible production is $P = 4500$ barrels per day.

40. Let (a,b) denote the point where one of the two lines is tangent to the parabola. Then $b = 4a - a^2$, and the slope of the tangent line there is $4 - 2a$. As in the solution of Problem 39, we then have

$$4 - 2a = \dfrac{4a - a^2 - 5}{a - 2}.$$

The two solutions of this equation are $a = 1$ and $a = 3$. Thus one tangent line has slope 2 and the other has slope -2; their equations are $y - 5 = 2(x - 2)$ and $y - 5 = -2(x - 2)$, respectively.

Chapter 1 Miscellaneous Problems

4. $0 < 3x + 4 < 20:$

$$-4 < 3x < 16;$$
$$-4/3 < x < 16/3. \quad \text{Answer:} \quad (-4/3, 16/3).$$

10. $x \neq 2$.

16. $x^2 < 9$: $(-3, 3)$.

19. Let x denote the length of each of the three (equal) sides of the triangle. Draw an altitude of the triangle and apply the Pythagorean theorem to find that the altitude has length $h = (x\sqrt{3})/2$. Thus the area of the triangle is $A = xh/2 = (x^2\sqrt{3})/4$. But $x = P/3$, so

$$A = A(P) = \frac{\sqrt{3}}{36}P^2, \quad 0 < P < +\infty.$$

22. $y + 1 = -3(x - 4)$.

25. Rewrite $y - 2x = 10$ in the form $y = 2x + 10$. Because L is perpendicular to this line, L has slope $-1/2$.

28. $|x - y| = 1$ is satisfied if either $x - y = 1$ or $x - y = -1$. So the graph consists of the two parallel lines $y = x - 1$ and $y = x + 1$.

34.

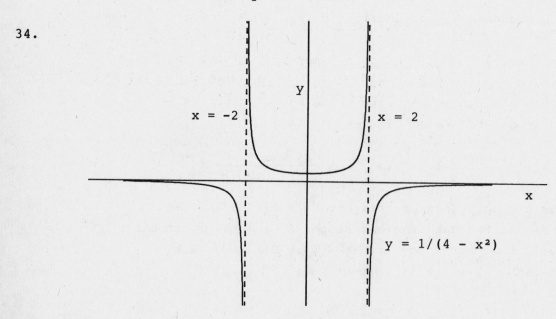

40. $f'(x) = -2 - 6x$; $f'(1) = -8$; $f(1) = -4$:
    $y + 4 = -8(x - 1)$.

8

43. $f'(x) = \lim\limits_{h \to 0} \dfrac{2(x + h)^2 + 3(x + h) - 2x^2 - 3x}{h}$

$= \lim\limits_{h \to 0} \dfrac{2x^2 + 4xh + 2h^2 + 3x + 3h - 2x^2 - 3x}{h}$

$= \lim\limits_{h \to 0} \dfrac{4xh + 2h^2 + 3h}{h}$

$= \lim\limits_{h \to 0} (4x + 2h + 3) = 4x + 3.$

46. $f'(x) = \lim\limits_{h \to 0} \dfrac{1}{h} \left(\dfrac{1}{2(x + h) + 1} - \dfrac{1}{2x + 1} \right)$

$= \lim\limits_{h \to 0} \dfrac{2x + 1 - 2x - 2h - 1}{h(2x + 2h + 1)(2x + 1)}$

$= \lim\limits_{h \to 0} \dfrac{-2h}{h(2x + 2h + 1)(2x + 1)}$

$= \lim\limits_{h \to 0} \dfrac{-2}{(2x + 2h + 1)(2x + 1)}$

$= \dfrac{-2}{(2x + 1)^2}.$

49. $f(x + h) - f(x) = \dfrac{x + h + 1}{x + h - 1} - \dfrac{x + 1}{x - 1}$

$= \dfrac{x^2 + xh + x - x - h - 1 - x^2 - xh + x - x - h + 1}{(x + h - 1)(x - 1)}$

$= \dfrac{-2h}{(x + h - 1)(x - 1)}.$

Section 2.1

1. $\lim\limits_{x \to 0} (3x^2 + 7x - 12)$

$= 3 \left(\lim\limits_{x \to 0} x \right)^2 + 7 \left(\lim\limits_{x \to 0} x \right) - \lim\limits_{x \to 0} 12$

$= (3)(0)^2 + (7)(0) - 12 = -12.$

4. $\left|(-2)^2 - 2\right|^5 = 2^5 = 32.$

7. $\dfrac{x + 1}{x^2 - x - 2} = \dfrac{1}{x - 2} \to -\dfrac{1}{3}$ as $x \to -1$.

10. $\dfrac{(1/y) - (1/3)}{y - 3} = \dfrac{3 - y}{3y(y - 3)} = -\dfrac{1}{3y} \to -\dfrac{1}{9}$

as $y \to 3$.

13. $\dfrac{8^{2/3}}{8 - \sqrt{16}} = \dfrac{4}{4} = 1.$

16. $\dfrac{1/(2 + h) - (1/2)}{h} = \dfrac{2 - (2 + h)}{2h(2 + h)} = \dfrac{-1}{2(2 + h)}$

$\to -\dfrac{1}{4}$ as $h \to 0.$

19. $|1 - 3| = 2.$

22. $\dfrac{3 - x^{1/2}}{9 - x} = \dfrac{3 - x^{1/2}}{(3 - x^{1/2})(3 + x^{1/2})} = \dfrac{1}{3 + \sqrt{x}}$

$\to \dfrac{1}{3 + \sqrt{9}} = \dfrac{1}{6}$ as $x \to 9.$

25. $\dfrac{x^2 - 16}{2 - x^{1/2}} = \dfrac{(x + 4)(x^{1/2} + 2)(x^{1/2} - 2)}{2 - x^{1/2}}$

$= -(x + 4)(x^{1/2} + 2) \to -(4 + 4)(2 + 2) = -32$

as $x \to 4.$

28. $(-3)^{6/3} = 9.$

34. $1/3$

37. $f'(x) = \lim_{h \to 0} \dfrac{1}{h} \left(\dfrac{1}{\sqrt{x + h}} - \dfrac{1}{\sqrt{x}} \right)$

$= \lim_{h \to 0} \dfrac{1}{h} \cdot \dfrac{x^{1/2} - (x + h)^{1/2}}{x^{1/2}(x + h)^{1/2}} \cdot \dfrac{x^{1/2} + (x + h)^{1/2}}{x^{1/2} + (x + h)^{1/2}}$

$$= \lim_{h \to 0} \frac{x - (x + h)}{h x^{1/2} (x + h)^{1/2} (\sqrt{x} + \sqrt{x + h})}$$

$$= \lim_{h \to 0} \frac{-1}{\sqrt{x} \sqrt{x + h} (\sqrt{x} + \sqrt{x + h})}$$

$$= \frac{-1}{\sqrt{x} \sqrt{x} (\sqrt{x} + \sqrt{x})} = -\frac{1}{2} x^{-3/2}.$$

40.
$$f(x + h) - f(x) = \sqrt{3x + 3h + 1} - \sqrt{3x + 1}$$

$$= \frac{3x + 3h + 1 - 3x - 1}{\sqrt{3x + 3h + 1} + \sqrt{3x + 1}},$$

so

$$f'(x) = \lim_{h \to 0} \frac{f(x + h) - f(x)}{h}$$

$$= \lim_{h \to 0} \frac{3}{\sqrt{3x + 3h + 1} + \sqrt{3x + 1}}$$

$$= \frac{3}{2\sqrt{3x + 1}}.$$

43. $1 + x^2 \geq 1$ for all x. So $0 \leq \dfrac{1}{1 + x^2} \leq 1$

for all x. Thus

$$0 \leq \frac{|x|}{1 + x^2} \leq |x| \quad \text{for all } x.$$

Therefore

$$\lim_{x \to 0} \frac{|x|}{1 + x^2} = 0 \quad \text{by the Squeeze Law.}$$

46. If $-1 \leq x \leq 1$, then $-2 \leq x \leq 0$ and $0 \leq x + 1 \leq 2$.
So $|x + 1| - |x - 1| = (x + 1) + (x - 1) = 2x$ if
$-1 \leq x \leq 1$. But $1 + (1 + |x + 2|^3)^{1/2} \geq 1$
for all x, so

$$-2x \leq \frac{|x + 1| - |x - 1|}{1 + (1 + |x + 2|^3)^{1/2}} \leq 2x$$

11

for $-1 \le x \le 1$. Therefore $g(x) \to 0$ as $x \to 0$.

49. If x is near the integer n, then $f(x) = n - 1$ for $x < n$ and $f(x) = n$ for $x > n$. So $f(x)$ has no limit as $x \to n$. On the other hand, if r is not an integer, then $n < r < n + 1$ for some integer n, and $f(x) = n$ if $n < x < n + 1$, so $f(x) \to n$ as $x \to r$.

52. If $3 < x < 4$, then $g(x) = 1 + 3 - 4 = 0$. If $2 < x < 3$, then $g(x) = 1 + 2 - 3 = 0$. Therefore $g(x) \to 0$ as $x \to 3$. But $g(3) = 1 + 3 - 3 = 1$, so $g(x)$ does not have limit $g(3)$ as $x \to 3$.

Section 2.2

1. $3 - 0 = 3$.

4. If $x < 4$, then $4 - x > 0$, so the limit is 0.

7. $\sqrt{5 \cdot (5 - 5)} = 0$.

10. $6 - x - x^2 = (3 + x)(2 - x)$, so $3 + x > 0$ and $2 - x > 0$ for $x > -3$. So the limit is zero.

13. If $x > 3$, then $x^2 - 6x + 9 = (x - 3)^2 > 0$ and $x - 3 > 0$, so

$$\frac{(x^2 - 6x + 9)^{1/2}}{x - 3} = \frac{|x - 3|}{x - 3} \to 1 \quad \text{as} \quad x \to 3^+.$$

16. If $x < 7$ then $x - 7 < 0$, so $(7 - x)/|x - 7| = 1$. So the limit is 1.

19. $\{(5 - x)^2\}^{1/2} = |5 - x| = x - 5$ for $x > 5$, so the limit is -1.

22. $f(x) \to +\infty$ as $x \to 3^-$, $f(x) \to -\infty$ as $x \to 3^+$.

25. $1 - x^2$ is near -3 if x is near -2. So $f(x) \to +\infty$ as $x \to -2^-$ while $f(x) \to -\infty$ as $x \to -2^+$.

28. The numerator $x + 1$ of $f(x)$ is near -2 for x near -3, while the denominator $(x + 3)^2 > 0$ for all $x \neq -3$. So $f(x) \rightarrow -\infty$ as $x \rightarrow -3$.

31. If x is an even integer then $f(x) = 3$; if x is an odd integer then $f(x) = 1$. But if n is an integer, then $f(x) \rightarrow 2$ as $x \rightarrow n$.

34. If n is an integer and $2n - 1 < x < 2n$, then

$$n - \frac{1}{2} < \frac{x}{2} < n,$$

so $f(x) = n - 1$. If $2n < x < 2n + 1$ then

$$n < \frac{x}{2} < n + \frac{1}{2},$$

so $f(x) = n$. So $f(x) \rightarrow n - 1$ as $x \rightarrow 2n^-$ and $f(x) \rightarrow n$ as $x \rightarrow 2n^+$.

If $2n + 1 < x < 2n + 2$, then

$$n + \frac{1}{2} < \frac{x}{2} < n + 1,$$

so $f(x) = n$. So $f(x) \rightarrow n$ as $x \rightarrow (2n + 1)^+$; previous work shows that $f(x) \rightarrow n$ as $x \rightarrow (2n + 1)^-$.

Section 2.3

1. $(f + g)(x) = (x + 1) + (x^2 + 2x - 3) = x^2 + 3x - 2$; domain: $(-\infty, +\infty)$. $(fg)(x) = (x + 1)(x^2 + 2x - 3)$; domain: $(-\infty, +\infty)$. $(f/g)(x) = (x + 1)/(x^2 + 2x - 3)$; domain: All real numbers other than $x = -3$ and $x = 1$.

4. $(f + g)(x) = \sqrt{x + 1} + \sqrt{5 - x}$; domain: $-1 \leq x \leq 5$. $(fg)(x) = (5 + 4x - x^2)^{1/2}$; domain: Same. $(f/g)(x) = \sqrt{(x + 1)/(5 - x)}$; domain: $-1 \leq x < 5$.

7. $f(g(x)) = -17$; domain: $(-\infty, +\infty)$. $g(f(x)) = 17$; domain: Same.

10. $f(g(x)) = x + 4 - 4 = x$; domain: $(-\infty, +\infty)$. $g(f(x)) = (x^3 - 4 + 4)^{1/3} = x$; domain: Same.

16. $h(x) = (4x - 6)^{4/3} = f(g(x))$ where $f(x) = x^{4/3}$, $g(x) = 4x - 6$.

22. $h(x) = x^2 = f(g(x)) = 1 + g(x):$ $g(x) = x^3 - 1$.

25. $h(x) = (x + 2)^{1/2} = f(g(x)) = (g(x) - 2)^{1/2}:$ $g(x) = x + 4$.

28. $f(g(x)) = x + 6$ for $x \geq -3$, so f and g are not inverses of each other.

31. $y = 13x - 5:$ $y + 5 = 13x$, $x = \frac{1}{13}(y + 5)$. So $f^{-1}(x) = \frac{1}{13}(x + 5)$.

34. $y = x^2 - 4$, $0 \leq x \leq 2$, $-4 \leq t \leq 0:$ $y + 4 = x^2$, $x = \sqrt{y + 4}$. So $f^{-1}(x) = \sqrt{x + 4}$, $-4 \leq x \leq 0$.

37. $f(x)$ has domain and range $(-\infty, +\infty)$; let

$$g(x) = \frac{1}{a}(x - b), \quad -\infty < x < +\infty.$$

Then $g(f(x)) = x$ and $f(g(x)) = x$ for all x.

40. It is clear that every increasing function is also a one-to-one function.

Section 2.4

1. The cube root of every real number exists and is unique, so the domain of f is the set of all real numbers. By an argument like the one in Example 2, f is continuous on the set of all real numbers as well.

4. Continuous on its domain, $x \neq 5$.

7. Continuous on its domain, $x \neq 5$.

10. Because $x^4 \geq 0$ for all x, $x^4 + 4 > 0$ for all x, and so $(x^4 + 4)^{1/4}$ exists for all x. By Theorem 1,

14

f is continuous on its domain, the set of all real numbers.

13. Continuous on its domain, all x other than 0 and 1.

16. We require $1 - x^2$ and $4 - x^2$ to have the same sign, and for $4 - x^2$ to be nonzero. If $x^2 \leq 1$ and $x^2 \leq 4$, this implies that $x^2 \leq 1$, so $-1 \leq x \leq 1$. If $x^2 \geq 1$ and $x^2 \geq 4$, then $x^2 \geq 4$; however, $x^2 \neq 4$, so $x > 2$ or $x < -2$. So the domain of f consists of the three intervals $(-\infty, -4)$, $[-1, 1]$, and $(4, +\infty)$, and f is continuous there.

19. $f(x) = \dfrac{x - 2}{x^2 - 4} = \dfrac{x - 2}{(x + 2)(x - 2)} = \dfrac{1}{x + 2}$ provided $x \neq 2$. It is clear that f is discontinuous at both 2 and -2, cannot be made continuous at -2 because it has no limit there, but can be made continuous at $x = 2$ simply by defining $f(2)$ to be $1/4$, its limit at 2.

22. If $x > 1$, then $f(x) = 1/(x - 1)^2$, so f is discontinuous at $x = 1$ and cannot be made continuous there.

25. The function f is discontinuous at $x = 0$ because it is not defined there. If we define $f(0)$ to be 0, then f will be continuous at $x = 0$ as well because its limit at $x = 0$ will be its value there.

28. Minimum value -1 at $x = -1$ because $f(x)$ is an increasing function. It has no maximum value.

31. Minimum value 0 at $x = 2$, maximum value 2 at $x = 4$.

34. The maximum of $f(x)$ occurs when its denominator is minimal -- that is, when $x = 0$. It has no minimum value because $f(x)$ becomes arbitrarily small positive for $|x|$ large.

37. Let $f(x) = x^3 - 3x^2 + 1$. Then f is continuous, $f(0) = 1$, and $f(1) = -1$. Therefore $f(x) = 0$ for some x, $0 < x < 1$ (approximately 0.6527).

40. Let $f(x) = x^5 - 5x^3 + 3$. Then f is continuous

because $f(x)$ is a polynomial. Also $f(-3) = -105 < 0$ and $f(-2) = 11 > 0$. Therefore $f(x) = 0$ for some x, $-3 < x < -2$ (approximately -2.291164).

43. Let $f(x) = x^2 - a$ where $a > 0$. Then $f(0) = -a < 0$ and $f(a + 1) = a^2 + a + 1 > 0$. Because $f(x)$ is a polynomial, it is continuous, and thus has the intermediate value property. Therefore $f(r) = 0$ for some r, $0 < r < a + 1$. Consequently $r^2 = a$, and so every positive number has a square root.

46. If r is not an integer, then $n < r < n + 1$ where n is an integer, and $f(x) = x - n$ for all x near r. So f is continuous at non-integers. If r is an integer, then $f(x)$ is near zero but positive for $x > r$ and close to r, but $f(x)$ is near 1 for $x < r$ and close to r. So the left-hand and right-hand limits of f are unequal at integers; therefore f is not continuous at any integer but continuous at every non-integer.

NOTE:

For technical reasons, we will use the symbol $\sim$ for "approximately equal to," the Greek letter ξ in place of theta, and -- as you have already noticed -- braces in many places where the preferred usage is square brackets.

49. Let $f(x) = x^4 + 2x - 1$. Then:
    $f(0) = -1$, $f(0.5) = 0.0625$;
    $f(0.25) \sim -0.49609$, $f(0.5) = 0.0625$;
    $f(0.375) \sim -0.23022$, $f(0.5) = 0.0625$;
    $f(0.4375) \sim -0.08836$, $f(0.5) = 0.0625$;
    $f(0.46875) \sim -0.01422$, $f(0.5) = 0.0625$;
    $f(0.46875) \sim -0.01422$, $f(0.484375) \sim 0.02380$;
    $f(0.46875) \sim -0.01422$, $f(0.4765625) \sim 0.00470$;
    $f(0.4736525) \sim -0.00478$, $f(0.4765625) \sim 0.00470$;
    $f(0.474609375) \sim -0.00004$, $f(0.4767625) \sim 0.00470$;
    $f(0.474609375) \sim -0.00004$, $f(0.4755859375) \sim 0.00233$;
    $f(0.474609375) \sim -0.00004$, $f(0.47509765625) \sim 0.00114$;
    $f(0.474609375) \sim -0.00004$, $f(0.474853515625) \sim 0.00006$;
Answer: Approximately 0.47. (A better approximation is 0.47462662.)

Section 2.5

1. $2\pi/9$, $-3\pi/2$, $7\pi/4$, $7\pi/6$, $-5\pi/6$

4. (a) $k\pi$, k an integer; (b) $x = \dfrac{\pi}{2} + 2k\pi$, k an integer; (c) $x = 2k\pi - \dfrac{\pi}{2}$, k an integer.

7. $\sin x = -3/5$, $\cos x = -4/5$; use the relations in (3) to obtain the other values.

10. Write $\tan(x + y)$ as $\dfrac{\sin(x + y)}{\cos(x + y)}$. Expand the numerator and denominator using Eqs. (6) and (7) of the text. Divide each term in both numerator and denominator by $\cos x \cos y$ and simplify to obtain the desired result.

13. Use Eqs. (6) and (7) of the text.

16. $\sin^2 x = \cos^2 x$:

$$\sin^2 x = 1 - \sin^2 x;$$

$$2\sin^2 x = 1;$$

$$\sin x = + \frac{1}{2}\sqrt{2}$$

(because $0 \leqq x \leqq \pi$, $\sin x \geqq 0$);

$$x = \pi/4,\ 3\pi/4.$$

19. $8\sin^2 x \cos^2 x = 1$:

$$4\sin^2 x \cos^2 x = 1/2;$$

$$(2\sin x \cos x)^2 = 1/2;$$

$$\sin^2 2x = 1/2.$$

Now $0 \leqq 2x \leqq 2\pi$, so the sine function takes on both positive and negative values:

$$\sin 2x = \frac{1}{2}\sqrt{2} \quad \text{or} \quad \sin 2x = -\frac{1}{2}\sqrt{2};$$

17

$$2x = \pi/4, \quad 3\pi/4, \quad 5\pi/4, \quad 7\pi/4;$$

$$x = \pi/8, \quad 3\pi/8, \quad 5\pi/8, \quad 7\pi/8.$$

22. If $u \to 1$ as $x \to 0$, then $u^2 \to 1$ as well.

25. Divide each term in numerator and denominator by x.

28. $\displaystyle \lim_{x \to 0} \frac{\sin 2x}{x \cos 3x}$

$$= \lim_{x \to 0} \frac{\sin 2x}{2x} \cdot \frac{2}{\cos 3x} = 2.$$

31. Replace $x/3$ by u, then apply Theorem 2 of the text.

34. $\displaystyle \lim_{x \to 0} \frac{\tan 3x}{\tan 5x}$

$$= \lim_{x \to 0} \frac{3}{5} \cdot \frac{\tan 3x}{3x} \cdot \frac{5x}{\tan 5x} = \frac{3}{5}.$$

37. Multiply numerator and denominator by $1 + \cos \xi$.

40. $\displaystyle \lim_{x \to 0} \frac{\tan 2x}{3x}$

$$= \lim_{x \to 0} \frac{2}{3} \cdot \frac{\tan 2x}{2x} = \frac{2}{3}.$$

43. Replace $x/2$ by u.

46. $-1 \le \sin u \le 1$ for all u. So

$$-x^2 \le x^2 \sin \frac{1}{x^2} \le x^2$$

for all x. But $x^2 \to 0$ as $x \to 0$, so the limit of the expression caught in the squeeze is also zero.

52. $\displaystyle f'(0) = \lim_{h \to 0} \frac{f(0 + h) - f(0)}{h}$

$$= \lim_{h \to 0} \frac{1}{h} h^2 \sin \frac{1}{h}$$

$$= \lim_{h \to 0} h \sin \frac{1}{h}.$$

Now apply the squeeze law to deduce that the last limit is zero.

Section 2.6

1. Given $\varepsilon > 0$, choose $\delta = \varepsilon$. Suppose that $0 < |x - a| < \delta$.
    Here we have $f(x) = x$ and $L = a$, so $|f(x) - L| = |x - a|$
    $< \delta = \varepsilon$. Thus $|f(x) - L| < \varepsilon$. Therefore, by definition,
    $\lim\limits_{x \to a} x = a$.

4. Take $f(x) = 2x + 1$, $a = -3$, and $L = -5$. Given
    $\varepsilon > 0$, let $\delta = \varepsilon/2$.

7. Given $\varepsilon > 0$, let $\delta = \varepsilon/k$ where you will choose a
    suitably large positive integer k later in the proof so
    that the inequalities will work. Then go back through the
    proof and replace k by this integer. Write it neatly
    and turn it in for a perfect grade. This is a standard
    technique in ε-δ proofs.

8. Suppose first that $a > 0$. Given $\varepsilon > 0$, choose δ to be
    the minimum of $a/3$ and $8a^5/27$. Okay, why? Here's why.
    We need

$$\left| \frac{1}{x^2} - \frac{1}{a^2} \right| < \varepsilon,$$

which would hold provided

$$\left| \frac{a^2 - x^2}{a^2 x^2} \right| < \varepsilon.$$

This would follow from

$$\frac{|a + x||a - x|}{a^2 x^2} < \varepsilon,$$

which in turn would follow from

$$|x - a| < \frac{a^2 x^2 \varepsilon}{|x + a|}.$$

This means that we must control the values of both $|x + a|$ and a^2x^2. For the former, we insure that $|x + a|$ is not large by keeping x close to a: We require that

$$\frac{a}{2} < x < \frac{3a}{2}$$

by making sure that $\delta < a/2$. If so, then it is easy to show that

$$\frac{1}{4}a^2 < x^2 < \frac{3}{4}a^2$$

and also that

$$\frac{2}{3a} < \frac{1}{x + a} < \frac{2}{5a}.$$

It then follows that

$$|x - a| < \frac{27}{8}a^5\epsilon.$$

So it suffices to insure also that $\delta \leq 8a^5\epsilon/27$. Thus we choose δ to be the minimum of $a/3$ and $8a^5\epsilon/27$. The desired inequalities then follow.

10. The desired inequality

$$\left| \frac{1}{\sqrt{x}} - \frac{1}{\sqrt{a}} \right| < \epsilon$$

follows from

$$| \sqrt{a} - \sqrt{x} | < \epsilon\sqrt{ax},$$

and we keep x from becoming negative or zero (or even too close to zero) by insuring that $a/2 < x < 3a/2$. We obtain the last displayed inequality from

$$|a^{1/2} + x^{1/2}||a^{1/2} - x^{1/2}| < \epsilon(ax)^{1/2}(a^{1/2} + x^{1/2});$$

that is,

$$|x - a| < \varepsilon\sqrt{ax}\,(\sqrt{a} + \sqrt{x}).$$

What will suffice is that

$$\delta < \varepsilon\sqrt{ax}\,(\sqrt{a} + \sqrt{x}),$$

and this can be assured by choosing $\delta < a\varepsilon/2$, as this implies the last inequality. So choose δ to be the minimum of $a/2$ and $a\varepsilon/2$.

13. First deal with the case $L > 0$. The desired inequality follows from $|f(x) - L| < \varepsilon L f(x)$. But $f(x)$ can be forced to lie between $L/2$ and $3L/2$ by choosing δ sufficiently small, and now the choice of δ should be easy: Merely insure that $\delta < L^2 \varepsilon/2$.

16. Let $\varepsilon = \frac{1}{2} f(a)$. Note that $f(x) \to f(a)$ as $x \to a$ because f is continuous at $x = a$. Now choose δ such that $|f(x) - f(a)| < \varepsilon$ if $0 < |x - a| < \delta$. For such x, we have

$$-\varepsilon < f(x) - 2\varepsilon < \varepsilon,$$

so $\varepsilon < f(x) < 3\varepsilon$. Therefore $f(x) > 0$ if x is in the interval $(a - \delta, a + \delta)$.

Chapter 2 Miscellaneous Problems

1. $0^2 - 3 \cdot 0 + 4 = 4$.

4. $(1 + 1 - 1)^{17} = 1$.

7. $\dfrac{x^2 - 1}{1 - x} = -(x + 1) \to -2$ as $x \to 1$.

10. $\dfrac{4 - x^2}{3 + x} \to \dfrac{4}{3}$ as $x \to 0$.

13. $(16)^{3/4} = 8$.

16. $x - (x^2 - 1)^{1/2} = \dfrac{x^2 - (x^2 - 1)}{x + (x^2 - 1)^{1/2}}$

$= \dfrac{1}{x + (x^2 - 1)^{1/2}} \to 1$ as $x \to 1^+$.

19. $|(2 - x)^2|^{1/2} = |2 - x| = x - 2$ for $x > 2$, so the fraction and its limit are equal to -1.

22. $\sqrt{9 - 9} = 0$.

25. The numerator approaches 4 while the denominator approaches 0 through positive values, so the limit is $+\infty$.

28. For $x \neq 1$, the fraction is equal to $\dfrac{1}{x - 1}$, and its denominator approaches 0 through negative values, so the limit is $-\infty$.

31. $\dfrac{\sin 3x}{x} = \dfrac{3 \sin 3x}{3x} \to 3$ as $x \to 0$.

34. $\dfrac{\tan 2x}{\tan 3x} = \dfrac{2}{3} \cdot \dfrac{\tan 2x}{2x} \cdot \dfrac{3x}{\tan 3x} \to \dfrac{2}{3}$ as $x \to 0$.

37. Multiply numerator and denominator by $1 + \cos 3x$ to obtain

$$\frac{\sin^2 3x}{2x^2(1 + \cos 3x)}$$

$$= \frac{9}{2} \cdot \frac{\sin^2 3x}{(3x)^2} \cdot \frac{1}{1 + \cos 3x},$$

which approaches $9/4$ as $x \to 0$.

40. $x^2 \cot^2 3x = \dfrac{(3x)^2}{(\sin 3x)^2} \cdot \dfrac{(\cos 3x)^2}{9} \to 1/9$ as $x \to 0$.

43. $y = (x^3 - 1)^{-5}$, $x \neq 1$, $y \neq 0$:

$$x^3 - 1 = y^{-1/5};$$
$$x = (1 + y^{-1/5})^{1/3}.$$
$$f^{-1}(x) = (1 + x^{-1/5})^{1/3}, \quad x \neq 0.$$

46. $(1 + \sqrt{x}\,)^2 = 1 + 2\sqrt{x} + x;$

$$2 + (1 + \sqrt{x}\,)^2 = 3 + 2\sqrt{x} + x;$$

$$f(x) = 2 + x^2.$$

49. Every rational function is continuous wherever its denominator is nonzero. Here,

$$f(x) = \frac{(x - 1)(x + 2)}{(x - 1)(x + 3)} = \frac{x + 2}{x + 3}$$

provided $x \neq 1$. If we define $f(1)$ to be $3/4$, then f will be continuous at $x = 1$, but f cannot be made continuous at $x = -3$.

52. Let $f(x) = x^3 - 3x^2 + 1$. Then $f(-1) = -3$, $f(0) = 1$, $f(1) = -1$, and $f(3) = 1$. Because $f(x)$ is a polynomial, it is continuous everywhere, so has the intermediate value property on every interval. Therefore $f(x_1) = 0$ for some number x_1 in $(-1, 0)$, $f(x_2) = 0$ for some number x_2 in $(0, 1)$, and $f(x_3) = 0$ for some number x_3 in $(1, 3)$. (The actual values are approximately $x_1 = -0.532088886$, $x_2 = 0.652703645$, and $x_3 = 2.879385242$.)

Section 3.1

1. Here, $a = 0$, $b = 4$, and $c = -5$. So $f'(x) = 4$.

4. Here, $a = 0$, $b = -49$, and $c = 16$. So $f'(x) = -49$.

7. Here, $a = 5$, $b = 3$, and $c = 0$. So $dz/du = 10u + 3$.

10. $du/dt = 14t + 13$.

13. $f(x + h) - f(x) = (x + h)^2 + 5 - x^2 - 5 = 2xh + h^2.$

16. $f'(x) = \displaystyle\lim_{h \to 0} \frac{f(x + h) - f(x)}{h}$

$$= \lim_{h \to 0} \frac{1}{h}\left(\frac{1}{3 - (x + h)} - \frac{1}{3 - x} \right)$$

23

$$= \lim_{h \to 0} \frac{3 - x - 3 + (x + h)}{h(3 - x - h)(3 - x)}$$

$$= \lim_{h \to 0} \frac{1}{(3 - x - h)(3 - x)} = \frac{1}{(3 - x)^2}.$$

19. $f(x + h) - f(x) = \dfrac{x + h}{1 - 2(x + h)} - \dfrac{x}{1 - 2x}$

$$= \frac{(x + h)(1 - 2x) - x(1 - 2x - 2h)}{(1 - 2x - 2h)(1 - 2x)}$$

$$= \frac{h}{(1 - 2x - 2h)(1 - 2x)}.$$

22. $v = ds/dt = -32t + 160$; $v = 0$ when $t = 5$; $s = 425$ when $t = 5$.

25. $v = ds/dt = -20 - 10t$; $v = 0$ when $t = -2$; $s = 120$ when $t = -2$.

28. $ds/dt = -32t + 128$; $ds/dt = 0$ when $t = 4$; $s_{max} = s(4) = 281$ (ft).

31. Let r denote the radius of the circle. Then $A = \pi r^2$ and $C = 2\pi r$, so $r = C/(2\pi)$. Thus $A = C^2/(4\pi)$, so the rate of change of A with respect to C is $dA/dC = C/(2\pi)$.

34. Note that

$$V = 10\left(1 - \frac{t}{50} + \frac{t^2}{10,000}\right)$$

$$= 10 - \frac{1}{5}t + \frac{1}{1000}t^2.$$

Thus $V'(t) = -\dfrac{1}{5} + \dfrac{1}{500}t$. The rate at which the water is leaking out after 1 minute has passed is $V'(60) = -2/25$ (gal/sec) -- if you prefer, -4.8 gal/min. The average rate of change of V from $t = 0$ until $t = 100$ is

24

$$\frac{V(100) - V(0)}{100 - 0} = \frac{0 - 10}{100} = -\frac{1}{10}$$

and this is equal to the instantaneous rate of change at that time t satisfying

$$V'(t) = -\frac{1}{10}.$$

That is,

$$-\frac{1}{5} + \frac{1}{500} t = -\frac{1}{10},$$

so the instantaneous rate of change of V is equal to its average rate of change at time t = 50 (sec).

37. On our graph, the tangent line at the point (20,810) has slope m_1 approximately 0.6, and the tangent line at (40,2686) has slope m_2 approximately 0.9. A line of slope 1 on our graph corresponds to a velocity of 125 ft/sec (because the line through (0,0) and (10,1250) has slope 1), and thus we estimate the velocity of the car at time t = 20 to be about (0.6)(125) = 75 ft/sec, and at time t = 40 it is traveling at about (0.9)(125) = 112.5 ft/sec. The method is crude, as you can see by the fact that the answer in the back of the text is quite different.

40. A right circular cylinder of radius r and height h has volume $V = \pi r^2 h$ and total surface area S obtained by adding the areas of its top, bottom, and curved side: $S = 2\pi r^2 + 2\pi rh$. We are given h = 2r in this problem, so $V = 2\pi r^3$ and $S = 6\pi r^2$. Now $dV/dr = 6\pi r^2 = S$, so the rate of change of volume with respect to radius is indeed equal to total surface area.

43. Let V(t) denote the volume (in cm^3) of the snowball at time t (in hours), and let r(t) denote its radius (in cm) then. From the data given in the problem, r = 12 - t. The volume of the snowball is

$$V = \frac{4}{3} \pi r^3 = \frac{4}{3} \pi (12 - t)^3$$

$$= \frac{4}{3} \pi (1728 - 432t + 36t^2 - t^3),$$

so its instantaneous rate of change is

$$V'(t) = \frac{4}{3} \pi (-432 + 72t - 3t^2)$$

$$= -576\pi + 96\pi t - 4t^2.$$

Therefore its rate of change of volume when $t = 6$ is -144π cm^3/hr. Its average rate of change of volume from $t = 3$ to $t = 9$ in cm^3/hr is

$$\frac{V(9) - V(3)}{9 - 3} = \frac{36\pi - 972\pi}{6} = - \frac{936\pi}{6} = -156\pi.$$

46. Because

$$P(t) = 100 + 4t + \frac{3}{10} t^2,$$

we have

$$P'(t) = 4 + \frac{3}{5} t.$$

The year 1975 corresponds to $t = 5$, so the rate of change of P then was $P'(5) = 7$ (thousands per year). The average rate of change of P from 1973 ($t = 3$) to 1978 ($t = 8$) was

$$\frac{P(8) - P(3)}{8 - 3} = \frac{151.2 - 114.7}{5} = 7.3$$

thousands per year.

Section 3.2

4. $g'(x) = (2x^2 - 1)(3x^2) + (4x)(x^3 + 2) = 10x^4 - 3x^2 + 8x.$

7. $f(y) = 4y^3 - y$: $f'(y) = 12y^2 - 1.$

10. $f'(t) = \dfrac{0 - (1)(-2t)}{(4 - t^2)^2} = \dfrac{2t}{(4 - t^2)^2}.$

13. By first multiplying the two factors of $g(t)$:

$$g'(t) = 5t^4 + 4t^3 + 3t^2 + 4t.$$

By applying the product rule:

$$g'(t) = (t^2 + 1)(3t^2 + 2t) + (t^3 + t^2 + 1)(2t).$$

Of course both answers are the same.

16. $f(x) = 2x - 3 + 4x^{-1} - 5x^{-2}$, so

$$f'(x) = 2 - \frac{4}{x^2} + \frac{10}{x^3} = \frac{2x^3 - 4x + 10}{x^3}.$$

22. $h'(x) = \dfrac{(2x - 5)(6x^2 + 2x - 3) - (2)(2x^3 + x^2 - 3x + 17)}{(2x - 5)^2}$

$$= \frac{8x^3 - 28x^2 - 10x - 19}{(2x - 5)^2}.$$

25. First rewrite the function in the form $g(x) = \dfrac{x^3 - 2x^2}{2x - 3}$. Then

$$g'(x) = \frac{(2x - 3)(3x^2 - 4x) - (2)(x^3 - 2x^2)}{(2x - 3)^2}$$

$$= \frac{4x^3 - 13x^2 + 12x}{(2x - 3)^2}.$$

28. $\dfrac{dy}{dx} = -3x^{-2} + 8x^{-3}.$

34. $y = \dfrac{x^2}{x^2 - 4}$ for $x \neq 0$. So

$$\frac{dy}{dx} = \frac{(x^2 - 4)(2x) - (x^2)(2x)}{(x^2 - 4)^2} = -\frac{8x}{(x^2 - 4)^2}.$$

37. $y = \dfrac{10x^6}{15x^5 - 4}$ for $x \neq 0$.

40. $y = x^{-1} + 10x^{-2}$, so $dy/dx = -x^{-2} - 20x^{-3}$.

43. $dy/dx = -(x - 1)^2$; the slope at P is -1. An equation of the tangent line is $y - 1 = -(x - 2)$.

46. $y = \dfrac{x^2}{x - 1}$ for $x \neq 0$. So

$$\frac{dy}{dx} = \frac{(x - 1)(2x) - x^2}{(x - 1)^2} = \frac{x^2 - 2x}{(x - 1)^2}.$$

The slope at P is therefore 0, and the line has equation $y = 4$.

49. $\dfrac{dy}{dx} = \dfrac{3x^2 + 6x}{(x^2 + x + 1)^2}.$

52. $W = \dfrac{2 \times 10^9}{R^2} = (2 \times 10^9)R^{-2}.$ So $\dfrac{dW}{dR} = \dfrac{-4 \times 10^9}{R^3}$;

when $R = 3960$, $\dfrac{dW}{dR} = -\dfrac{62,500}{970,299}$ pounds per mile. Thus W decreases at about 1.03 ounces per mile.

55. Let (a, a^3) be the point of tangency. The slope of the tangent line can be computed using dy/dx at $x = a$ and also by using the two points known to be on the line. We thereby find that

$$3a^2 = \frac{a^3 - 5}{a - 1}.$$

This leads to the equation $2a^3 - 3a^2 + 5 = 0$; that is,

$$(a + 1)(2a^2 - 5a + 5) = 0.$$

The quadratic factor has negative discriminant, so the only real solution of the cubic equation is $a = -1$. The point of tangency is $(-1, -1)$, the slope there is 3 and the equation of the line in question is therefore $y = 3x + 2$.

58. Let $(a, 1/a)$ be a point of tangency. The slope of the tangent there is $-1/a^2$, so $-1/a^2 = -2$. Thus there are two possible values for a: $+\frac{1}{2}\sqrt{2}$ and $-\frac{1}{2}\sqrt{2}$. These lead to the equations of the two lines:

$$y = -2x + 2\sqrt{2} \qquad \text{and} \qquad y = -2x - 2\sqrt{2}.$$

61. Take n = 3 in Eq. (15) and $u_1(x) = u_2(x) = u_3(x) = f(x)$.
     Then

$$D_x\{f(x)\}^3 = f'(x)f(x)f(x) + f(x)f'(x)f(x) + f(x)f(x)f'(x)$$

$$= 3\{f(x)\}^2 f'(x).$$

64. With $f(x) = x^2 + x + 1$ and $n = 100$, we obtain
     $D(x^2 + x + 1)^{100} = 100(x^2 + x + 1)^{99}(2x + 1)$.

Section 3.3

1. $f(x) = (x^3 + 1)^{1/2}$, so $f'(x) = \dfrac{1}{2}(x^3 + 1)^{-1/2}(3x^2)$.

4. $f(x) = \dfrac{x}{(1 + x^4)^{1/2}}$, so

$$f'(x) = \frac{(1 + x^4)^{1/2} - (x/2)(1 + x^4)^{-1/2}(4x^3)}{1 + x^4}$$

$$= \frac{1 - x^4}{(1 + x^4)^{3/2}}.$$

10. $f'(t) = 5(t^2 + \{1 + t\}^4)^4 D_t(t^2 + \{1 + t\}^4)$

$$= 5(t^2 + \{1 + t\}^4)^4(2t + 4\{1 + t\}^3).$$

13. $f'(t) = \dfrac{1}{2}\left(\dfrac{t^2 + 1}{t^2 - 1}\right)^{-1/2} \dfrac{(t^2 - 1)(2t) - (2t)(t^2 + 1)}{(t^2 - 1)^2}$

$$= \frac{1}{2}\left(\frac{t^2 - 1}{t^2 + 1}\right)^{1/2} \frac{-4t}{(t^2 - 1)^2}$$

$$= -\frac{2t}{(t^2 + 1)^{1/2}(t^2 - 1)^{3/2}}.$$

16. $g'(z) = \dfrac{2z(1 + z^2)^{1/2} - (1/2)z^2(1 + z^2)^{-1/2}(2z)}{1 + z^2}$

$$= \frac{2z(1 + z^2) - z^3}{(1 + z^2)^{3/2}} = \frac{z^3 + 2z}{(1 + z^2)^{3/2}}.$$

19. $f'(x) = \frac{1}{3}(1 - x^2)^{-2/3}(-2x) = -\frac{2x}{3(1 - x^2)^{2/3}}.$

22. $\underline{A}$ solution is not $\underline{the}$ solution, but here is one of many:

$$g(t) = t^{-2}\{t - (1 + t^2)^{1/2}\}, \quad so$$

$$g'(t) = -2t^{-3}\{t - (1 + t^2)^{1/2}\} + t^{-2}\{1 - t(1 + t^2)^{-1/2}\}.$$

25. $g'(t) = -2(1 + \frac{1}{t})(\frac{1}{t^2})(3t^2 + 1)^{1/2}$

$$+ \frac{1}{2}(3t^2 + 1)^{-1/2}(6t)(1 + \frac{1}{t})^2.$$

28. $h'(z) = 4(z - 1)^3(z + 1)^6 + 6(z - 1)^4(z + 1)^5$

$$= 2(z - 1)^3(z + 1)^5(5z - 1).$$

31. $h'(y) = y^{-10/3}\{y^{5/3}\{\frac{1}{2}(1 + y)^{-1/2} + \frac{1}{2}(1 - y)^{-1/2}\}$

$$- \frac{5}{3}y^{2/3}\{(1 + y)^{1/2} + (1 - y)^{1/2}\}\}.$$

34. $f'(x) = 3x^2\left(1 - \frac{1}{x^2 + 1}\right)^{1/2}$

$$+ \frac{1}{2}x^3\left(1 - \frac{1}{x^2 + 1}\right)^{-1/2}\frac{2x}{(x^2 + 1)^2}.$$

37. $\frac{dy}{dx} = \frac{1}{2}x^{-1/2} - \frac{3}{2}x^{1/2} = \frac{1 - 3x}{2x^{1/2}};$

$\frac{dx}{dy} = \frac{2x^{1/2}}{1 - 3x}.$ So there is a horizontal tangent

where $x = 1/3$ (there, $y = -\frac{2}{3}\sqrt{1/3}$) and a vertical

tangent at $(0,0)$.

40. $\dfrac{dy}{dx} = \dfrac{(2x^2 - 5)x}{\{(1 - x^2)(4 - x^2)\}^{1/2}}$ and

$\dfrac{dx}{dy} = \dfrac{\{(1 - x^2)(4 - x^2)\}^{1/2}}{x(2x^2 - 5)}$.

So there is a horizontal tangent at $(0,2)$ and vertical tangents at $(1,0)$ and at $(-1,0)$ (not at $(2,0)$ nor at $(-2,0)$ because y is undefined there).

43. Whether $y = + (1 - x^2)^{1/2}$ or $y = - (1 - x^2)^{1/2}$, it follows easily that $dy/dx = - x/y$. The slope of the tangent is -2 when $x = 2y$, so from $x^2 + y^2 = 1$ we see that $x^2 = 4/5$.

46. Let $Q(a,a^2)$ be a point on the parabola $y = x^2$ where a line through $P(3,10)$ is normal to the parabola. Then, as in the solution to Problem 45, we find that

$$\dfrac{a^2 - 10}{a - 3} = - \dfrac{1}{2a} .$$

This yields the cubic equation $2a^3 - 19a - 3 = 0$, and after a little computation we find one of its small integral roots to be $r = -3$. So $a + 3$ is a factor of the cubic; we solve

$$(a + 3)(2a^2 - 6a - 1) = 0.$$

We already know the obvious solution $a = -3$, and the quadratic formula yields the other two solutions --

$$a = 3 + \sqrt{11} \quad \text{and} \quad a = 3 - \sqrt{11}.$$

The equations of the three lines are, with each of these values of a, $y - 10 = - \dfrac{1}{2a} (x - 3)$.

Section 3.4

1. $f'(x) = 3$, so the only candidates for extrema are the two end points -2 and 3. Now $f(-2) = -4 < 11 = f(3)$, so the minimum value of f is -4 and its maximum value is 11.

31

4. $f'(x) = 2x$; $f'(0) = 0$. $f(0) = 3$ (minimum), $f(5) = 28$ (maximum).

7. $f'(x) = 3x^2 - 3$; $f'(-1) = 0 = f'(1)$. Now $f(-2) = -2 = f(1)$ (minimum), $f(-1) = 2$, and $f(4) = 52$ (maximum).

10. $f'(x) = 2x - \dfrac{16}{x^2}$; $f'(x) = 0$ when $x^3 = 8$ -- that is, when $x = 2$. $f(1) = 17$ (maximum), $f(2) = 12$ (minimum), and $f(3) = 43/3$.

13. $f'(x) = -12 - 18x$; $f'(-2/3) = 0$. $f(-1) = 8$, $f(-2/3) = 9$ (maximum), and $f(1) = -16$ (minimum).

16. $f(x) = 3x^2 + 1 > 0$ for all x. $f(-1) = -2$ (minimum) and $f(2) = 10$ (maximum).

19. $f'(7/3)$ does not exist and $f'(x)$ is never zero.

22. $f'(x) = 2 - \dfrac{1}{2x^2}$; there are no points in the domain of f at which $f'(x) = 0$. $f(1) = 2.5$ (minimum) and $f(4) = 8.125$ (maximum).

25. $f'(x) = \dfrac{(x + 1)(x - 3)}{(x^2 + 3)^2}$.

28. $f'(x) = \dfrac{4 - 2x^2}{(4 - x^2)^{1/2}}$; $f'(x) = 0$ when $x = \sqrt{2}$ ($x = -\sqrt{2}$ is not in the domain of f). $f(0) = 0 = f(2)$ (minimum) and $f(\sqrt{2}) = 2$ (maximum).

31. If $A \ne 0$, then $f'(x) = A$ is never zero, but because f is continuous it must have global extrema. Therefore they occur at the end points. If $A = 0$, then f is a constant function, and its maximum and minimum value B occurs at every point of the interval, including the two end points.

1.   With $x > 0$, $y > 0$,   and $x + y = 50$,   we are to maximize
the product $P = xy$.   Now $P = P(x) = x(50 - x) = 50x - x^2$,
$0 < x < 50$ ($x < 50$ because $y > 0$).   The product is not
maximal if we let $x = 0$ or $x = 50$,   so we adjoin the end
points to the domain of   P;   thus the continuous function
$P(x) = 50x - x^2$ has a global maximum on the closed
interval $0 \leq x \leq 50$,   and the maximum does not occur
at either end point. Because P is differentiable, the
maximum must occur at a point where $P'(x) = 0$:

$$50 - 2x = 0,$$

so that $x = 25$.   Because this is the only critical point
of $P(x)$,   it follows that $x = 25$ maximizes $P(x)$.   When
$x = 25$, $y = 50 - x = 25$,   so the two positive real numbers
with sum   50   and maximum possible product are   25   and   25.

4.   If the side of the pen parallel to the wall has length x   and
the two perpendicular sides each have length y,   then we are
to maximize area $A = xy$ given $x + 2y = 600$.   Thus

$$A = A(y) = y(600 - 2y), \quad 0 \leq y \leq 300.$$

As usual, adjoining the end points to the domain is allowed
because the maximum that we seek occurs at neither.   Therefore
the maximum occurs at an interior critical point; we have
$A'(y) = 600 - 4y$,   so the only critical point of $A(y)$ is
$y = 150$.   When $y = 150$,   we have $x = 300$,   so the maximum
possible area that can be enclosed is   45,000   square meters.

7.   If the two numbers are x and y,   then we are to minimize
$S = x^2 + y^2$ given $x > 0$, $y > 0$, and $x + y = 48$.   So
$S(x) = x^2 + (48 - x)^2$, $0 \leq x \leq 48$.   Here we adjoin
the end points to assure the existence of a maximum, but we
must test the values of S at these end points because it is
not immediately clear that neither $S(0)$ nor $S(48)$ yields
the maximum of $S(x)$ on this domain. It is best to compute
$S'(x) = 2x - 2(48 - x)$ without expansion of $(48 - x)^2$
by the binomial formula; the only interior critical point of
$S(x)$ is thus at $x = 24$, for which $y = 24$ as well.

10. Draw a cross section of the circular log -- a circle of radius r. Inscribe in this circle a cross section of the beam -- a rectangle of width w and height h. Draw a diagonal of the rectangle; the Pythagorean theorem yields $w^2 + h^2 = 4r^2$. The strength S of the beam is given by $S = kwh^2$ where k is a positive constant. Because $h^2 = 4r^2 - w^2$, we have

$$S = S(w) = kw(4r^2 - w^2) = k(4wr^2 - w^3)$$

with natural domain $0 < w < 2r$. We adjoin the end points to this domain because $S = 0$ when $w = 0$ and when $w = 2r$, clearly not the maximum of S. Next, $S'(w) = k(4r^2 - 3w^2)$ is zero when $3w^2 = 4r^2$, and the corresponding (positive) value of w yields the maximum of S (we know that $S(w)$ must have a maximum for $0 \leqq w \leqq 2r$ because of the continuity of S on this interval, and we also know that the maximum does not occur at either end point; therefore there is only one possible location for the maximum). At maximum, $h^2 = 4r^2 - w^2 = 3w^2 - w^2 = 2w^2$, so $h = w\sqrt{2}$ describes the shape of the beam of greatest strength.

13. If the rectangle has sides x and y, then $x^2 + y^2 = 256$ by the Pythagorean theorem. The area of the rectangle is then

$$A(x) = x(256 - x^2)^{1/2}, \quad 0 \leqq x \leqq 16.$$

The suggestion of Problem 12 is useful -- we maximize

$$f(x) = \{A(x)\}^2 = x^2(256 - x^2) = 256x^2 - x^4.$$

The only solutions of $f'(x) = 0$ are $x = 0$ and $x = 8\sqrt{2}$.

16. Let $P(x,0)$ be the lower right-hand corner point of the rectangle. The rectangle then has base $2x$, height $4 - x^2$, and thus area

$$A = A(x) = 2x(4 - x^2) = 8x - 2x^3, \quad 0 \leqq x \leqq 2.$$

Now $A'(x) = 8 - 6x^2$; $A'(x) = 0$ when $x = \frac{2}{3}\sqrt{3}$. Because $A(0) = 0$, $A(2) = 0$, and $A(\frac{2}{3}\sqrt{3}) > 0$, the maximum possible area is $\frac{32}{9}\sqrt{3}$.

34

19. Let x be the length of the edge of each of the twelve small squares. Then the three cross-shaped pieces each will form boxes with base length 1 - 2x and height x, so each of the three will have volume $x(1 - 2x)^2$. Each of the two small cubical boxes will have edge x and thus volume x^3. So the total volume of all five boxes will be

$$V(x) = 3x(1 - 2x)^2 + 2x^3$$

$$= 14x^3 - 12x^2 + 3x, \quad 0 \leq x \leq \frac{1}{2}.$$

Now $V'(x) = 42x^2 - 24x + 3$; $V'(x) = 0$ when

$$14x^2 - 8x - 1 = 0.$$

The quadratic formula gives the two solutions $\frac{1}{14}(4 + \sqrt{2})$ and $\frac{1}{14}(4 - \sqrt{2})$. These are approximately 0.3867 and 0.1847, respectively, and each lies in the domain of V. Now $V(0) = 0$, $V(0.5) = 0.25$, $V(0.1847) = 0.2329$, and $V(0.3867) = 0.1752$ (the last two values are approximations). Therefore, to maximize V, one must cut each of the three large squares into four smaller squares of side length 1/2 each, and form the resulting twelve squares into two cubes. At maximum volume there will be only two boxes, not five.

22. See Figure 3.21 of the text. Suppose that the pen measures x (horizontal) by y (vertical). Then it has area A = xy. Case 1: $x \geq 10$, $y \geq 5$. Then

$$x + (x - 10) + y + (y - 5) = 85, \quad \text{so} \quad x + y = 50.$$

Therefore

$$A = A(x) = x(50 - x) = 50x - x^2, \quad 10 \leq x \leq 45.$$

Then $A'(x) = 0$ when x = 25; $A(25) = 625$. Note also that $A(10) = 400$ and that $A(45) = 625$.

Case 2: $0 \leq x \leq 10$, $y \geq 5$. Then

$$x + y + (y - 5) = 85, \quad \text{so that} \quad x + 2y = 90.$$

Therefore

35

$$A = A(x) = x\frac{90 - x}{2} = \frac{1}{2}(90x - x^2)$$

with domain $0 \leq x \leq 10$. Here, $A'(x) = 0$ when $x = 45$, but 45 doesn't lie in the domain of A. Note that $A(0) = 0$ and that $A(10) = 400$.

Case 3: $x \geq 10$, $0 \leq y \leq 5$. Then

$$x + (x - 10) + y = 85, \quad \text{so that} \quad 2x + y = 95.$$

Therefore

$$A = A(y) = y\frac{95 - y}{2} = \frac{1}{2}(95y - y^2)$$

with domain $0 \leq y \leq 5$. In this case, $A'(y) = 0$ when $y = 47.5$, but 47.5 isn't in the domain of A. Note that $A(0) = 0$ and that $A(5) = 225$.

Conclusion: The area of the pen is maximized when the pen is square, 25 meters on each side (the maximum from Case 1).

25. Suppose that n presses are used, $1 \leq n \leq 8$. The total cost of the poster run would then be

$$C(n) = 5n + (10 + 6n)\frac{50,000}{3600n}$$

$$= 5n + \frac{125}{9}(\frac{10}{n} + 6)$$

dollars. Temporarily assume that n can take on any real number value between 1 and 8. Then

$$C'(n) = 5 + \frac{125}{9}(-10n^{-2});$$

$C'(n) = 0$ when $n = \frac{5}{3}\sqrt{10}$, approximately 5.27

presses. But an integral number of presses must be used, so the actual number that will minimize the cost is either 5 or 6, unless the minimum occurs at one of the two end points. But the values in question are (approximately) $C(1) = 227$, $C(5) = 136.1$, $C(6) = 136.5$, and $C(8) = 141$. So to minimize cost and thereby maximize profit, five presses should be used.

28. We assume that each one-cent increase in price reduces sales by 50 wieners per night. Let x be the amount, in cents, by which the price is increased. The resulting profit is

$$P(x) = (50 + x)(5000 - 50x) - 25(5000 - 50x) - 100,000$$

$$= (25 + x)(5000 - 50x) - 100,000$$

$$= 25,000 + 3750x - 50x^2, \quad -50 \leq x.$$

Because $P(x) < 0$ for large x and for $x = -50$, P will be maximized where $P'(x) = 0$:

$$P'(x) = 2750 - 100x; \quad P'(x) = 0 \quad \text{when} \quad x = 37.5.$$

Now $P(37) = 953$, $P(37.5)$ is approximately 953.13, and $P(38) = 953$. Therefore profit is maximized when the selling price is either 87 or 88 cents, and will be $953.

31. Draw an isosceles triangle with horizontal base, representing a cross section of the cone through its axis. Inscribe a rectangle with vertical and horizontal sides; this represents a cross section of the cylinder through its axis. Let x be the radius of the cylinder and y its height. By similar triangles in your figure,

$$\frac{H}{R} = \frac{y}{R - x}, \quad \text{so that} \quad y = \frac{H}{R}(R - x).$$

We are to maximize the volume $V = \pi x^2 y$ of the cylinder, so we write

$$V = V(x) = \pi x^2 \frac{H}{R}(R - x) = \pi \frac{H}{R}(Rx^2 - x^3),$$

$0 \leq x \leq R$. Because $V(0) = 0 = V(R)$, V is maximized when $V'(x) = 0$; this leads to the equation $2xR = 3x^2$ and thus to the results $x = \frac{2}{3}R$ and $y = \frac{1}{3}H$.

34. Let (x,y) be the coordinates of the corner of the rectangle in the first quadrant. Then (by symmetry) the area of the rectangle is $A = (2x)(2y) = 4xy$. But from the equation of the ellipse we find that

$$y = \frac{3}{5}(25 - x^2)^{1/2},$$

so

$$A = A(x) = \frac{12}{5} x (25 - x^2)^{1/2}, \qquad 0 \leq x \leq 5.$$

We can simplify the algebra by maximizing instead

$$f(x) = \frac{25}{144} A^2 = 25x^2 - x^4;$$

$$f'(x) = 50x - 4x^3;$$

$$f'(x) = 0 \quad \text{when} \quad x = 0 \quad \text{and when} \quad x = \frac{5}{2}\sqrt{2}.$$

The value of $A(x)$ there is 30, while $A(0) = 0 = A(5)$. So the rectangle of maximum area has base $2x = 5\sqrt{2}$ and height $2y = 3\sqrt{2}$.

37. Let x and y be the two numbers. Then $x \geq 0$, $y \geq 0$, and $x + y = 16$. We are to find both the maximum and the minimum values of $x^{1/3} + y^{1/3}$. Because $y = 16 - x$, we seek the extrema of

$$f(x) = x^{1/3} + (16 - x)^{1/3}, \qquad 0 \leq x \leq 16.$$

Now

$$f'(x) = \frac{1}{3} x^{-2/3} - \frac{1}{3} (16 - x)^{-2/3}$$

$$= \frac{1}{3x^{2/3}} - \frac{1}{3(16 - x)^{2/3}};$$

$f'(x) = 0$ when $(16 - x)^{2/3} = x^{2/3}$, so that $16 - x = x$, and thus $x = 8$. Now $f(0) = 16^{1/3} = f(16)$, which is approximately 2.52, while $f(8) = 4$.

40. It suffices to minimize $x^2 + y^2$ given $y = (3x - 4)^{1/3}$. Let

$$f(x) = x^2 + (3x - 4)^{2/3}.$$

Then

$$f'(x) = 2x + (3x - 4)^{-2/3}.$$

38

Now $f'(x) = 0$ when

$$2x + \frac{1}{(3x - 4)^{2/3}} = 0;$$

$$2x(3x - 4)^{2/3} = -1;$$

$$8x^3(3x - 4) = -1.$$

By inspection, $x = 1$ is a solution of the last equation. Given that there is exactly one point on the given graph that is closest to the origin, we have found it: $(1,-1)$.

43. Set up a coordinate system in which the island is located at $(0,2)$ and the village at $(6,0)$, and let $(x,0)$ be the point at which the boat lands. It is clear that $0 \le x \le 6$. The trip involves the land distance $6 - x$ traveled at 20 kph and the water distance $(4 + x^2)^{1/2}$ traveled at 10 kph. The total time of the trip is then given by

$$T = T(x) = \frac{1}{10}(4 + x^2)^{1/2} + \frac{1}{20}(6 - x),$$

$0 \le x \le 6$. Now

$$T'(x) = \frac{x}{10(4 + x^2)^{1/2}} - \frac{1}{20}.$$

Thus $T'(x) = 0$ when $3x^2 = 4$; because $x \ge 0$, we choose the solution $x = \frac{2}{3}\sqrt{3}$. The value of T there is

$$\frac{1}{10}(3 + \sqrt{3}) \sim 0.473,$$

while $T(0) = 0.5$ and $T(6) = \frac{1}{10}\sqrt{10} \sim 0.632$. Therefore the boater should make landfall at $\frac{2}{3}\sqrt{3}$ km from the point on the shore closest to the island.

46. (a) $T = \frac{1}{c}(a^2 + x^2)^{1/2} + \frac{1}{v}\{(s - x)^2 + b^2\}^{1/2}.$

(b) $T'(x) = \frac{x}{c(a^2 + x^2)^{1/2}} - \frac{s - x}{v\{(s - x)^2 + b^2\}^{1/2}}.$

39

T'(x) = 0 when

$$\frac{x}{c(a^2 + x^2)^{1/2}} = \frac{s - x}{v\{(s - x)^2 + b^2\}^{1/2}} \, ;$$

$$\frac{x}{(a^2 + x^2)^{1/2}} \; \frac{\{(x - s)^2 + b^2\}^{1/2}}{s - x} = \frac{c}{v} \, ;$$

$$(\sin \alpha)(\csc \beta) = \frac{c}{v} \, ;$$

$$\frac{\sin \alpha}{\sin \beta} = \frac{c}{v} = n.$$

49. Let the horizontal piece of wood have length $L_1 = 2x$ and the vertical piece have length $L_2 = y + z$ where y is the length of the part above the horizontal piece and z is the length of the part below it. Then

$$y = (4 - x^2)^{1/2} \quad \text{and} \quad z = (16 - x^2)^{1/2}.$$

Also

$$y + z = \frac{x^2}{y} + \frac{x^2}{z} \, .$$

We multiply each side of the last equation by yz to obtain

$$y^2 z + yz^2 = x^2 z + x^2 y,$$

so that

$$yz(y + z) = x^2(y + z);$$

$$x^2 = yz;$$

$$x^4 = y^2 z^2 = (4 - x^2)(16 - x^2);$$

$$x^4 = 64 - 20x^2 + x^4;$$

$$20x^2 = 64;$$

$$x = \frac{4}{5}\sqrt{5} \, .$$

With this value of x, we find that

$$y = \frac{2}{5}\sqrt{5} \quad \text{and} \quad z = \frac{8}{5}\sqrt{5}.$$

Therefore $L_1 = \frac{8}{5}\sqrt{5}$ and $L_2 = \frac{10}{5}\sqrt{5}$ for maximum area.

Section 3.6

1. $f(x) = 3(\sin x)^2$, so $f'(x) = 6\sin x \cos x$.

4. $f'(x) = x^{1/2}\cos x + \frac{1}{2}x^{-1/2}\sin x$.

10. $g'(t) = 3(2 - \cos^2 t)(2\cos t \sin t)$.

16. $h'(\xi) = \dfrac{2\xi \cos \xi \sin \xi + 3\cos^2 \xi}{\xi^4}$.

22. $g'(t) = \frac{1}{2}t^{-1/2}\cos^3 3t - 9t^{1/2}\cos^2 3t \sin 3t$

28. $f'(x) = 4\sin 2x \cos 2x \sin^3 3x \sin^4 4x$

$$+ \ 9\sin^2 2x \sin^2 3x \cos 3x \sin^4 4x$$

$$+ \ 16\sin^2 2x \sin^3 3x \sin^3 4x \cos 4x.$$

34. The area A of the rectangle is $4xy$, but $x = \cos \xi$ and $y = \sin \xi$, so

$$A = A(\xi) = 4\sin \xi \cos \xi, \quad 0 \leq \xi \leq \pi/2.$$

Now $A'(\xi) = 4(\cos^2 \xi - \sin^2 \xi) = 4\cos 2\xi$, so $A'(\xi) = 0$ when $\cos 2\xi = 0$ where $0 \leq 2\xi \leq \pi$. It follows that $2\xi = \pi/2$, so $\xi = \pi/4$. But $A(0) = 0 = A(\pi/2)$ and $A(\pi/4) = 2$, so the latter is the largest possible area of a rectangle inscribed in the unit circle.

37. The figure at the top of the next page shows a cross section of the sphere-with-cone through the axis of the cone and a diameter of the sphere. Note that $h = r \tan \xi$ and that

$$\cos \xi \;=\; \frac{R}{h - R} \cdot$$

Therefore

$$h \;=\; R \,+\, R \sec \xi,$$

and thus

$$r \;=\; \frac{R \,+\, R \sec \xi}{\tan \xi} \,.$$

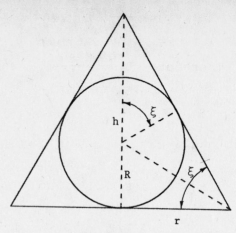

Now $V = \frac{1}{3}\pi r^2 h,$ so for $0 < \xi < \pi/2$ we have

$$V \;=\; V(\xi) \;=\; \frac{1}{3}\,\pi R^3\, \frac{(1 \,+\, \sec \xi)^3}{\tan^2 \xi}\,.$$

Therefore

$$V'(\xi) \;=\; \frac{\pi R^3}{3\tan^4 \xi}\,\{(\tan^2 \xi)(1 \,+\, \sec \xi)^2 \sec \xi \tan \xi$$

$$-\; (1 \,+\, \sec \xi)^3 (2\tan \xi \sec^2 \xi)\}.$$

For $V'(\xi) = 0$ we must have either $\sec \xi = -1$ (that is, $\xi = \pi,$ which we reject), or $\sec \xi = 0$ (which has no solutions), or $\tan \xi = 0$ (so that either $\xi = 0$ or $\xi = \pi,$ which we also reject), or -- writing $\sec^2 \xi - 1$ in place of $\tan^2 \xi$ --

$$3(\sec^2 \xi \,-\, 1) \,-\, 2\sec \xi \,-\, 2\sec^2 \xi \;=\; 0;$$

$$\sec^2 \xi \,-\, 2\sec \xi \,-\, 3 \;=\; 0.$$

Therefore $\sec \xi = 3$ or $\sec \xi = -1.$ We reject the latter as before, and find that $\sec \xi = 3,$ so that ξ is about 0.9449 (radians). The resulting minimum volume of the cone is $\frac{8}{3}\pi R^3.$

40. See the figure at the top of the next page, in which $r = 15$ (cm). The area of the small triangle is $2r^2 \cos^3 \xi \sin \xi$ and the area of the rectangle is

$(2r - 4r\cos^2\xi)(2r\cos\xi\sin\xi)$

$= 4r^2(1 - 2\cos^2\xi)(\sin\xi\cos\xi).$

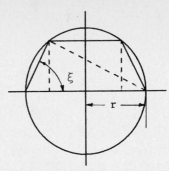

Therefore (after simplifications) the area of the hexagon is

$$A = A(\xi) = 8r^2\sin^3\xi\cos\xi,$$

$0 \leq \xi \leq \pi/2.$ After more simplifications we find that

$$\frac{dA}{d\xi} = 8r^2(\sin^2\xi)(4\cos^2\xi - 1).$$

Now $dA/d\xi = 0$ when $\sin\xi = 0$ and when $\cos\xi = 1/2$. When $\sin\xi = 0$, $A = 0$; also, $A(0) = 0 = A(\pi/2)$. Therefore A is maximal when $\cos\xi = 1/2$: $\xi = \pi/3$. When this happens, we find that $\alpha = 2\pi/3$ and also that $\beta = \pi - \xi = 2\pi/3$. Therefore the figure of maximal area is a regular hexagon.

43. The values you obtain in part (a) should be similar to the ones shown in the table that follows.

$\xi°$	$\dfrac{\sin\xi°}{\xi}$
10	0.017364818
5	0.017431149
1	0.017452406
0.5	0.017453071
0.1	0.017453284
0.05	0.017453290
0.01	0.017453292

For part (b), replace $\xi°$ by $\dfrac{\xi\pi}{180}$ (radians), then compute the limit. You should obtain $\pi/180$, which is approximately 0.0174533, in accord with the data above.

Section 3.7

1. $u = 2x - x^2$, $r = 1/2$.

4. $u = x^2 - 4x + 1$, $r = 3/2$; $f'(x) = \dfrac{3}{2}(x^2 - 4x + 1)^{1/2}(2x - 4)$.

7. $u = \dfrac{x + 1}{x^2 - 16}$, $r = 4$.

10. $\dfrac{dy}{dx} = \dfrac{dy}{du} \cdot \dfrac{du}{dx}$

$\qquad = -\dfrac{1}{2}u^{-2} + \dfrac{2}{3}u^{-3}$ (2)

$\qquad = -(2x + 1)^{-2} + \dfrac{4}{3}(2x + 1)^{-3}$.

16. $\dfrac{dy}{dx} = -\dfrac{2x^4 - 4x + 8}{(2x^3 + x^2 - 4x)^2}$.

22. $\dfrac{dy}{dx} = \dfrac{-2x \sin 2x - \cos 2x}{x^2}$.

25. $\dfrac{dy}{dx} = (2\cos 2x)(\cos 3x) + (\sin 2x)(-3\sin 3x)$

$\qquad = 2\cos 2x \cos 3x - 3\sin 2x \sin 3x$.

28. $y = \{\cos(x^{1/2})\}^{1/2}$:

$\qquad \dfrac{dy}{dx} = \dfrac{1}{2}\{\cos(x^{1/2})\}^{-1/2}\{-\sin(x^{1/2})\}\{\dfrac{1}{2}x^{-1/2}\}$

$\qquad\qquad = -\dfrac{1}{4}x^{-1/2}\{\sec(x^{1/2})\}^{1/2}\sin(x^{1/2})$.

34. $y = \{\cos(x^3)\}^3$:

$\qquad \dfrac{dy}{dx} = 3\{\cos(x^3)\}^2\{-\sin(x^3)\}\{3x^2\}$

$\qquad\qquad = -9x^2\cos^3(x^3)\sin(x^3)$.

40. $\dfrac{dy}{dx} = 2x\cos(1/x) - \dfrac{x^2}{x^2}\cos(1/x) = (2x - 1)\cos(1/x)$.

46. $\dfrac{dy}{dx} = \{\cos(1 + \sqrt{\sin x})\}\{\dfrac{1}{2}(\sin x)^{-1/2}\cos x\}$.

49. If the circle has area A and radius r, then $A = \pi r^2$.
If t denotes time (in seconds), then we are given dr/dt = 2
at the time in question. But

$$\frac{dA}{dt} \;=\; \frac{dA}{dr} \cdot \frac{dr}{dt}$$

$$=\; (2\pi r)(2) \;=\; 4\pi r,$$

so when r = 10 (inches), the area of the circle is increasing
at 40π square inches per second.

52. Let x denote the length of each side of the triangle. Then
its altitude is $x\sqrt{3}$, so its area is $A = \frac{1}{2}x^2\sqrt{3}$.
Therefore the rate of change of its area with respect to time
t (in seconds) is

$$\frac{dA}{dt} \;=\; x\sqrt{3}\;\frac{dx}{dt}\,.$$

We are given x = 10 and dx/dt = 2, so at that point the
area is increasing at $20\sqrt{3}$ square inches per second.

55. G'(t) = {f'(h(t))}h'(t).   When t = 1, h(t) = 4 and
h'(t) = -6.   But f'(4) = 3, so G'(1) = (3)(-6).

58. Let V denote the volume of the balloon and r its radius at
time t (in seconds). We are given $dV/dt = 200\pi$.   Now

$$\frac{dV}{dt} \;=\; \frac{dV}{dr} \cdot \frac{dr}{dt} \;=\; 4\pi r^2\,\frac{dr}{dt}\,.$$

When r = 5, we have $200\pi = (4\pi)(25)(dr/dt)$, and so
dr/dt = 2.   Answer: When r = 5 (cm), the radius of the
balloon is increasing at 2 cm/sec.

61. Let V denote the volume of the snowball and A its surface
area at time t (in hours).   Then

$$\frac{dV}{dt} \;=\; kA \qquad \text{and} \qquad A \;=\; cV^{2/3}$$

(the latter because A is proportional to r^2 while V is
proportional to r^3).   Therefore

$$\frac{dV}{dt} = \alpha V^{2/3} \quad \text{and thus} \quad \frac{dt}{dV} = \beta V^{-2/3}$$

(α and β are constants). From the last equation we may conclude that $t = \gamma V^{1/3} + \delta$ for some constants γ and δ, so that $V = V(t) = (Pt + Q)^3$ for some constants P and Q. From the information $500 = V(0) = Q^3$ and $250 = V(1) = (P + Q)^3$, we find that $Q = 5\sqrt[3]{4}$ and that $P = (-5)(\sqrt[3]{4} - \sqrt[3]{4})$. Now $V(T) = 0$ when $PT + Q = 0$; it turns out that

$$T = \frac{2^{1/3}}{2^{1/3} - 1},$$

approximately 4.8473. Therefore the snowball finishes melting at about 2:50:50 P.M. of the same day.

Section 3.8

In Problems 1 - 46, y' is an abbreviation for dy/dx.

1. $2x - 2yy' = 0$: $y' = \dfrac{x}{y}$.

4. $3x^2 + 3y^2y' = 0$: $y' = -\dfrac{x^2}{y^2}$.

7. $\dfrac{2}{3}x^{-1/3} + \dfrac{2}{3}y^{-1/3}y' = 0$: $y' = -\sqrt[3]{y/x}$.

10. $2(x^2 + y^2)(2x + 2yy') = 4xy' + 4y$:

$$\{(2x^2 + 2y^2)(2y) - 4x\}y' = 4y - 4x(x^2 + y^2);$$

$$\frac{dy}{dx} = \frac{y - x^3 - xy^2}{x^2y + y^3 - x}.$$

13. $x^2y' + 2xy = 1$, so $y' = \dfrac{1 - 2xy}{x^2}$. At $(2,1)$ the tangent has slope $-\dfrac{3}{4}$ and thus equation

$$y - 1 = -\frac{3}{4}(x - 2).$$

16. $-\dfrac{1}{(x + 1)^2} - \dfrac{y'}{(y + 1)^2} = 0$:

$$y' = -\frac{(y + 1)^2}{(x + 1)^2}.$$

At $(1,1)$ the tangent line has slope -1 and thus equation $y - 1 = -(x - 1)$.

19. $-3x^{-4} - 3y^{-4}y' = 0$: $y' = -\dfrac{y^4}{x^4}$.   At $(1,1)$ the tangent line has slope -1 and thus equation

$$y - 1 = -(x - 1).$$

22. Here we have $y^5 + 5xy^4y' + 5x^4y + x^5y' = 0$, so

$$y' = -\frac{y^5 + 5x^4y}{x^5 + 5xy^4}.$$

A fraction can be zero only when its numerator is zero, so $y' = 0$ only if

$$y^5 + 5x^4y = y(y^4 + 5x^4) = 0.$$

This will hold only if $y = 0$ or if $y^4 + 5x^4 = 0$, so in either case $y = 0$. But there are no points on the graph of $xy^5 + x^5y = 1$ corresponding to $y = 0$. Therefore the graph has no horizontal tangents.

25. Here we obtain

$$y' = \frac{2 - x}{y - 2},$$

so horizontal tangents can occur only if $x = 2$ and $y \neq 2$. When $x = 2$, the equation $x^2 + y^2 = 4x + 4y$ becomes $y^2 - 4y - 4 = 0$, which yields $y = 2 + \sqrt{8}$ and $y = 2 - \sqrt{8}$. Thus we obtain two points at which the tangent line is horizontal.

28. Here,

$$\frac{dy}{dx} = \frac{y - 2x}{2y - x} \quad \text{and} \quad \frac{dx}{dy} = \frac{2y - x}{y - 2x}.$$

47

For horizontal tangents, $y = 2x$, and from the original equation $x^2 - xy + y^2 = 9$ it follows upon substitution of $y = 2x$ that $x^2 = 3$. So the tangent line is horizontal at $(\sqrt{3}, 2\sqrt{3})$ and at $(-\sqrt{3}, -2\sqrt{3})$. For vertical tangents, $x = 2y$, and (as above) it turns out at $y^2 = 3$; there are vertical tangents at $(2\sqrt{3}, \sqrt{3})$ and $(-2\sqrt{3}, -\sqrt{3})$.

31. We maximize $f(x,y) = x^2 + y^2$ given $(x^2 + y^2)^2 = 4xy$. Implicit differentiation leads to $y' = -x/y = -y/x$. Thus we have either $x^2 = y^2$, $x = 0$, or $y = 0$. In the latter cases we are dealing with the origin itself, certainly not the answer. The equation of the lemniscate shows that x and y cannot have opposite signs, so $x = y$, which yields the two farthest points: $(1,1)$ and $(-1,-1)$.

34. $1 - y' = 0$ and $2x + y + xy' + 2yy' = 0$:

$$1 = y' = -\frac{2x + y}{x + 2y}.$$

It follows that $y = -x$, so that $x^2 = 16 = y^2$. We obtain the two critical points $(4,-4)$ and $(-4,4)$, and the result that the maximum value of $x - y$ is 8 and its minimum value is -8.

37. We are to minimize $(x - 2)^2 + (y - 2)^2$ given the constraint $x^3 + y^3 = 6xy$. First show that the method of auxiliary variables leads to

$$y' = \frac{2y - x^2}{y^2 - 2x} = -\frac{x - 2}{y - 2}.$$

Then show that the equation $x^2y + 4y = xy^2 + 4x$ follows. The trick for solving this equation is to write it in the form

$$x^2y - xy^2 = 4x - 4y,$$

so that

$$xy(x - y) = 4(x - y).$$

Thus $y = x$ or $xy = 4$. With the aid of the equation of the folium, you discover the critical points $(0,0)$ and $(3,3)$ when

48

$y = x$, and critical points corresponding to the two solutions of $x^3 = 12 + 4\sqrt{5}$, $x^3 = 12 - 4\sqrt{5}$ when $xy = 4$, approximately $(2.756, 1.451)$ and $(1.451, 2.756)$. The corresponding values of $(x - 2)^2 + (y - 2)^2$ are 8, 2, and about 0.8735, so both the latter points are closest to the point $(2,2)$.

40. Let x be the radius of the cylinder (also one side of the rectangle) and y its height (the other side of the rectangle). Maximize $\pi x^2 y$ given $x + y = 18$: $2xy + x^2 y' = 0$ and $1 + y' = 0$. Thus $y' = -1$, and so the maximum occurs at a solution of $2xy = x^2$; surely not $x = 0$, so that $x = 2y$. From the constraint we find $y = 6$ and $x = 12$, so the maximum possible volume is $\pi(12)^2(6) = 864\pi$.

43. Let x be the length of the two ends (perpendicular to the wall) and thus also the length of the divider; let y be the length of the side parallel to the wall. Maximize area $A = xy$ given $3x + y = 600$. The method yields the equations

$$y + xy' = 0 \qquad \text{and} \qquad 3 + y' = 0,$$

and so $y = 3x = 300$: $x = 100$, $y = 300$, and the maximum possible area is $30,000$ square meters.

46. Draw a cross section of the sphere-with-cylinder through the axis of the cylinder, which of course coincides with a diameter of the sphere. Let x denote the radius of the cylinder and y its height. Your cross section shows a circle with an inscribed rectangle; draw a diagonal of the rectangle. This is also a diameter of the sphere, so it has length $2R$. Thus by the Pythagorean theorem, $4x^2 + y^2 = 4R^2$. This will be the constraint on maximizing the volume $V = \pi x^2 y$ of the inscribed cylinder. The method of auxiliary variables yields

$$8x + 2yy' = 0 \qquad \text{and} \qquad x^2 y' + 2xy = 0,$$

so that

$$y' = -\frac{4x}{y} = -\frac{2xy}{x^2}.$$

Consequently $4x^3 = 2xy^2$. Because $x \neq 0$ at the maximum, we find that the condition $2x^2 = y^2$ clearly maximizes V, and so $y = x\sqrt{2}$.

49. Maximize the volume $V = \frac{1}{3}\pi r^2 h$ of the cone given the constraint $r^2 + h^2 = 100$. Choosing r as the independent variable and h as the dependent variable yields the equations

$$\frac{2}{3}\pi rh + \frac{1}{3}\pi r^2 \frac{dh}{dr} = 0,$$

$$2r + 2h\frac{dh}{dr} = 0;$$

$$\frac{dh}{dr} = -\frac{r}{h} = -\frac{2rh}{r^2};$$

so $r^3 = 2rh^2$. Because $r \neq 0$ at maximum, we find that $r^2 = 2h^2$, and it follows that the dimensions

$$h = \frac{10}{3}\sqrt{3}, \quad r = \frac{10}{3}\sqrt{6}$$

yield the maximum volume $V = \frac{2000}{27}\pi\sqrt{3}$.

Section 3.9

1. $2x\frac{dx}{dt} + 2y\frac{dy}{dt} = 0; \quad y = -x\frac{dx/dt}{dy/dt}$

$$= -\frac{(3)(-4)}{6} = 2.$$

4. $2(\sin x \cos x)\frac{dx}{dt} - 2(\cos y \sin y)\frac{dy}{dt} = 0;$

$$x = y = \frac{\pi}{4} \quad \text{and} \quad \frac{dx}{dt} = 0.1.$$

Therefore

$$2\frac{1}{2}(0.1) = 2\frac{1}{2}\frac{dy}{dt}, \quad \text{and so} \quad \frac{dy}{dt} = 0.1.$$

7.   Suppose that the pile has height h = h(t) at time t (sec)
     and radius r = r(t).   We are given h = 2r, and we know
     that the volume of the pile at time t is

$$V \;=\; V(t) \;=\; \frac{\pi}{3}\, r^2 h \;=\; \frac{2}{3}\, \pi r^3.$$

Now $\dfrac{dV}{dt} \;=\; \dfrac{dV}{dr}\,\dfrac{dr}{dt}$,   so $10 \;=\; 2\pi r^2\,\dfrac{dr}{dt}$.

When h = 5,   r = 2.5;   at that time,

$$\frac{dr}{dt} \;=\; \frac{10}{2\pi(5/2)^2} \;=\; \frac{20}{25\pi} \;=\; \frac{4}{5\pi}\,,$$

approximately 0.25465 feet per second.

10. In the diagram below, x is the distance from the ostrich to the
     street light and u is the distance from the tip of the ostrich's
     shadow to the base of the street light.

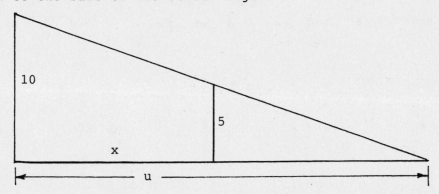

We are to find du/dt and

$$D_t\,(u - x) \;=\; \frac{du}{dt} \;-\; \frac{dx}{dt}\,.$$

Now $\dfrac{u}{10} \;=\; \dfrac{u - x}{5}$,   so u = 2x.   Therefore

$$\frac{du}{dt} \;=\; 2\,\frac{dx}{dt} \;=\; (2)(-4) \;=\; -8;$$

$$\frac{du}{dt} \;-\; \frac{dx}{dt} \;=\; -8 \;-\; (-4) \;=\; -4.$$

Answers: (a) +8 ft/sec;   (b) +4 ft/sec.

13. Let r denote the radius of the balloon and V its volume at time t (in seconds). Then

$$V = \frac{4}{3} \pi r^3, \quad \text{so} \quad \frac{dV}{dt} = 4\pi r^2 \frac{dr}{dt}.$$

We are to find dr/dt when r = 10, and we are given the information that dV/dt = 100π.   Therefore

$$100\pi = 4\pi(10)^2 \frac{dr}{dt},$$

and so at the time in question the radius is increasing at the rate of dr/dt = 1/4 = 0.25 centimeters per second.

16. Locate the observer at the origin and the balloon at (300,y) where y = y(t) is its altitude.   Let ξ be the angle of elevation of the balloon (in radians) from the observer's point of view.   Then $\tan \xi = \frac{y}{300}$, and we are given dξ/dt = π/180 rad/sec. Here we are to find dy/dt when ξ = π/4; y = 300 tan ξ, so

$$\frac{dy}{dt} = (300 \sec^2 \xi) \frac{d\xi}{dt}.$$

Substitution of the known values of ξ and dξ/dt yields the answer

$$\frac{dy}{dt} = (300)(2) \frac{\pi}{180} = \frac{10\pi}{3},$$

approximately 10.472 ft/sec.

19. Here we take a = 10, so that $V = \frac{1}{3} \pi y^2 (30 - y)$.
So

$$-100(0.1337) = \frac{dV}{dt} = \pi(20y - y^2) \frac{dy}{dt}.$$

Thus $\frac{dy}{dt} = - \frac{13.37}{\pi y (20 - y)}$.

Substitution of y = 7 and y = 3 yields the two answers.

22. Let x be the length of the base of the rectangle and y its
     height. We are given $dx/dt = +4$ and $dy/dt = -3$, with
     units in centimeters and seconds. The area of the rectangle is
     $A = xy$, so

$$\frac{dA}{dt} = x\frac{dy}{dt} + y\frac{dx}{dt} = -3x + 4y.$$

     Therefore when $x = 20$ and $y = 12$, we have $dA/dt = -12$,
     so the area of the rectangle is decreasing at 12 cm^2/sec.

25. Locate the radar station at the origin and the rocket at $(4,y)$
     at time t, with y in miles and t in hours. The distance
     z between the station and the rocket satisfies the equation
     $y^2 + 16 = z^2$, so

$$2y\frac{dy}{dt} = 2z\frac{dz}{dt}.$$

     When $z = 5$, we have $y = 3$, and because $dz/dt = 3600$ it
     follows that $dy/dt = 6000$ mph.

28. Let x be the distance between the Pinta and the island at
     time t and y the distance between the Niña and the island
     then. We know that $x^2 + y^2 = z^2$ where $z = z(t)$ is
     the distance between the two ships, so

$$2z\frac{dz}{dt} = 2x\frac{dx}{dt} + 2y\frac{dy}{dt}.$$

     When $x = 30$ and $y = 40$, $z = 50$.   It follows from the last
     equation that $dz/dt = -25$ then.   Answer: They are drawing
     closer at 25 mph then.

31. Let r be the radius of the water surface at time t and h
     the height of the water remaining at time t.   If Q is the
     amount of water remaining in the tank at time t, then because
     the water forms a cone, $Q = Q(t) = \frac{1}{3}\pi r^2 h$.   But by similar
     triangles, $r/h = 3/5$, so $r = 3h/5$.   Thus

$$Q(t) = \frac{1}{3}\pi\frac{9}{25}h^3 = \frac{3}{25}\pi h^3.$$

     We are given $dQ/dt = -0.02$ when $h = 3$.   This implies that when h = 3,

$$-0.02 = \frac{dQ}{dt} = \frac{9}{25} \pi h^2 \frac{dh}{dt}.$$

So at the time in question,

$$\frac{dh}{dt} = -\frac{1}{50} \frac{25}{81\pi} = -\frac{1}{162\pi},$$

approximately -0.001965 ft/sec, about -0.0236 in./sec.

34. Let x denote the distance between the ship and A, y the distance between the ship and B, h the perpendicular distance from the position of the ship to the line AB, u the distance from A to the foot of this perpendicular, and v the distance from B to the foot of the perpendicular. At the time in question, we know that x = 10.4, dx/dt = 19.2, y = 5, and dy/dt = -0.6. From the right triangles involved, we see that

$$u^2 + h^2 = x^2 \quad \text{and} \quad (12.6 - u)^2 + h^2 = y^2.$$

Therefore

$$x^2 - u^2 = y^2 - (12.6 - u)^2. \qquad (*)$$

We take x = 10.4 and y = 5 in this equation; it follows that u = 9.6 and that v = 12.6 - u = 3. From (*), we know that

$$x\frac{dx}{dt} - u\frac{du}{dt} = y\frac{dy}{dt} + (12.6 - u)\frac{du}{dt},$$

so

$$\frac{du}{dt} = \frac{1}{12.6} (x\frac{dx}{dt} - y\frac{dy}{dt}).$$

From the data given, du/dt is approximately 16.0857. Also h = $(x^2 - u^2)^{1/2}$ = 4, h(dh/dt) = x(dx/dt) - u(du/dt), so

$$4\frac{dh}{dt} = (10.4)(19.2) - (9.6)(16.0857),$$

and therefore dh/dt is approximately 11.3143. Finally, $\frac{dh/dt}{du/dt}$ is approximately 0.7034, so the ship is sailing a course about $35° 7'$ north <u>or</u> south of east at a speed of $\{(du/dt)^2 + (dy/dt)^2\}^{1/2} \sim 19.67$ mph. It is located 9.6 miles east and four miles north or south of A, or 10.4 miles from A at a bearing of either $67° 22' 48''$ or $112° 37' 12''$.

37. Let r denote the radius of the conical pile and h its height. Then $r = 3h$, and so the volume of the pile is $V = 3\pi h^3$. We are given $dV/dt = 120\pi$, so

$$120\pi = \frac{dV}{dt} = 9\pi h^2 \frac{dh}{dt}.$$

When $h = 20$, we therefore have $120\pi = 3600\pi \frac{dh}{dt}$, and thus when the pile is 20 feet high, its altitude is increasing at 1/30 of a foot per second -- two feet per minute.

3.10

The equals mark will be used throughout this section in many places where it is obvious that an approximation is the intent. Your results may differ in the last decimal place or two because of differences in calculators or method of solution.

1. $x_0 = 2.2$; we use $f(x) = x^2 - 5$. Then
    $x_1 = 2.236363636$,
    $x_2 = 2.236067997$,
    $x_3 = 2.236067978$,
    $x_4 = 2.236067978$.

4. Let $f(x) = x^{3/2} - 10$. Then $x_0 = 4.628863603$. From the iterative formula

$$x \longleftarrow x - \frac{x^{3/2} - 10}{(3/2)x^{1/2}}$$

we obtain
    $x_1 = 4.641597575$,
    $x_2 = 4.641588834$,
    $x_3 = 4.641588834$.

7. $x_0 = -0.5$; $x_1 = -0.81$, $x_2 = -0.74496$, $x_2 = -0.74024$, $x_3 = -0.7402217826$, $x_4 = -0.7402217821 = x_5$.

10. Let $f(x) = x^2 - \sin x$. Then $f'(x) = 2x - \cos x$. The interpolation formula in (4) yields $x_0 = 0.7956861008$, and the iterative formula

$$x \longleftarrow x - \frac{x^2 - \sin x}{2x - \cos x}$$

(with calculator in <u>radian</u> mode) yields these results:

$$x_1 = 0.8867915207,$$
$$x_2 = 0.8768492470,$$
$$x_3 = 0.8767262342,$$
$$x_4 = 0.8767262154 = x_5.$$

13. With $x_0 = 2.188405797$ and the iterative formula

$$x \longleftarrow x - \frac{x^4(x + 1) - 100}{x^3(5x + 4)},$$

we get $x_1 = 2.36$, $x_2 = 2.339638357$, $x_3 = 2.339301099$, $x_4 = 2.339301008 = x_5$.

16. Because $7\pi/2$ (approximately 10.9956) and 4π (approximately 12.5663) are the nearest discontinuities of $f(x) = x + \tan x$, this function has the intermediate value property on the interval $11 \leq x \leq 12$. Because $f(11) = -214.95$ and $f(12) = 11.364$, the equation $f(x) = 0$ has a solution in that interval. We obtain $x_0 = 11.94978618$ by interpolation, and the iteration

$$x \longleftarrow = x - \frac{x + \tan x}{1 + \sec^2 x}$$

of Newton's method yields the successive approximations

$$x_1 = 7.457596948,$$
$$x_2 = 6.180210620,$$
$$x_3 = 3.157913273,$$
$$x_4 = 1.571006986;$$

after many more iterations we arrive at the answer 2.028757838 of Problem 15. The problem is caused by the fact that $f(x)$ is generally a very large number, so the above iteration tends to alter the value of x excessively. A little experimentation yields the fact that $f(11.08)$ is approximately -0.736577 and $f(11.09)$ is approximately 0.531158. We begin anew on the better interval $11.08 \leq x \leq 11.09$, and obtain

$$x_0 = 11.08581018,$$
$$x_1 = 11.08553759,$$
$$x_2 = 11.08553841 = x_3.$$

19. $x_0 = 1.538461538,$ $x_1 = 1.932798309,$ $x_2 = 1.819962709,$
    $x_3 = 1.802569044,$ $x_4 = 1.802191039,$ $x_5 = 1.802190864,$
    $x_6 = 1.802190864.$ Slow convergence because $f'(x_6)$ is large.

22. (b) With $x_0 = 1.5$ we obtain the successive approximations
    $1.610123,$ $1.586600,$ $1.584901,$ $1.584893,$ and $1.584893.$

25. Here we take $x \longleftarrow (\{(ax)^{1/2}\}^{1/2})^{1/2}$ (it converges more
    rapidly than the equally correct $x \longleftarrow (a/x^3)^{1/4}$). With
    $x_0 = 1$ and $a = 10$, we obtain $1.333521,$ $1.382372,$ $...,$ and
    after several more iterations $1.389495494.$

In the remaining problems, we will take advantage of the following facts
about real zeros of polynomials with real coefficients. Suppose that

$$P(x) = a_n x^n + a_{n-1} x^{n-1} + ... + a_2 x^2 + a_1 x + a_0$$

is a polynomial of degree n. Then $P(x) = 0$ has no more than n
real solutions. Every solution lies between $-M$ and M, where

$$M = |a_n|(|a_n| + |a_{n-1}| + ... + |a_2| + |a_1| + |a_0|).$$

---

28. $-2.414213562,$ $0.4142135624,$ and 2

34. 0.8241323123 and -0.8241323123

40. For graphical reasons the smallest positive solution of $f(x) = 0$
    (where $f(x) = x - \tan x$) is between π and $3\pi/2$. With
    initial guess $x = 4.5$ we obtain $4.493613903,$ $4.493409655,$
    $4.493409458,$ and $4.493409458.$

43. From the given formula and the figure to the right we obtain first the equation

$$\frac{1}{3} \pi (1 + x)^2 (3 - 1 - x)$$

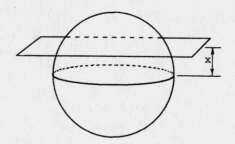

$$= \frac{2}{3} \pi (1 - x)^2 (3 - 1 + x),$$

and it follows that

$$(1 + x)^2 (2 - x)$$

$$= 2(1 - x)^2 (2 + x).$$

We expand the squared terms, collect like powers of x, and the equation $3x^3 - 9x + 2 = 0$ follows. With $x_0 = 0.25$, Newton's method yields the sequence 0.2259259259, 0.2260737086, 0.2260737138, 0.2260737138.   To four places, x = 0.2261.

Chapter 3 Miscellaneous Problems

1. $\dfrac{dy}{dx} = 2x - \dfrac{6}{x^3}$.

4. $\dfrac{dy}{dx} = \dfrac{5}{2} (x^2 + 4x)^{3/2} (2x + 4) = 5(x + 2)(x^2 + 4x)^{3/2}$.

7. $\dfrac{dy}{dx} = 4(3x - \dfrac{1}{2} x^{-2})^3 (3 + x^{-3})$.

10. $y = (5x^6)^{-1/2}$: $\dfrac{dy}{dx} = -\dfrac{1}{2} (5x^6)^{-3/2} (30x^5)$

$$= -\frac{15x^5}{5x^6 (5x^6)^{1/2}} = -\frac{3}{x(5x^6)^{1/2}}.$$

13. $\dfrac{dy}{dx} = \dfrac{dy}{du} \dfrac{du}{dx} = \dfrac{-2u}{(1 + u^2)^2} \dfrac{-2x}{(1 + x^2)^2}$.

Now $1 + u^2 = 1 + \dfrac{1}{(1 + x^2)^2} = \dfrac{x^4 + 2x^2 + 2}{(1 + x^2)^2}$.

So

$$\frac{dy}{du} = (-2u) \frac{1}{(1 + u^2)^2} = \frac{-2}{1 + x^2} \cdot \frac{(1 + x^2)^4}{(x^4 + 2x^2 + 2)^2}$$

$$= \frac{-2(1 + x^2)^3}{(x^4 + 2x^2 + 2)^2} .$$

Therefore

$$\frac{dy}{dx} = \frac{-2(1 + x^2)^3}{(x^4 + 2x^2 + 2)^2} \cdot \frac{-2x}{(1 + x^2)^2} = \frac{4x(1 + x^2)}{(x^4 + 2x^2 + 2)^2} .$$

16. $\dfrac{dy}{dx} = \dfrac{15x^4 - 8x}{2(3x^5 - 4x^2)^{1/2}} .$

19. $2x^2 y \dfrac{dy}{dx} + 2xy^2 = 1 + \dfrac{dy}{dx} ,$ so

$$\frac{dy}{dx} = \frac{1 - 2xy^2}{2x^2 y - 1} .$$

22. $\dfrac{dy}{dx} = \dfrac{(x^2 + \cos x)(1 + \cos x) - (x + \sin x)(2x - \sin x)}{(x^2 + \cos x)^{26}}$

$$= \frac{1 - x^2 - x \sin x + \cos x + x^2 \cos x}{(x^2 + \cos x)^2} .$$

28. $\dfrac{dy}{dx} = \dfrac{3(1 + x^{1/2})^2}{2x^{1/2}} (1 - 2x^{1/3})^4$

$$+ 4(1 - 2x^{1/3})^3 (-\frac{2}{3} x^{-2/3})(1 + x^{1/2})^3.$$

31. $\dfrac{dy}{dx} = (\sin^3 2x)(2)(\cos 2x)(-\sin 3x)(3) + (\cos^2 3x)(3 \sin^2 2x)(2 \cos 2x)$

$$= 6(\cos 3x \sin^2 2x)(\cos 3x \cos 2x - \sin 2x \sin 3x)$$

$$= 6 \cos 3x \cos 5x \sin^2 2x.$$

34. $(x + y)^3 = (x - y)^2,$ so

$$3(x + y)^2 (1 + \frac{dy}{dx}) = 2(x - y)(1 - \frac{dy}{dx}); \quad \text{thus}$$

59

$$\frac{dy}{dx} = \frac{2(x - y) - 3(x + y)^2}{3(x + y)^2 + 2(x - y)}$$

$$= \frac{2(x + y)^{3/2} - 3(x + y)^2}{3(x + y)^2 + 2(x + y)^{3/2}}$$

$$= \frac{2 - 3(x + y)^{1/2}}{2 + 3(x + y)^{1/2}} .$$

37. $1 = (2\cos 2y)\dfrac{dy}{dx}$, so $\dfrac{dy}{dx} = \dfrac{1}{2\cos 2y}$.

Because dy/dx is undefined at $(1, \pi/4)$, there is probably a vertical tangent there; sure enough, $dx/dy = 0$ at $(1, \pi/4)$. Therefore the tangent line has equation $x = 1$.

40. $V(x) = \dfrac{1}{3}\pi(36x^2 - x^3)$:

$$V'(x) = \frac{1}{3}\pi(72x - 3x^2) = \pi x(24 - x).$$

Now $\dfrac{dV}{dt} = \dfrac{dV}{dx}\dfrac{dx}{dt}$; when $x = 6$, $36\pi = -(180\pi)\dfrac{dx}{dt}$,

so $dx/dt = -1/3$ inches per second. Answer: At $1/3$ in/sec.

43. $g(x) = x^{-1/2}$, $f(x) = x^2 + 25$.

46. $g(x) = x^{10}$, $f(x) = \dfrac{x + 1}{x - 1}$.

$$h'(x) = -\frac{20(x + 1)^9}{(x - 1)^{11}} .$$

49. $\dfrac{dV}{dS}\dfrac{dS}{dr} = \dfrac{dV}{dr}$. Now $V = \dfrac{4}{3}\pi r^3$ and $S = 4\pi r^2$, so

$$\frac{dV}{dS}(8\pi r) = 4\pi r^2; \quad \text{therefore} \quad \frac{dV}{dS} = \frac{r}{2} = \frac{1}{4}\sqrt{S/\pi} .$$

52. Current production per well: 200 (bbl/day). Number of new wells: x $(x \geq 0)$. Production per well: $200 - 5x$. Total production:

$$T = T(x) = (20 + x)(200 - 5x), \quad 0 \leq x \leq 40.$$

60

$T(x) = 4000 + 100x - 5x^2$, so $T'(x) = 100 - 10x$. $T'(x) = 0$ when $x = 10$. $T(0) = 4000$, $T(40) = 0$, and $T(10) = 4500$. So $x = 10$ maximizes $T(x)$. Answer: Ten new wells should be drilled, thereby increasing total production from 4000 bbl/day to 4500 bbl/day.

55. Let one sphere have radius r and the other have radius s. We are to find the extrema of

$$A = 4\pi(r^2 + s^2) \quad \text{given} \quad \frac{4}{3}\pi(r^3 + s^3) = V,$$

a constant. The method of auxiliary variables:

$$\frac{dA}{dr} = 4\pi(2r + 2s\frac{ds}{dr});$$

$dA/dr = 0$ yields $ds/dr = -(r/s)$.

$$\frac{4}{3}\pi(3r^2 + 3s^2\frac{ds}{dr}) = 0,$$

so

$$3r^2 + 3s^2(-r/s) = 0;$$

$$r^2 - rs = 0.$$

Therefore $r = 0$ or $r = s$. Also, ds/dr is undefined when $s = 0$. So we check these three critical points. If $r = 0$ or if $s = 0$, then there is only one sphere, with radius and surface area

$$r = (3V/4\pi)^{1/3} \quad \text{and} \quad A = (36\pi V^2)^{1/3},$$

respectively. If $r = s$, then there are two spheres of equal size, each with radius and surface area

$$r = \frac{1}{2}(3V/\pi)^{1/3} \quad \text{and} \quad A = (72\pi V^2)^{1/3},$$

respectively. Therefore, for maximum surface area, make two equal spheres. For minimum surface area, make only one sphere.

58. Let x denote the length of the two sides of the corral that are perpendicular to the wall. There are two cases to consider.

Case 1: Part of the fence is used. Let y be the length of the side of the corral parallel to the fence. Then $y = 400 - 2x$, and we are to maximize area

$$A = xy = x(400 - 2x), \quad 150 \le x \le 200.$$

Then $A'(x) = 400 - 4x$; $A'(100) = 0$, but $x = 100$ is not in the domain of A. Note that $A(150) = 15,000$ and that $A(200) = 0$.

Case 2: All of the fence is used. Let y be the length of fence added to one end of the wall, so that the side parallel to the wall has length $100 + y$. Then $100 + 2y + 2x = 400$, so that $y = 150 - x$. We are to maximize area

$$A = xy = x(150 - x), \quad 0 \le x \le 150.$$

In this case $A'(x) = 0$ when $x = 125$. Now $A(150) = 15,000$, $A(0) = 0$, and $A(125) = 15,625$.

Answer: The maximum area is 15,625 square feet; to attain it, use all the existing wall and build a square corral.

61. Let x be the width of the base of the box, so that the base has length 2x; let y be the height of the box. Then the volume of the box is $V = 2x^2 y$, and in order that its total surface area be 54 square feet, we require $2x^2 + 6xy = 54$. Therefore the volume of the box is given by

$$V = V(x) = 2x^2 \frac{27 - x^2}{3x} = \frac{2}{3}(27x - x^3),$$

$0 < x \le 3\sqrt{3}$. Now $V'(x) = 0$ when $x^2 = 9$, so that $x = 3$. Also $V(0) = 0$, so even though $x = 0$ is not in the domain of $V(x)$, the continuity of $V(x)$ implies that $V(x)$ is near zero for x near zero. Finally, $V(3\sqrt{3}) = 0$, so $V(3) = 36$ (cubic feet) is the maximum possible volume of the box.

64. The square of the length of PQ is a function of x, say

$$G(x) = (x - x_0)^2 + (y - y_0)^2,$$

which we are to minimize given the constraint

$$C(x) = y - f(x) = 0.$$

Now

$$\frac{dG}{dx} = 2(x - x_0) + 2(y - y_0)\frac{dy}{dx}$$

and

$$\frac{dC}{dx} = \frac{dy}{dx} - f'(x).$$

When both vanish, $f'(x) = dy/dx = -(x - x_0)/(y - y_0)$. The line containing P and Q has slope

$$(y - y_0)/(x - x_0) = -\frac{1}{f'(x)},$$

and therefore it is normal to the graph at Q.

67. As the diagram to the right suggests, we are to minimize the sum of the lengths of the two diagonals. Fermat's principle of least time may be applied here, so we know

that the angles at which the roads meet the shore are equal, and thus so are the tangents of those angles:

$$\frac{x}{1} = \frac{6 - x}{2}.$$

It then follows that the pier should be built two miles from the point on the shore nearest the first town and four miles from the point on the shore nearest the second town. A short computation is sufficient to show that this is actually the global minimum.

70. Write v for v_0 throughout. We have

$$R = R(\xi) = \frac{v^2}{16}\sqrt{2}\,(\cos\xi\sin\xi - \cos^2\xi)$$

for $\frac{\pi}{4} \le \xi \le \frac{\pi}{2}$. Now

$$R'(\xi) = \frac{v^2}{16}\sqrt{2}\,(\cos^2\xi - \sin^2\xi + 2\sin\xi\cos\xi);$$

$R'(\xi) = 0$ when $\cos 2\xi + \sin 2\xi = 0$, so that $\tan 2\xi = -1$.

It follows that $\xi = 3\pi/8$ (67.5°). This yields the maximum range because $R(\pi/4) = 0 = R(\pi/2)$.

73. Iterate $x \longleftarrow x - \dfrac{x^5 - 75}{5x^4}$. Results: $x_0 = 2.20379147$,

2.39896311, 2.37206492, 2.37144094, 2.37144061. Answer: 2.3714.

76. Linear interpolation gives $x_0 = -1/3$. We iterate

$$x \longleftarrow x - \frac{x^3 - 4x - 1}{3x^2 - 4}$$

to obtain the sequence of improving approximations -0.2525252525, -0.2541011930, -0.2541016884. Answer: -0.2541.

79. Linear interpolation gives $x_0 = -0.5854549279$. If you got -0.9996955062 instead, it's because your calculator was set in degree mode rather than radian mode. Note also that a quick look at the graphs of $y = -x$ and $y = \cos x$ shows that the equation $x + \cos x = 0$ has exactly one solution in the interval $-2 \le x \le 0$. We use the Newton's method formula: We iterate

$$x \longleftarrow x - \frac{x + \cos x}{1 - \sin x}$$

and obtain -0.7451929664, -0.7390933178, -0.7390851332, -0.7390851332. Answer: -0.7391.

82. Let $f(x) = 5(x + 1) - \cos x$. Then $f'(x) = 5 + \sin x$, and we iterate the Newton's method formula

$$x \longleftarrow x - \frac{f(x)}{f'(x)}.$$

Linear interpolation yields the initial estimate -0.8809986055, and successive approximations are -0.8712142932, -0.8712215145, and -0.8712215145. Answer: -0.8712.

85. Let $f(x) = x^5 - 3x^3 + x^2 - 23x + 19$. Then $f(-3) = -65$, $f(0) = 19$, $f(1) = -5$, and $f(3) = 121$. So there are at least three, and at most five, real solutions. Newton's method

produces three real solutions, specifically -2.2722493355,
0.8012614801, and 2.309976541. If one (laboriously) divides
the polynomial $f(x)$ by $(x - r_1)(x - r_2)(x - r_3)$ where r_1,
r_2, and r_3 are these three real solutions, one obtains the
quotient polynomial $x^2 + (0.38874466)x + 3.770552031$, which has
no real zeros -- the quadratic formula yields the two complex roots
$-0.194372333 + (1.932038153)i$ and $-0.194372333 - (1.932038153)i$.
Consequently we have found all three real solutions.

88. We factor:
$$z^{3/2} - x^{3/2} = (z^{1/2})^3 - (x^{1/2})^3$$

$$= (z^{1/2} - x^{1/2})(z + z^{1/2}x^{1/2} + x)$$

and

$$z - x = (z^{1/2})^2 - (x^{1/2})^2$$

$$= (z^{1/2} - x^{1/2})(z^{1/2} + x^{1/2}).$$

Therefore

$$\frac{z^{3/2} - x^{3/2}}{z - x} = \frac{z + z^{1/2}x^{1/2} + x}{z^{1/2} + z^{1/2}}$$

$$\rightarrow \frac{3x}{2x^{1/2}} = \frac{3}{2}x^{1/2} \quad \text{as} \quad z \rightarrow x.$$

91. The balloon has volume $V = \frac{4}{3}\pi r^3$ and surface area $A = 4\pi r^2$
where r is its radius, and V, A, and r are all functions of
time t. We are given $dV/dt = +10$, and we are to find dA/dt
when $r = 5$.

$$\frac{dV}{dt} = 4\pi r^2 \frac{dr}{dt}, \quad \text{so} \quad 10 = 4\pi(25)\frac{dr}{dt}.$$

Thus

$$\frac{dr}{dt} = \frac{10}{100\pi} = \frac{1}{10\pi}.$$

Also

$$\frac{dA}{dt} = 8\pi r \frac{dr}{dt},$$

so at the time in question,

$$\frac{dA}{dt} = (8\pi)(4)\frac{1}{10\pi} = 4.$$

Answer: At 4 square inches per second.

94. Let x denote the distance from plane A to the airport, y the distance from plane B to the airport, and z the distance between the two aircraft. Then

$$z^2 = x^2 + y^2 + (3-2)^2 = x^2 + y^2 + 1$$

and $\frac{dx}{dt} = -500.$ Now

$$2z\frac{dz}{dt} = 2x\frac{dx}{dt} + 2y\frac{dy}{dt},$$

and when $x = 2$, we have $y = 2$; therefore $z = 3$ at that time. Therefore, at that time,

$$(3)(-600) = (2)(-500) + (2)\frac{dy}{dt},$$

and thus $\frac{dy}{dt} = -400.$ Answer: Its speed is 400 mph.

97. Write b for x_0 and c for y_0, so that $P = P(b,c)$. The straight line through $P(b,c)$ and $Q(a,a^2)$ has slope

$$\frac{a^2 - c}{a - b} = 2a,$$

a consequence of the two-point formula for slope and the fact that the line is tangent to the parabola $y = x^2$ at $Q(a,a^2)$. Hence $a^2 - 2ab + c = 0$. Think of this as a quadratic equation in the unknown a. It has two real solutions when the discriminant $b^2 - c > 0$, and this establishes the conclusion in Part (b). There are no real solutions when $b^2 - c < 0$, and this is enough to establish the conclusion in Part (c). What if $b^2 - c = 0$?

Section 4.2

4. $dy = -\dfrac{1}{(x - x^{1/2})^2}(1 - \dfrac{1}{2}x^{-1/2})\,dx.$

10. $dy = (x^2\cos x + 2x\sin x)\,dx.$

66

16. $dy = -3(1 + \cos 2x)^{1/2}(\sin 2x)dx.$

22. Let $f(x) = x^{1/2}$. Then $f'(x) = \frac{1}{2}x^{-1/2}$. Take $x = 100$ and $\Delta x = 2$ in the linear approximation formula to obtain

$$\sqrt{102} = f(x + \Delta x) \sim f(x) + f'(x)\Delta x$$

$$= (100)^{1/2} + \frac{2}{2\sqrt{100}} = 10.1.$$

25. Let $f(x) = x^{1/4}$; then $f'(x) = \frac{1}{4}x^{-3/4}$. Let $x = 16$ and let $\Delta x = -1$. Then

$$(15)^{1/4} = f(x + \Delta x)$$

$$\sim f(x) + f'(x)\Delta x$$

$$= (16)^{1/4} + \frac{1}{4(16)^{3/4}}(-1)$$

$$= 2 - \frac{1}{32} = \frac{63}{32} = 1.96875.$$

The true value is approximately 1.96798967.

28. Let $f(x) = \sin x$; then $f'(x) = \cos x$. Let $x = \pi/6$ and let $\Delta x = \pi/90$ (2°). Then

$$\sin(32°) = \sin(x + \Delta x)$$

$$\sim \sin x + (\cos x)\Delta x = \sin(\pi/6) + (\pi/90)\cos(\pi/6)$$

$$= \frac{1}{2} + \frac{\pi}{180}\sqrt{3} \sim 0.53023.$$

Note that the first approximation involves the mathematical error in using the tangent line to approximate the value of the function, while the second approximation involves calculator roundoff error.

31. Let $f(x) = \sin x$; then $f'(x) = \cos x$. Let $x = \pi/2$ and let $\Delta x = -\pi/90$ (-2°). Then

$$\sin(88°) = \sin(x + \Delta x)$$

$$\sim \sin x + (\cos x)\Delta x = \sin(\pi/2) - (\pi/90)\cos(\pi/2)$$

$$= 1 - 0 = 1.00000.$$

The true value is approximately 0.99939.

34. $\frac{2}{3}x^{-1/3}dx + \frac{2}{3}y^{-1/3}dy = 0$:

$$y^{-1/3}dy = -x^{-1/3}dx;$$

$$\frac{dy}{dx} = -x^{-1/3}y^{1/3} = -(y/x)^{1/3}.$$

37. Given: $x\sin y = 1$.

$$x(\cos y)dy + (\sin y)dx = 0;$$

$$x(\cos y)dy = -(\sin y)dx;$$

$$\frac{dy}{dx} = -\frac{\sin y}{x\cos y} = -\frac{\tan y}{x}.$$

40. The relationship between the surface area A and the radius r of the sphere is $A = 4\pi r^2$, and hence $dA = 8\pi r\, dr$. Thus $\Delta A \sim 8\pi r\, \Delta r$. With $r = 5$ and $\Delta r = 0.2$ we obtain $\Delta A \sim 8\pi(5)(0.2) = 8\pi \sim 25.1327$ square inches. The true value is approximately 25.6354 square inches.

46. With circumference C and radius r, we have $C = 2\pi r$. So, given $\Delta r = +10$, $\Delta C \sim 20\pi$ (feet). Thus the wire should be lengthened approximately 63 feet.

49. With surface area S and radius r, we have $S = 2\pi r^2$, so that $dS = 4\pi r\, dr \sim 4\pi(100)(0.01) = 4\pi$. That is, $\Delta S \sim 12.57$ square meters.

Section 4.3

1. $f'(x) > 0$ for all x, so f is increasing for all x.

68

4. $f'(x) = 8x + 8 = 8(x + 1)$. Therefore f is increasing for
    $x > -1$ and decreasing for $x < -1$.

7. $f'(x) = 4x^3 - 4x = 4x(x + 1)(x - 1)$. The intervals on which
    $f'(x)$ cannot change sign are $x < -1$, $-1 < x < 0$, $0 < x < 1$,
    and $1 < x$. Because $f'(-2) = -24$, $f'(-0.5) = 1.5$,
    $f'(0.5) = -1.5$, and $f'(2) = 24$, we may conclude that f is
    increasing if $-1 < x < 0$ or if $x > 1$, decreasing for $x < -1$
    and for $0 < x < 1$.

10. Note that f is continuous for all x, as is

    $$f'(x) = \frac{2x^2 + 1}{(x^2 + 1)^{1/2}} \; ;$$

    also, $f'(x) > 0$ for all x. Hence f is increasing for all x.

13. After simplifications,

    $$f'(x) = \frac{2(x - 1)(x - 3)}{(x^2 - 3)^2} \; .$$

    The intervals on which $f'(x)$ cannot change sign are $x < -\sqrt{3}$,
    $-\sqrt{3} < x < 1$, $1 < x < \sqrt{3}$, $\sqrt{3} < x < 3$, and $3 < x$. Now
    $f'(-2) = 30$, $f'(0) = 2/3$, $f'(1.5) = -8/3$, $f'(2) = -2$, and
    $f'(4) = 6/169$. Therefore f is increasing for $x < -\sqrt{3}$,
    $-\sqrt{3} < x < 1$, and $3 < x$; f is decreasing for $1 < x < \sqrt{3}$
    and for $\sqrt{3} < x < 3$.

16. $f(-3) = 81 - 81 = 0 = f(3)$, f is continuous everywhere, and
    $f'(x) = 18x - 4x^3$ exists for all x, including all x in the
    interval $(-3,3)$. Thus f satisfies the hypotheses of Rolle's
    theorem. To find what value or values c might assume, we solve
    the equation $f'(c) = 0$ to obtain the three values $c = 0$,
    $c = \frac{3}{2}\sqrt{2}$, and $c = -\frac{3}{2}\sqrt{2}$. All three of these numbers
    lie in the interval $(-3,3)$, so these are the three possible
    values for the number c whose existence is guaranteed by Rolle's
    theorem.

19. On the interval $(-1,0)$, $f'(x) = 1$; on the interval $(0,1)$,
    we have $f'(x) = -1$. Because f is not differentiable at

$x = 0$, it does not satisfy the hypotheses of Rolle's theorem, so there is no guarantee that the equation $f'(x) = 0$ has a solution -- and, indeed, it has no solution in $(-1,1)$.

22. It is clear that f satisfies the hypotheses of the mean value theorem, for every polynomial is continuous and differentiable everywhere. To find c, we solve

$$f'(c) = \frac{f(1) - f(-1)}{1 - (-1)} :$$

thus $3c^2 = 2/2 = 1$, with the two solutions $c = 1/\sqrt{3}$ and $c = -1/\sqrt{3}$. Both these numbers lie in the interval $-1 \leq x \leq 1$, so each is an answer to the problem.

25. First, $f'(x) = \frac{2}{3}(x - 1)^{-1/3}$ is defined on $(1,2)$; moreover, f is continuous for $1 \leq x \leq 2$ (the only "problem point" is $x = 1$). To find c, we solve

$$f'(c) = \frac{2}{3(c - 1)^{1/3}} = \frac{f(2) - f(1)}{2 - 1} = \frac{1 - 0}{1} = 1.$$

This leads to the equation $(c - 1)^{1/3} = 2/3$, and thereby $c = 35/27$. Note that $35/27$ does lie in the given interval.

28. Because f is not differentiable at $x = 1$, the hypotheses of the mean value theorem do not hold. The only values of $f'(x)$ are 1 (for $x > 1$) and -1 (for $x < 1$). Neither of these is equal to the average slope of f on the interval $0 \leq x \leq 3$:

$$\frac{f(3) - f(0)}{3 - 0} = \frac{3 - 2}{3} = \frac{1}{3},$$

so the conclusion of the theorem also fails to hold.

31. Let $f(x) = x^5 + 2x - 3$. Then $f'(x) = 5x^4 + 2$, so $f'(x) > 0$ for all x. This means that f is an increasing function, and therefore f can have at most one zero in any interval. To show that f has at least one zero in the interval $0 \leq x \leq 1$, it is sufficient to notice that $f(1) = 0$.

34. Because $f'(0)$ does not exist, the function $f(x) = x^{2/3}$ does not satisfy the hypotheses of the mean value theorem on the given

interval. But consider the equation

$$f'(c) = \frac{f(27) - f(-1)}{27 - (-1)} ; \tag{*}$$

that is,

$$\frac{2}{3c^{1/3}} = \frac{9 - 1}{28} = \frac{2}{7} ,$$

which leads to $c^{1/3} = 7/3$, and thus to $c = 343/27$, which is approximately 12.7. Because $-1 < c < 27$, there is indeed a number c in $(-1, 27)$ satisfying Eq. (*) above.

37. Proof: Suppose that $f'(x)$ is a polynomial of degree $n - 1$ on the interval $I = \{x \mid a \le x \le b\}$. Then $f'(x)$ has the form

$$f'(x) = a_{n-1}x^{n-1} + a_{n-2}x^{n-2} + \dots + a_2 x^2 + a_1 x + a_0$$

where $a_{n-1} \ne 0$. Note that $f'(x)$ is the derivative of the function

$$g(x) = \frac{1}{n} a_{n-1}x^n + \dots + \frac{1}{2} a_1 x^2 + a_0 x.$$

By Corollary 2, $f(x)$ and $g(x)$ can differ only by a constant, and this is sufficient to establish that $f(x)$ must also be a polynomial, and one of degree n because the coefficient of x^n in $f(x)$ is nonzero.

40. Let $f(x) = x^7 + x^5 + x^3 + 1$. Then $f(-1) = -2$, $f(1) = 4$, and $f'(x) = 7x^6 + 5x^4 + 3x^2$. Now $f'(x) > 0$ for all x except that $f'(0) = 0$, so f is increasing on the set of all real numbers. This information together with the fact that f (continuous) has the intermediate value property establishes that the equation $f(x) = 0$ has exactly one solution (approximately -0.79130272).

43. The average slope of the graph of f on the given interval is

$$\frac{f(2) - f(-1)}{2 - (-1)} = \frac{5 - (-1)}{3} = 2$$

and f satisfies the hypotheses of the mean value theorem there. Therefore $f'(c) = 2$ for some number c, $-1 < c < 2$. This

71

implies that the tangent line to the graph of f at the point (c,f(c)) has slope 2 and is therefore parallel to the line with equation y = 2x because the latter line also has slope 2.

Section 4.4

1. f'(x) = 2x - 4; x = 2 is the only critical point. Because f'(x) > 0 for x > 2 and f'(x) < 0 for x < 2, it follows that f(2) = 1 is the global minimum value of f(x).

4. f'(x) = 3x² - 3 = 3(x + 1)(x - 1), so x = 1 and x = -1 are the only critical points. If x < -1 or if x > 1, then f'(x) > 0, while f'(x) < 0 on (-1,1). So f(-1) = 7 is a local maximum value while f(1) = 3 is a local minimum.

7. f'(x) = -6(x - 5)(x + 2); f'(x) < 0 if x < -2 and if x > 5, while f'(x) < 0 for -2 < x < 5. Hence f(-2) = -58 is a local minimum value of f(x) and f(5) = 285 is a local maximum value.

10. f'(x) = 15x²(x + 1)(x - 1), so f'(x) > 0 if x < -1 and if x > 1, while f'(x) < 0 on (-1,0) and on (0,1). Therefore f(0) = 0 is not an extremum of f(x), but f(-1) = 2 is a local maximum value and f(1) = -2 is a local minimum value.

13. Here,

$$f'(x) = 2x - \frac{2}{x^2} = \frac{2(x^3 - 1)}{x^2}$$

$$= \frac{2(x - 1)(x^2 + x + 1)}{x^2}.$$

Because x² + x + 1 > 0 for all x, the only critical point is x = 1; note that f is not defined at x = 0. Also f'(x) has the sign of x - 1, so f'(x) > 0 for x > 1 and f'(x) < 0 for 0 < x < 1 and for x < 0. Consequently f(1) = 3 is a local minimum value of f(x). It is not a global minimum; check the behavior of f(x) for x negative and near zero.

16. Because $f'(x) = \frac{1}{3} x^{-2/3}$, f'(x) > 0 for all x except

72

for x = 0, where f is continuous but f'(x) is not defined.
Consequently f has no extrema.   Examination of the behavior of
f(x) and f'(x) for x near zero makes it clear that the graph
of f has a vertical tangent at (0,4).

19. Let us minimize

$$g(x) = (x - 3)^2 + (3 - 2x - 2)^2$$

$$= (x - 3)^2 + (1 - 2x)^2,$$

the square of the distance of (x,y) on the line 2x + y = 3
from the point (3,2).   We have

$$g'(x) = 2(x - 3) - 4(1 - 2x) = 10x - 10,$$

so x = 1 is the only critical point of g(x).   If x > 1 then
g'(x) > 0, while g'(x) < 0 for x < 1.   Thus x = 1 minimizes
g(x), and so the point on the line 2x + y = 3 closest to the
point (3,2) is (1,1).   As an independent check, note that the
slope of the line segment joining (3,2) and (1,1) is 1/2,
while the slope of the line 2x + y = 3 is -2, so the segment
and the line are perpendicular, as implied by a theorem from plane
geometry.

22. If the radius of the base of the pot is r and its height is h
(inches), then we are to minimize the total surface area A given
the constraint $\pi r^2 h = 125$.   Thus $h = 125/(\pi r^2)$, and so

$$A = \pi r^2 + 2\pi rh = A(r) = \pi r^2 + \frac{250}{r}, \quad r > 0.$$

Now

$$A'(r) = 2\pi r - \frac{250}{r^2};$$

A'(r) = 0 when $r^3 = 125/\pi$, so that $r = 5/\sqrt[3]{\pi}$.   The latter
point is the only value of r at which A'(r) can change sign
(for r > 0), and it is easy to see that A'(r) is positive when
r is large positive, while A'(r) is negative when r is near
zero.   Therefore we have located the global minimum of A(r), and
it occurs when the pot has radius $r = 5/\sqrt[3]{\pi}$ inches and
height $h = 5/\sqrt[3]{\pi}$ inches. Thus the pot will have its radius
equal to its height, each approximately 3.414 inches.

73

25. If the sides of the rectangle are x and y, then $xy = 100$, so that $y = 100/x$. Therefore the perimeter of the rectangle is

$$P = P(x) = 2x + \frac{200}{x}, \quad 0 < x.$$

Then

$$P'(x) = 2 - \frac{200}{x^2};$$

$P'(x) = 0$ when $x = 10$ (-10 is not in the domain of $P(x)$). Now $P'(x) < 0$ on $(0,10)$ and $P'(x) > 0$ for $x > 10$, and so $x = 10$ minimizes $P(x)$. A little thought about the behavior of $P(x)$ for x near zero and for x large makes it clear that we have found the global minimum value for P: $P(10) = 40$. When $x = 10$, also $y = 10$, so the rectangle of minimal perimeter is indeed a square.

28. Let r denote the radius of the can and h its height (in centimeters). We are to minimize its total surface area $A = 2\pi r^2 + 2\pi rh$ given the constraint $xr^2h = V = 16\pi$. First we note that $h = V/(\pi r^2)$, so we minimize

$$A = A(r) = 2\pi r^2 + \frac{2V}{r}, \quad r > 0.$$

Now

$$A'(r) = 4\pi r - \frac{2V}{r^2};$$

$A'(r) = 0$ when $4\pi r^3 = 2V = 32\pi$ -- that is, when $r = 2$. Now $A(r)$ is decreasing on $(0,2)$ and increasing for $r > 2$, so the global minimum of $A(r)$ occurs when $r = 2$, for which $h = 4$.

31. Let $(x,y) = (x,x^2)$ denote an arbitrary point on the curve. The square of its distance from $(0,2)$ is then

$$f(x) = x^2 + (x^2 - 2)^2.$$

Now $f'(x) = 2x(2x^2 - 3)$, and therefore $f'(x) = 0$ when $x = 0$, when $x = -\sqrt{3/2}$, and when $x = +\sqrt{3/2}$. Now $f'(x) < 0$ if $x < -\sqrt{3/2}$ and if $0 < x < \sqrt{3/2}$; $f'(x) > 0$ if $-\sqrt{3/2} < x < 0$ and if $x > \sqrt{3/2}$. Therefore $x = 0$ yields a local maximum for f; the other two zeros of $f'(x)$ yield its global minimum. Answer: There are exactly two points on the curve that are nearest $(0,2)$; they are $(+\sqrt{3/2}, 3/2)$ and $(-\sqrt{3/2}, 3/2)$.

34. Let y be the height of the cylindrical part and x the length of the radii of both the cylinder and the hemisphere. The total surface area is

$$A = \pi x^2 + 2\pi xy + 2\pi x^2 = 3\pi x^2 + 2\pi xy.$$

But the can must have volume $V = \pi x^2 y + \frac{2}{3}\pi x^3$, so

$$y = \frac{1000 - (2\pi x^3)/3}{\pi x^2}.$$

Therefore

$$A = A(x) = \frac{5}{3}\pi x^2 + \frac{2000}{x}, \quad x > 0.$$

Thus

$$\frac{dA}{dx} = \frac{10}{3}\pi x - \frac{2000}{x^2}.$$

Now $dA/dx = 0$ when $x = (600/\pi)^{1/3} \sim 5.7588$. Because $dA/dx < 0$ for smaller values of x and $dA/dx > 0$ for larger values, we have found the point at which $A(x)$ attains its global minimum value. After a little arithmetic, we find that $y = x$, so the radius of the hemisphere and the radius and height of the cylinder should all be equal to $(600/\pi)^{1/3}$ to attain minimal surface area.

This argument contains the implicit assumption that $y > 0$. If $y = 0$, then

$$x = (1500/\pi)^{1/3} \sim 7.8159, \quad \text{for which}$$

$$A = (150)(18\pi)^{1/3} \sim 575.747 \text{ cubic inches.}$$

But with $x = y = (600/\pi)^{1/3}$, we have

$$A = (100)(45\pi)^{1/3} \sim 520.940 \text{ cubic inches.}$$

So the solution in the first paragraph indeed yields the dimensions of the can requiring the least amount of material.

37. If the pyramid has base edge length x and altitude y, then its volume is $V = \frac{1}{3}x^2 y$. From Fig. 4.20 we see also that

$$\frac{2y}{x} = \tan \xi \quad \text{and} \quad \frac{a}{y-a} = \cos \xi$$

where ξ is the angle that each side of the pyramid makes with its base. It follows, successively, that

$$\left(\frac{a}{y-a}\right)^2 = \cos^2 \xi;$$

$$\sin^2 \xi = 1 - \cos^2 \xi = \frac{(y-a)^2 - a^2}{(y-a)^2}$$

$$= \frac{y^2 - 2ay}{(y-a)^2} = \frac{y(y-2x)}{(y-a)^2}.$$

$$\sin \xi = \frac{\{y(y-2a)\}^{1/2}}{y-a}.$$

$$y = \frac{x}{2}\frac{\sin \xi}{\cos \xi} = \frac{x}{2}\frac{\{y(y-2a)\}^{1/2}}{y-a}\frac{y-a}{a};$$

$$2y = \frac{x}{a}\sqrt{(y-2a)}.$$

$$x^2 = \frac{4a^2 y^2}{y(y-2a)}.$$

Therefore

$$V = \frac{1}{3}x^2 y = V(y) = \frac{4a^2 y^2}{3(y-2a)}, \quad y > 2a.$$

Now

$$\frac{dV}{dy} = \frac{24a^2 y(y-2a) - 12a^2 y^2}{9(y-2a)^2};$$

The condition $dV/dy = 0$ then implies that $2(y-2a) = y$, and thus that $y = 4a$. Consequently the minimum volume of the pyramid is

$$V(4a) = \frac{(4a^2)(16a^2)}{(3)(2a)} = \frac{32}{3}a^3.$$

The ratio of the volume of the smallest pyramid to that of the sphere is then

$$\frac{32/3}{4\pi/3} \;=\; \frac{32}{4\pi} \;=\; \frac{8}{\pi}.$$

Section 4.5

4. $f'(x) = 6x^2 + 6x - 12 = 6(x + 2)(x - 1)$ is positive for $x > 1$ and for $x < -2$, negative for $-2 < x < 1$. So there is a local maximum at $(-2, 20)$, a local minimum at $(1, -7)$. There are intercepts at (about) $(-3.312, 0)$, $(1.812, 0)$, and (exactly) $(0, 0)$; the graph is shown below, on the left.

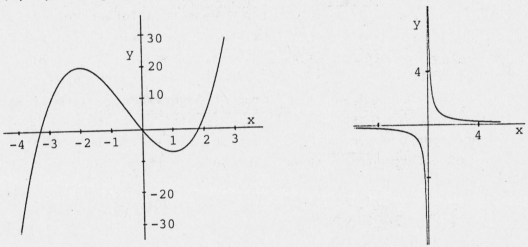

10. $f'(x) = 2(x - 2)(2x + 3)(4x - 1)$: Local minima at $(-1.5, 0)$ and at $(2, 0$, local maximum at $(0.25, 37.515625)$.

16. $f'(x) = -1/x^2$ is negative for all $x \neq 0$, so the function is decreasing for all $x \neq 0$; there is an infinite discontinuity at $x = 0$. There are no extrema and no intercepts. The graph is shown above, on the right.

22. $f'(x) = 3(x - 1)^2$ is positive except at $x = 1$, so the graph is increasing for all x; there are no extrema, and the intercepts are at $(0, -1)$ and $(1, 0)$.

28. $f'(x) = 4x^2(x - 3)$, so f is increasing for $x > 3$, decreasing for $x < 3$. So there is a local (and global) minimum at $(3, -27)$; $(0, 0)$ and $(4, 0)$ are the only intercepts. There is a horizontal tangent at $(0, 0)$ but no extremum there.

34. After simplifications, we find that

$$f'(x) = \frac{2 - 3x}{3x^{2/3}(2 - x)^{1/3}},$$

so $f'(x) = 0$ when $x = 2/3$ and $f'(x)$ does not exist at $x = 0$ and at $x = 2$. The graph is increasing for $x < 2/3$ and for $x > 2$, decreasing for $2/3 < x < 2$. There is a vertical tangent at $(0,0)$, which is not an extremum. There's a horizontal tangent at $(2/3, 1.058)$ (ordinate approximate), which is a local maximum. There is a cusp at $(2,0)$, which is also a local minimum. Note that $f(x) \sim x$ for $|x|$ large; this aids in constructing the global sketch of the graph.

40. Let $f(x) = x^5 - 5x^3 - 20x + 17$. We seek solutions of $f(x) = 0$. Now $f'(x) = 5(x^2 + 1)(x + 2)(x - 2)$, so f is increasing for $x > 2$ and for $x < -2$, decreasing for $-2 < x < 2$. Also $f(-3) = -31$, $f(-2) = 65$, $f(2) = -31$, and $f(3) = 65$. Because f has the intermediate value property everywhere, there is at least one zero of $f(x)$ for $x < -2$, at least one in $(-2,2)$, and at least one for $x > 2$. But the increasing-decreasing structure of the graph shows that there is at most one zero in each of those three intervals. Therefore $f(x) = 0$ has precisely three solutions. (They are approximately -2.859047924, 0.754757713, and 2.636263512.)

This seems a good spot to introduce Descartes' Rule of Signs. In a sequence of nonzero numbers, such as

-3, -5, 2, 4, -1, 6, 6, 6, -2, -2, 12
          *   *   *   *   *

there are five <u>sign</u> <u>changes</u>, marked with asterisks. If some terms of such a sequence are zero, they are simply disregarded in counting the number of sign changes; thus the sequence

2, 0, 0, -3, -4, 0, 0, 0, 2, 3, -4, 0, 0
             *   *   *

has three sign changes. <u>Descartes'</u> <u>Rule</u> <u>of</u> <u>Signs</u> is a classical theorem that states that the number of positive real roots of a polynomial equation with real coefficients, in the form

$$p(x) = a_0 x^n + a_1 x^{n-1} + \ldots + a_{n-1}x + a_n = 0,$$

is never greater than the number of sign changes in the sequence

$$a_0, \quad a_1, \quad a_2, \quad \ldots, \quad a_{n-1}, \quad a_n,$$

and if less, then is less by an even number. For example, the equation

$$f(x) = x^5 - 5x^3 - 20x + 17 = 0$$

has the sequence 1, 0, -5, 0, -20, 17 of coefficients, which has two sign changes. Consequently this equation has either two or zero positive solutions. If we replace x by -x, we can (usually) count the number of negative solutions as well:

$$f(-x) = -x^5 + 5x^3 + 20x + 17 = 0$$

has one sign change, and therefore exactly one positive solution, whose negative is a (in fact, the <u>only</u>) negative solution of the original equation. So the original equation has exactly one negative real solution and either zero or two positive real solutions. This, together with the intermediate value property of continuous functions, gives an alternative method of showing that the equation of Problem 40 has exactly three real solutions.

Section 4.6

1. $8x^3 - 9x^2 + 6$, $24x^2 - 18x$, $48x - 18$

4. $2t + \dfrac{1}{2}(t+1)^{-1/2}$, $2 - \dfrac{1}{4}(t+1)^{-3/2}$, $\dfrac{3}{8}(t+1)^{-5/2}$

10. $\dfrac{8z}{(x^2+4)^2}$, $\dfrac{32 - 24z^2}{(x^2+4)^3}$, $\dfrac{96z^3 - 384z}{(z^2+4)^4}$

16. Given: $x^2 + y^2 = 4$.

$$2x + 2yy' = 0, \quad \text{so} \quad y' = -\frac{x}{y}.$$

$$y'' = -\frac{y - xy'}{y^2} = -\frac{y + (x^2/y)}{y^2}$$

$$= -\frac{y^2 + x^2}{y^3} = -\frac{4}{y^3}.$$

22. $\sin^2 x + \cos^2 y = 1$:

$$2\sin x \cos x - 2y'\sin y \cos y = 0;$$

$$y' = \frac{\sin x \cos x}{\sin y \cos y}.$$

$\dfrac{d^2 y}{dx^2}$ can be simplified (with the aid of the original equation) to

$$\frac{\cos^2 x \sin^2 y - \sin^2 x \cos^2 y}{\sin^3 y \cos^3 y}.$$

28. $f'(x) = 4x^3$; $f''(x) = 12x^2$. The only critical point and the only possible inflection point is $(0,0)$. The second derivative does not identify this point as a local maximum or minimum, and it is not an inflection point because f'' does not change sign there. (It is, of course, the location of the global minimum of f.)

34. Given: $f(x) = 12x - x^3$. Then $f'(x) = 3(2 - x)(2 + x)$ and $f''(x) = -6x$. So the graph is increasing for $-2 < x < 2$ and decreasing for $|x| > 2$, concave upward for $x < 0$ and concave downward for $x > 0$. It follows immediately that $(-2,-16)$ is a local minimum, $(2,16)$ is a local maximum, and $(0,0)$ is an inflection point. The intercepts are $(-2\sqrt{3},0)$, $(0,0)$, and $(2\sqrt{3},0)$. The graph is shown below on the left.

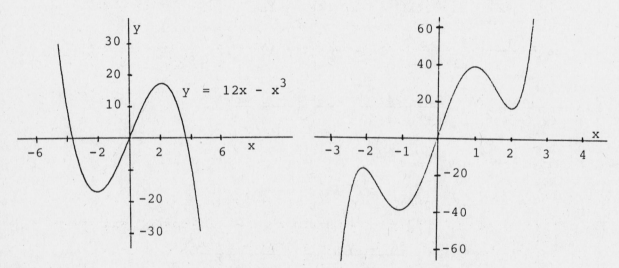

40. Given: $f(x) = 3x^5 - 25x^3 + 60x$. Then

$$f'(x) = 15x^4 - 75x^2 + 60 = 15(x^2 - 4)(x^2 - 1)$$

80

and

$$f''(x) = 60x^3 - 150x = 30x(2x^2 - 5).$$

Thus the critical points occur where $x = -1$, $x = 1$, $x = -2$, and $x = 2$. The possible inflection points occur where $x = 0$, $x = -\sqrt{5/2}$, and $x = \sqrt{5/2}$. The graph is shown on the previous page on the right.

46. Given: $f(x) = x^{2/3}(5 - 2x)$. Then

$$f'(x) = \frac{10 - 10x}{3x^{1/3}}$$

and

$$f''(x) = -\frac{20x + 10}{9x^{4/3}}.$$

If $|x|$ is large, then $f(x) \sim -2x^{5/3}$, which (because the exponent $5/3$ has odd numerator and odd denominator) acts rather like $-2x^3$ for $|x|$ large (at least qualitatively). This aids in determining the behavior of $f(x)$ for $|x|$ large. The graph is shown below.

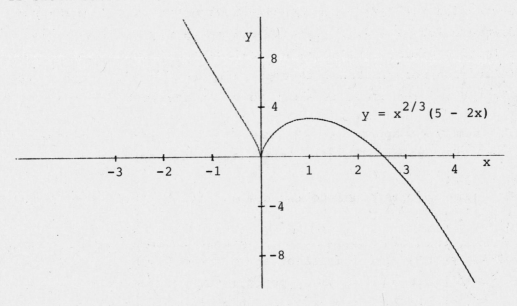

52. $f'(x) = \cos x$, $f''(x) = -\sin x$, $f^{(3)}(x) = -\cos x$, and $f^{(4)}(x) = \sin x = f(x)$. It is now clear that

$$f^{(n+4)}(x) = f^{(n)}(x)$$

for all $n \geq 0$ (we interpret $f^{(0)}(x)$ to mean $f(x)$).

81

55. If $f(x) = ax^3 + bx^2 + c + d$ with $a \neq 0$, then $f'(x)$ and $f''(x)$ exist for all x, and $f''(x) = 6ax + 2b$. The latter is zero when and only when $x = -b/3a$, and this is the abscissa of an inflection point because $a \neq 0$. Therefore the graph of a cubic polynomial has exactly one inflection point.

58. If $f''(c) < 0$, then (from the given formula for $f''(x)$ and with the suggested choice of h) we would have

$$f(c + h) - 2f(c) + f(c - h) < 0,$$

and therefore

$$\frac{f(c - h) + f(c + h)}{2} < f(c).$$

The left-hand member of the last inequality is the ordinate of the midpoint of the chord joining $(c-h, f(c-h))$ and $(c+h, f(c+h))$, and is smaller than the ordinate of the point on the curve having the same abscissa c. This means that at least one point of the chord is below the curve, and thereby we obtain a contradiction.

Section 4.7

1. $\dfrac{x}{x + 1} = \dfrac{1}{1 + (1/x)} \rightarrow 1$ as $x \rightarrow +\infty$.

4. The numerator approaches -2 as $x \rightarrow 1$, while the denominator approaches zero. Therefore this limit does not exist.

7. The numerator is equal to the denominator for all $x \neq -1$, so the limit is 1.

10. Divide each term in numerator and denominator by $x^{3/2}$, the highest power of x that appears in any term. The numerator then becomes $2x^{-1/2} + x^{-3/2}$, which approaches 0 as $x \rightarrow +\infty$; the denominator becomes $x^{-1/2} - 1$, which approaches -1 as $x \rightarrow +\infty$. Therefore the limit is 0.

13. $\dfrac{4x^2 - x}{x^2 + 9} = \dfrac{4 - (1/x)}{1 + (9/x^2)} \rightarrow 4$ as $x \rightarrow +\infty$, so the answer is $\sqrt{4} = 2$.

16. $\lim\limits_{x \to -\infty} \{2x - (4x^2 - 5x)^{1/2}\} = \lim\limits_{x \to -\infty} \dfrac{4x^2 - (4x^2 - 5x)}{2x + (4x^2 - 5x)^{1/2}}$

$= \lim\limits_{x \to -\infty} \dfrac{5}{2 + \{4 - (5/x)\}^{1/2}} = \dfrac{5}{4}.$

19. Here we have

$$f'(x) = -\frac{6}{(x + 2)^3}$$

and

$$f''(x) = \frac{18}{(x + 2)^4}.$$

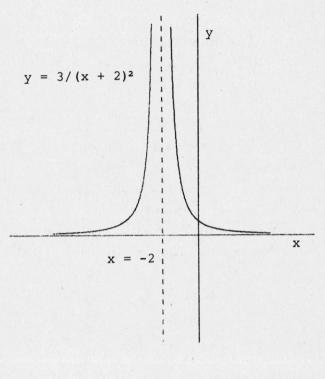

$y = 3/(x + 2)^2$

$x = -2$

The graph is increasing and concave upward for $x < -2$, decreasing and concave upward for $x > -2$. There are no extrema and no inflection points; the y-intercept is $(0, 3/4)$. The line $x = -2$ is a vertical asymptote and the x-axis is a horizontal asymptote. The graph appears to the right.

22. First,

$$f'(x) = -\frac{2}{(x - 1)^2}$$

and

$$f''(x) = \frac{4}{(x - 1)^3}.$$

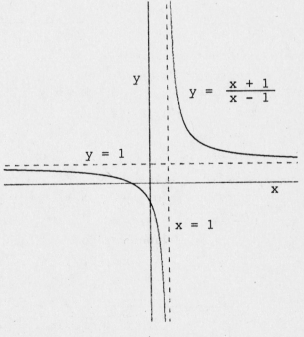

$y = \dfrac{x + 1}{x - 1}$

$y = 1$

$x = 1$

The graph is decreasing and concave downward if $x < 1$, decreasing and concave upward if $x > 1$. There are no extrema and no inflection points; the y-intercept is $(0, -1)$. The line $x = 1$ is a vertical asymptote and the line $y = 1$ is a horizontal asymptote. See the graph above, right.

83

25. $f'(x) = - \dfrac{2x}{(x^2 - 9)^2}$;

$f''(x) = \dfrac{6(x^2 + 3)}{(x^2 - 9)^3}$.

The graph is increasing for
x < 0 (except at x = -3)
and decreasing for x > 0
(except at x = 3). It is
concave upward if x < -3
and if x > 3, concave
downward on (-3,3). The
only extremum is the local
maximum and y-intercept at
the point (0,-1/9), and
there are no points of
inflection. The x-axis is a
horizontal asymptote and the
lines x = -3 and x = 3
are vertical asymptotes.

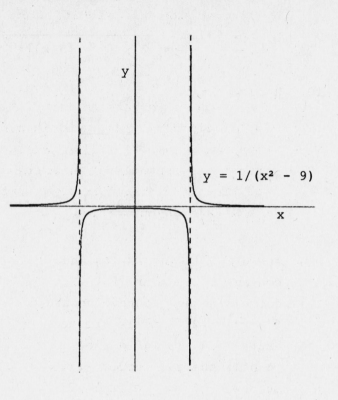

$y = 1/(x^2 - 9)$

28. $f'(x) = - \dfrac{2(2x - 1)(x + 1)}{x^2(x - 2)^2}$;

$f''(x) = \dfrac{2(4x^3 + 3x^2 - 6x + 4)}{(x^2 - 2x)^3}$.

The zeros of f'(x) occur at
-1 and 1/2, and the only
zero of f''(x) is (about)
x = -1.8517. The graph is
decreasing for x < -1, for
1/2 < x < 2, and for x > 2;
increasing for -1 < x < 0
and for 0 < x < 1/2. It
is concave downward for
x < 1.85* and on (0,2),
concave upward for x > 2
and on (-1.85*,0). The
line y = 2 is a horizontal
asymptote and the lines

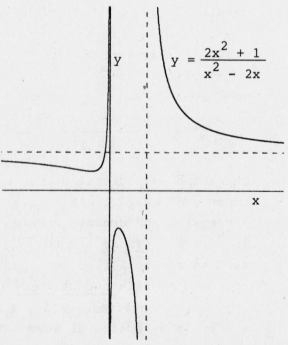

$y = \dfrac{2x^2 + 1}{x^2 - 2x}$

84

x = 0 and x = 2 are vertical asymptotes. There is a local
minimum at (-1,1), a local maximum at (1/2,-2), and a point
of inflection at (-1.85*,1.10*). (*Coordinates approximate.)

31. $f'(x) = \dfrac{x(x - 2)}{(x - 1)^2}$ and $f''(x) = \dfrac{2}{(x - 1)^3}$.

The graph is increasing for x < 0 and for x > 2, decreasing on
(0,1) and on (1,2). It is concave upward if x > 1, concave
downward if x < 1. The origin is a local maximum and the only
intercept, the only other extremum is a local minimum at (2,4),
and there are no inflection points. The lines y = x + 1 and
x = 1 are asymptotes.

34. $f'(x) = -\dfrac{2x}{(x^2 - 4)^2}$;

$f''(x) = \dfrac{6x^2 + 8}{(x^2 - 4)^3}$.

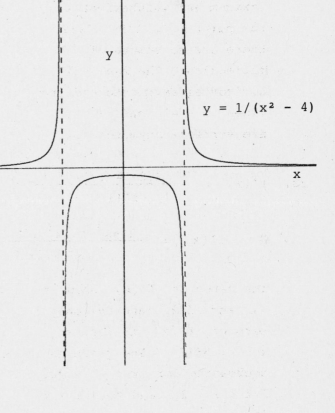

y = 1/(x² - 4)

The graph is increasing for
x < -2 and on (-2,0),
decreasing on (0,2) and
for x > 2. It is concave
upward if |x| > 2, concave
downward if |x| < 2. The
only intercept is at the
point (0,-1/4), which is
also a local maximum; there
are no other extrema and no
inflection points. The two
vertical lines x = -2 and
x = 2 are asymptotes, as is
the x-axis.

37. $f(x) = \dfrac{1}{x^2 - x - 2} = \dfrac{1}{(x + 1)(x - 2)}$:

$f'(x) = -\dfrac{2x - 1}{(x + 1)^2(x - 2)^2}$ and

$f''(x) = \dfrac{6(x^2 - x + 1)}{(x + 1)^3(x - 2)^3}$.

It is useful to notice the discontinuities at x = -1 and at
x = 2, that f(x) $\to$ 0 as x $\to$ +∞ and as x $\to$ -∞, and that
f(x) > 0 for x > 2 and for x < -1 while f(x) < 0 on the
interval (-1,2).   The denominator in f'(x) is never negative,
so the graph is decreasing for x > 1/2 (x $\neq$ 2) and increasing
for x < 1/2 (x $\neq$ -1).   The graph is concave upward for x > 2
and for x < -1, concave downward on (-1,2).   There are
no inflection points or intercepts, but there is a local maximum at
(1/2,-4/9).   The x-axis is a horizontal asymptote and the lines
x = -1 and x = 2 are vertical asymptotes.

40. $f'(x) = -\dfrac{x^2 + 1}{(x^2 - 1)^2}$;

$f''(x) = \dfrac{2x(x^2 + 3)}{(x^2 - 1)^3}$.

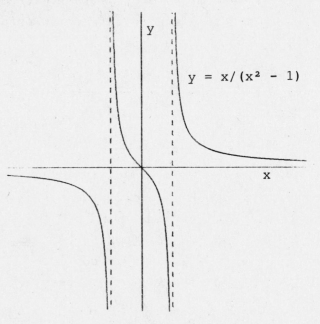

$y = x/(x^2 - 1)$

The graph is decreasing for
all x other than -1 and
1 (where f'(x) is not
defined); it is concave
upward for x > 1 and for
-1 < x < 0, concave
downward for 0 < x < 1 and
for x < -1.   The only
intercept is (0,0), which
is also an inflection point.
Note that f(x) $\to$ 0 as |x| $\to$ ∞, so the x-axis is a horizontal
asymptote; f(x) $\to$ +∞ as x $\to$ -1$^+$ and as x $\to$ +1$^+$, while
f(x) $\to$ -∞ as x $\to$ -1$^-$ and as x $\to$ +1$^-$, so the lines
|x| = 1 are vertical asymptotes.   There are no extrema.

43. The graph appears at the top of the next page.   To verify its
accuracy, note that

$$f'(x) = \frac{2(x^3 - 1)}{x^2} \qquad \text{and} \qquad f''(x) = \frac{2(x^3 + 2)}{x^3} .$$

So the graph is decreasing for 0 < x < 1 and for x < 0,
increasing for x > 1.   It is concave upward for x < -$\sqrt[3]{2}$ and
also for x > 0, concave downward for -$\sqrt[3]{2}$ < x < 0.   The only
intercept is at (-$\sqrt[3]{2}$,0); this is also the only inflection
point.   There is a local minimum at (1,3).   The y-axis is a
vertical asymptote.

86

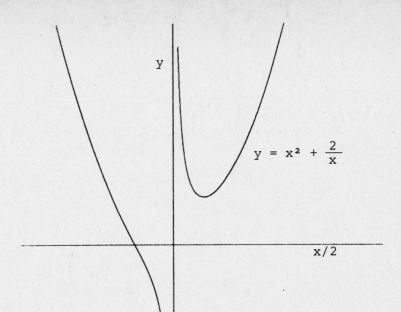

$$y = x^2 + \frac{2}{x}$$

$x/2$

Section 4.8

4. $\dfrac{1}{t}$ + C

10. $\dfrac{1}{5}(x + 1)^5$ + C

16. $\dfrac{1}{11}(t + 1)^{11}$ + C

22. Write $h(t) = 3t^2(2t^3 + 1)^{-1/2}$. Then its most general
    antiderivative is $(2t^3 + 1)^{1/2}$ + C.

28. $\dfrac{1}{5}\sin 5x$ + C

31. Write $h(x) = x(1 - x^2)^{1/2}$.

34. $-7(x + 77)^{-1}$ + C = $-\dfrac{7}{x + 77}$ + C

40. $\dfrac{1}{8}(1 + \sin x)^8$ + C

46. $2\sin\sqrt{x}$ + C

52. $\frac{2}{3}(x^2 + 1)^{3/2} + C$

58. $-\frac{1}{22}(1 - t^2)^{11} + C$

64. $-\frac{1}{4}\cos^4 x + C$

67. When $x = 100$, $(w)(100) = 100$ (tons); so because $w = \rho x$, $\rho = 1$. So

$$T_0 = \frac{x^2}{2y}; \quad \text{when } x = 100, \quad y = 20.$$

$$T_0 = \frac{(100)^2}{2(20)} = \frac{10,000}{40} = 250 \quad (\text{tons}).$$

Next, $(T_{100})^2 = (T_0)^2 + \rho^2 x^2 = (250)^2 + 100)^2$, and it follows that

$$T_{100} = 50\sqrt{29} \sim 269.26 \quad (\text{tons}).$$

Finally,

$$\tan \alpha = \frac{\rho x}{T_0} = \frac{(1)(100)}{250} = 0.4,$$

so

$$\alpha = \arctan\frac{2}{5} \sim 21.7°.$$

Section 4.9

1. From an initial antidifferentiation we see that

$$y = x^2 + x + C$$

for some constant C. The initial condition $y(0) = 3$ means that $y = 3$ when $x = 0$. We substitute this information to get

$$3 = 0 + 0 + C,$$

and thus find that $C = 3$. Therefore $y = x^2 + x + 3$.

4. $y = -\dfrac{1}{x} + 6$

10. $y = \dfrac{2}{3}(x + 5)^{3/2} - 21$

16. Write $y^{-1/2}\,dy = 1\,dx$.   Then $2y^{1/2} = x + C$.   But $y(0) = 4$, so $(2)(2) = C = 4$.   Therefore

$2y^{1/2} = x + 4$,   and thus $y(x) = \dfrac{1}{4}(x + 4)^2$.

22. $x(t) = -10t^2 - 15t + 5$

28. $v(t) = \dfrac{2}{3}t^{3/2} + v_0 = \dfrac{2}{3}t^{3/2}$ and

$x(t) = \dfrac{4}{15}t^{5/2} + x_0 = \dfrac{4}{15}t^{5/2}$

In the solutions for Problems 31 - 43, unless otherwise indicated, we will take the upward direction to be the positive direction, $s = s(t)$ for position (in feet) at time t (in seconds) with $s = 0$ corresponding to ground level, and $v(t)$ velocity at time t in ft/sec, $a = a(t)$ acceleration at time t in ft/sec^2. The initial position will be denoted by s_0 and the initial velocity by v_0.

31. Here it is more convenient to take the downward direction as the positive direction.   Thus

$$a(t) = +32, \qquad v(t) = +32t \quad (\text{because } v_0 = 0),$$

and

$$s(t) = 16t^2 \quad (\text{because } s_0 = 0).$$

The stone hits the bottom when $t = 3$, and at that time we have $s = s(3) = 144$.   Answer: The well is 144 feet deep.

34. First ball: $v_0 = 0$, $s_0 = 576$.   So $s(t) = -16t^2 + 576$.   The first ball strikes the ground at that $t > 0$ for which $s(t) = 0$: $t = 6$.   Second ball: The second ball must remain aloft from time $t = 3$ until time $t = 6$, thus for 3 seconds. Reset $t = 0$ as the time it is thrown downward. Then with initial velocity v_0, the second ball has velocity and position

$$v(t) = -32t + v_0$$

and

$$s(t) = -16t^2 + v_0 t + 576$$

at time t. We require that $s(3) = 0$; that is, that

$$0 = s(3) = -144 + 3v_0 + 576,$$

so that $v_0 = -144$. Answer: The second ball should be thrown straight downward with an initial velocity of 144 ft/sec.

37. With $v(t) = -32t + v_0$ and $s(t) = -16t^2 + v_0 t$, we have the maximum altitude $s = 225$ occurring when $v(t) = 0$; that is, when $t = v_0/32$. So

$$225 = s(v_0/32) = (-16)(v_0/32)^2 + (v_0)^2/32$$

$$= (v_0)^2/64.$$

It follows that $v_0 = +120$. So the initial velocity of the ball was 120 ft/sec.

40. Here s_0 will be the height of the building, so

$$v(t) = -32t - 25$$

and

$$s(t) = -16t^2 - 25t + s_0.$$

The velocity of impact is -153 ft/sec, so we can obtain the time of impact t by solving $v(t) = -153$: $t = 4$. At this time we also have $s = 0$:

$$0 = s(4) = (-16)(16) - (25)(4) + s_0,$$

so that $s_0 = 356$. Answer: The building is 356 feet high.

43. Because $v_0 = -40$, $v(t) = -32t - 40$. Thus

$$s(t) = -16t^2 - 40t + 555.$$

Now $s(t) = 0$ when $t = \frac{1}{4}(-5 + 2\sqrt{145}) \sim 4.77$ (sec).

The speed at impact is $|v(t)|$ for that value of t; that is, $16\sqrt{145} \sim 192.6655$ (ft/sec), over 131 miles per hour. For you trivia fans, Walter Johnson's catcher once caught a ball thrown from the top of the Washington monument. What was that catcher's name?

46. Let $x(t)$ denote the distance the car has traveled t seconds after the brakes are applied; let $v(t)$ denote its velocity and $a(t)$ its acceleration at time t during the braking. Then we are given $a = -40$, so $v(t) = -40t + 88$ (because 60 mph is the same speed as 88 ft/sec). The car comes to a stop when $v(t) = 0$; that is, when $t = 2.2$. The car travels the distance $x(2.2) = 96.8$. Answer: 96.8 feet.

49. Here's the calculation for the planet Jupiter. We begin with the general formula for the escape velocity v from a homogeneous spherical body of radius R and mass M,

$$v = \sqrt{2GM/R},$$

and the information that escape velocity from the earth is about

$$v_e = 11,174 \quad \text{(meters per second)}.$$

The velocity of escape v from Jupiter satisfies the equation

$$v^2 = 2GM/R$$

where M is the mass of Jupiter and R is its radius. So if M_e denotes the mass of the earth and R_e its radius, we have

$$(v/v_e)^2 = (2GM/R)/(2GM_e/R_e)$$

$$= (M/M_e)(R_e/R) = (315)/(11.3)$$

according to the table in the text. Thus $(v/v_e)^2 \sim 27.876$, which leads to $v/v_e \sim 5.2798$. Therefore escape velocity from Jupiter is approximately $v = (5.2798)(11,174) \sim 58,996$ meters per second, about 193,557 ft/sec, about 36.66 miles per second, about 131,971 miles per hour. <u>Careful</u>: Because the so-called <u>gravitational</u> <u>potential</u> of Jupiter is much greater than that of the earth (see Chapter 17), the amount of energy expended in escape from Jupiter would be far more than 5.2798 times that expended in escape from the earth.

52. $R = (0.00884)(0.206) \sim 0.000182$ meters -- less than 0.02 cm.

55. We begin with $dV/dt = -k\sqrt{y}$. Because $V = Ay$ and A is
constant, $dV/dt = A(dy/dt)$, and therefore

$$\frac{dy}{dt} = K\sqrt{y}$$

where $K = k/A$ is also constant. Thus

$$y^{-1/2}\, dy = K\, dt,$$

and an antidifferentiation yields

$$2y^{1/2} = Kt + C; \quad \text{thus} \quad y = (Bt + D)^2$$

where B and D are also constants. So $V(t) = A(Bt + D)^2$.
For simplicity in subsequent calculations, this last equation can
be written in the form

$$V(t) = V_0(bt + d)^2$$

where b and d are also constants. Now $V(0) = V_0$ and
$V(T) = 0$, so

$$V_0 d^2 = V_0$$

and

$$V_0(bT + d)^2 = 0.$$

It follows that $d^2 = 1$ and that $bT + d = 0$, so that
$b = -d/T$. Whether we take $d = 1$ or $d = -1$ makes no
difference; the result is the one given in Problem 55.

Section 4.10

1. (a) $C(400) = \$2200$;   (b) $C(400)/400 = \$5.50$;
(c) $C'(400) = \$3.00$;   (d) The cost of producing the 401st
item is $C(401) - C(400) = \$3.00$.

4. \$5020;   \$12.55;   \$0.025 (2.5 cents);   about 2.498 cents.

7. The average cost is

$$u(x) = (0.004)x + 40 + \frac{8000}{x};$$

$u'(x) = 0$ when

$$0.004 = \frac{8000}{x^2},$$

so that $x^2 = 2,000,000$. Consequently x is approximately 1414.21. If $x = 1415$, then $u(x)$ is about $51.31371; if $x = 1414$, then $u(x)$ is slightly smaller, about $51.31370. The minimum average cost is thus about $51.31.

10. The profit is $P(x) = 35x - 2000 - 15x - (0.02)x^2$

$$= 20x - 2000 - (0.02)x^2.$$

$$P'(x) = 20 - (0.04)x;$$

$P'(x) = 0$ when $x = 20/(0.04) = 500$. Because $y = P(x)$ is a parabola opening downward, $x = 500$ watches per week yields the absolute maximum of the profit function.

16. Cost: $C(x) = 1000 + 5x$. Current sales: 1000. Current price: 6000. With sales of x at price p, we assume that $p = Ax + B$ for some constants A and B. Therefore

$$6000 = 1000A + B$$

and

$$5950 = 1100A + B.$$

So $A = -0.05$ and $B = 6500$; $p = 6500 - (0.5)x$. Consequently the profit is

$$P(x) = px - 1000C(x)$$

$$= 6500x - (0.05)x^2 - 1,000,000 - 5000x$$

$$= 1500x - (0.05)x^2 - 10^6.$$

$P'(x) = 1500 - x;$ $P'(x) = 0$ when $x = 1500$. So $x = 1500$ and $p = 6500 - 750 = 5750$ yield the maximum profit. Answer: Offer a rebate of $250 per car.

1. $dy = \dfrac{3}{2}(4x - x^2)^{1/2}(4 - 2x)\,dx$

4. $dy = 2x\cos(x^2)\,dx$

10. Take $f(x) = x^{1/5}$; then $f'(x) = \dfrac{1}{5}x^{-4/5}$. Take $x = 32$ and $\Delta x = -2$. Then

$$(30)^{1/3} = f(x + \Delta x) \sim f(x) + f'(x)\,\Delta x$$

so $f'(x)$ exists for $1 < x < 3$ and f is continuous for $1 \le x \le 3$. So we are to solve

$$\frac{f(3) - f(1)}{3 - 1} = f'(c);$$

that is,

$$\frac{3 - (1/3) - 1 + 1}{2} = 1 + \frac{1}{c^2}.$$

After simplifications we find that $c^2 = 3$. Therefore, because $1 < c < 3$, $c = +\sqrt{3}$.

22. Here,

$$\frac{(1)^3 - (-2)^3}{1 - (-2)} = 3 = 3c^2,$$

so $c^2 = 1$. Because $+1$ is not in the interval $(-2, 1)$, only the answer $c = -1$ is correct.

25. $f'(x) = 2x - 6$ and $f''(x) = 2$. So the graph is increasing for $x > 3$, decreasing for $x < 3$, and always concave upward. Thus there is a global minimum at $(3, -5)$, no other extrema, and no inflection points. Because $f(x) \to +\infty$ as $x \to +\infty$ and as $x \to -\infty$, there are two x-intercepts; the y-intercept is at $(0, 4)$.

28. We begin by computing the first and second derivatives of f:

$$f'(x) = \frac{3(1-x)}{2x^{1/2}}$$

and

$$f''(x) = -\frac{3(x+1)}{4x^{3/2}}$$

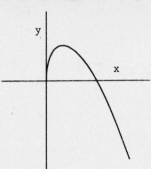

Next we note that $f(x)$ is continuous for $x \geq 0$, though $f'(0)$ is undefined. The graph is increasing for $x < 1$ and decreasing for $x > 1$; it is concave downward for all $x > 0$. The intercepts are $(0,0)$ and $(3,0)$. In sketching the graph -- shown above -- it helps to note that $f'(3) \sim -1.732$ and that $f'(x) \to -\infty$ as $x \to 0^+$.

34. $\frac{3}{2}(3y-1)^{-1/2}, \quad -\frac{9}{4}(3y-1)^{-3/2}, \quad \frac{81}{8}(3y-1)^{-5/2}$

40. $12(3-t)^{-5/2}, \quad 30(3-t)^{-7/2}, \quad 105(3-t)^{-9/2}$

46. $f(x) = 18x^2 - x^4$

$$= x^2(18 - x^2);$$

$$f'(x) = 36x - 4x^3$$

$$= 4x(3+x)(3-x);$$

$$f''(x) = 12(3 - x^2).$$

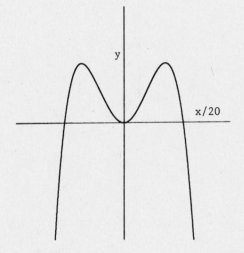

The graph appears to the right. There are global maxima at $(-3, 81)$ and $(3, 81)$ and a local minimum at $(0,0)$. The other two x-intercepts are at $(-3\sqrt{2}, 0)$ and $(3\sqrt{2}, 0)$. There are inflection points at $(-\sqrt{3}, 45)$ and $(\sqrt{3}, 45)$.

49. $f'(x) = \dfrac{4(3 - x)}{3(4 - x)^{2/3}}$ and $f''(x) = \dfrac{4(x - 6)}{9(4 - x)^{5/3}}$.

52. $f(x) = \dfrac{x}{(x - 2)(x + 1)}$,

$$f'(x) = -\frac{x^2 + 2}{(x^2 - x - 2)^2}, \quad \text{and}$$

$$f''(x) = \frac{2(x^3 + 6x - 2)}{(x + 1)^3(x - 2)^3}.$$

There are no critical points, but there is an inflection point at approximately $(0.3275, -0.1475)$. The graph is decreasing for all x other than -1 and 2, is concave upward on the interval $(-1, 0.3275)$ and if $x > 2$, and is concave downward on the interval $(0.3275, 2)$ and if $x < -1$. The asymptotes are $y = 0$, $x = 2$, and $x = -1$. The graph is shown below, left.

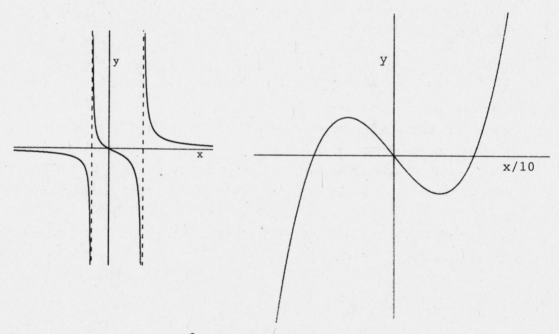

55. Here we have $f(x) = x^3(3x - 4)$, $f'(x) = 12x^2(x - 1)$, and $f''(x) = 12x(3x - 2)$. Hence there are intercepts at $(0,0)$ and $(4/3, 0)$; the graph is increasing for $x > 1$ and decreasing for $x < 1$; it is concave upward for $x > 2/3$ and for $x < 0$, concave downward on the interval $(0, 2/3)$. Consequently there is a global minimum at $(1, -1)$ and inflection points at $(0,0)$ and $(2/3, -16/27)$. There are no asymptotes, no other extrema, and $f(x) \to +\infty$ as $x \to +\infty$ and as $x \to -\infty$.

96

58. First, $f(x) = x(x^2 - 12)$, $f'(x) = 3(x + 2)(x - 2)$, and $f''(x) = 6x$. So there are intercepts at $(2\sqrt{3}, 0)$, $(0, 0)$, and $(-2\sqrt{3}, 0)$. The graph is increasing for $x > 2$ and for $x < -2$; it is decreasing on the interval $(-2, 2)$. It is concave upward for $x > 0$ and concave downward for $x < 0$. There is a local maximum at $(-2, 16)$, a local minimum at $(2, -16)$, and an inflection point at the origin. The graph is shown on the previous page (on the right).

61. Here, $f'(x) = 3(x + 1)(x - 1)$ and $f''(x) = 6x$.

64. $f(x) = \dfrac{x + 1}{x^2}$,

$f'(x) = -\dfrac{x + 2}{x^3}$,

$f''(x) = \dfrac{2(x + 3)}{x^4}$.

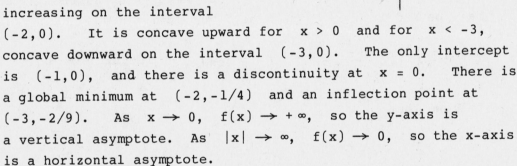

The graph is decreasing for $x > 0$ and for $x < -2$, increasing on the interval $(-2, 0)$. It is concave upward for $x > 0$ and for $x < -3$, concave downward on the interval $(-3, 0)$. The only intercept is $(-1, 0)$, and there is a discontinuity at $x = 0$. There is a global minimum at $(-2, -1/4)$ and an inflection point at $(-3, -2/9)$. As $x \to 0$, $f(x) \to +\infty$, so the y-axis is a vertical asymptote. As $|x| \to \infty$, $f(x) \to 0$, so the x-axis is a horizontal asymptote.

70. $-\dfrac{1}{2}\cos(1 + x^2) + C$

76. $y^{1/2}\, dy = 1\, dx$: $\dfrac{2}{3} y^{3/2} = x + C$.

$y(0) = 1$: $C = \dfrac{2}{3}$. $y^{3/2} = \dfrac{3}{2} x + 1$;

$y(x) = \left(\dfrac{3}{2} x + 1\right)^{2/3}$.

79. $y^{-2}\, dy = x\, dx$:

$$-y^{-1} = \frac{1}{2}x^2 + C = \frac{x^2 + 2C}{2};$$

$$y(x) = -\frac{2}{x^2 + 2C}.$$

$$1 = y(2) = -\frac{2}{4 + 2C}, \quad \text{so} \quad C = -3.$$

So $y(x) = \dfrac{2}{6 - x^2}$.

82. $y^{1/2}\,dy = x^{-1/2}\,dx$: $\quad \dfrac{2}{3}y^{3/2} = 2x^{1/2} + C.$

$$y(4) = 4: \quad \frac{16}{3} = 4 + C, \quad \text{so} \quad C = \frac{4}{3}.$$

$$y(x) = (2 + 3\sqrt{x})^{2/3}.$$

85. Let ξ be the angle that the ladder makes with the ground, let x be the distance from the foot of the ladder to the base of the wall, and let z be the total length of the ladder. Draw and so label a figure showing the wall 8 feet high and the building 4 feet beyond it. Then from the figure you can read that

$$x = \frac{8}{\tan \xi} \quad \text{and} \quad \cos \xi = \frac{4 + x}{z}.$$

It follows that

$$z = \frac{4}{\cos \xi} + \frac{8}{\sin \xi}.$$

Then

$$\frac{dz}{d\xi} = \frac{4 \sin \xi}{\cos^2 \xi} - \frac{8 \cos \xi}{\sin^2 \xi};$$

$dz/d\xi = 0$ when $\tan^3 \xi = 2$. It follows that $\xi \sim 51.56°$ and thus that $z \sim 16.65$ feet. The exact value of z at its maximum is $4(1 + \sqrt[3]{4})^{3/2}$ (feet).

88. We have acceleration $a = -22,500$, so velocity and position (in the usual coordinate system) are

$$v = (-22{,}500)t + v_0$$

and

$$s = (-11{,}250)t^2 + v_0 t + s_0.$$

Here we have $v_0 = 0$ and $s_0 = 450$, so

$$v(t) = (-22{,}500)t$$

and

$$x(t) = (-11{,}250)t^2 + 450.$$

The stone strikes the ground when $x(t) = 0$, and this equation has the positive solution $t = 1/5$. The impact speed of the stone is $|v(1/5)| = 4500$ ft/sec.

91. Let g denote the acceleration of gravity on the surface of the planet in question. Then

$$s = -\frac{1}{2}gt^2 + 20.$$

From the equation $0 = -\frac{1}{2}(4g) + 20$ we find that $g = 10$. So

$$s = -5t^2 \quad \text{and} \quad v = -10t$$

describe the behavior of the falling ball dropped at time $t = 0$. Now $s = 0$ when $t^2 = 40$, so the ball hits the ground after $2\sqrt{10}$ seconds. Its velocity then is $v(2\sqrt{10}) = -20\sqrt{10}$ feet per second. So the time aloft is approximately 6.3246 seconds and the impact speed is about 63.2456 ft/sec.

94. We found that

$$v^2 = (v_0)^2 + 2GM\left(\frac{1}{y} - \frac{1}{R}\right).$$

Now y_{max} occurs when $v = 0$, at which time

$$(v_0)^2 + 2GM\left(\frac{1}{y} - \frac{1}{R}\right) = 0.$$

If you solve this equation for y, you will find that

99

$$y = \frac{2GMR}{2GM - R(v_0)^2} .$$

Now $GM/R^2 = g$, so $GM = R^2 g$. Therefore:

(a) $\quad y_{max} = \dfrac{2R^2 g}{2Rg - (v_0)^2} \quad$ provided $v_0 < v_{esc}$.

(b) To reach a maximum altitude of 100 miles, we take $R = 3960$ (miles) as the radius of the earth, so that

$$y_{max} = (3960 + 100)(5280) = 21,436,800 \quad \text{(feet)}.$$

Because

$$2gR - (v_0)^2 = \frac{2gR^2}{y_{max}},$$

we find that $v_0 \sim 5741.0526$ ft/sec, approximately 3914.354 miles per hour.

(c) If $v_0 = (0.9)v_{esc}$, then $v_0 = (0.9)\sqrt{2gR}$. It follows that $y_{max} = \dfrac{100}{19} R$, about 20,842 miles.

97. $2y \dfrac{dy}{dx} = 3x^2 - 6x + 2$, so

$$\frac{dy}{dx} = \frac{3x^2 - 6x + 2}{2y} .$$

Now $dy/dx = 0$ when $x = 1 - \dfrac{1}{3}\sqrt{3}$. After lengthy simplifications, one can show that

$$\frac{d^2 y}{dx^2} = \frac{3x^4 - 12x^3 + 12x^2 - 4}{4y^3} .$$

The only zero of $d^2 y/dx^2$ in the domain is about 2.4679, and there the graph has the two values $|y| \sim 1.3109$.

Section 5.2

4. -231

10. $\dfrac{10^8}{4} + \dfrac{10^6}{2} + \dfrac{10^4}{4} = 25{,}502{,}500.$

13. $\dfrac{6n^5 + 15n^4 + 10n^3 - n}{30n^5} \to \dfrac{1}{5}$ as $n \to +\infty.$

16. $\dfrac{n(n - 1)}{30}(16n^3 + n^2 + n + 1)$

19. Take $x_i = i/n$ and $\Delta x = 1/n.$ Then $f(x_i) = (i/n)^2,$ and so

$$A_n = \sum_{i=1}^{n} (i/n)^2 (1/n) = \frac{1}{n^3} \sum_{i=1}^{n} i^2$$

$$= \frac{n(n + 1)(2n + 1)}{6n^3} = \frac{2n^2 + 3n + 1}{6n^2}.$$

The area is the limit of the last expression as $n \to +\infty,$ and so the area is $1/3.$

22. With inscribed rectangles, $x_i = 1 + \dfrac{2i}{n},$ and $\Delta x = \dfrac{2}{n},$ we obtain

$$L_n = 18 - \frac{4(n + 1)}{n} - \frac{4(n + 1)(2n + 1)}{3n^2}.$$

Therefore $A = \lim\limits_{n \to \infty} L_n = 18 - 4 - \dfrac{8}{3} = \dfrac{34}{3}.$

25. With $x_i = \dfrac{bi}{n}$ and $\Delta x = \dfrac{b}{n},$ we obtain

$$A_n = \frac{b^3(2n^2 + 3n + 1)}{6n^2},$$

and therefore $A = \lim\limits_{n \to \infty} A_n = \dfrac{1}{3} b^3.$

28. Proof: The formula holds when $n = 1.$ Suppose that it holds when $n = k$ for some integer $k \geq 1.$ Then

$$\sum_{i=1}^{k+1} i^2 = (k + 1)^2 + \sum_{i=1}^{k} i^2$$

$$= (k + 1)^2 + \frac{k(k + 1)(2k + 1)}{6}$$

$$= \frac{6k^2 + 12k + 6 + 2k^3 + 3k^2 + k}{k}$$

$$= \frac{2k^3 + 9k^2 + 13k + 6}{6} = \frac{(k + 1)(k + 2)(2k + 3)}{6}$$

$$= \frac{(k + 1)\{(k + 1) + 1\}\{2(k + 1) + 1\}}{6} .$$

Therefore, by induction, the formula holds for all $n \geqq 1$.

31. With $x_i = \dfrac{bi}{n}$ and $\Delta x = \dfrac{b}{n}$, we find that

$$A_n = \frac{hb}{2} + \frac{hb}{2n} .$$

Therefore $A = \dfrac{1}{2} bh.$

34. By the formula in Eq. (10),

$$\sum_{i=1}^{n} i^k = \frac{1}{k + 1} n^{k+1} + \frac{1}{2} n^k + \{\text{lower powers of } n\}.$$

The desired result now follows after division of all terms by n^{k+1} and then evaluation of the limit as $n \to +\infty$.

37. Proof: $f_k(n) = \dfrac{1}{k + 1} n^{k+1} + \{\text{terms of lower degree}\}.$ So the term of largest degree in $f_r(n)$ is the product of the two terms of largest degree in $f_p(n)$ and $f_q(n)$. That is,

$$\left(\frac{1}{p + 1} n^{p+1} \right)\left(\frac{1}{q + 1} n^{q+1} \right) = \frac{1}{r + 1} n^{r+1} .$$

Let $a = p + 1$, $b = q + 1$, and $c = r + 1$. Consideration of the coefficients above leads to the equation $ab = c$ while

consideration of the exponents leads to the equation $a + b = c$.
Consequently $a + b = ab$. This implies that $a = b(a - 1)$
and that $b = a(b - 1)$. All these quantities are positive
integers, so b is a positive divisor of a and a is a positive
divisor of b. Therefore a and b are equal. Moreover, $a - 1$
is a positive divisor of a because $a = b(a - 1)$. The only
way this can happen is if $a - 1 = 1$, and therefore $a = b = 2$.
It follows that $p = q = 1$ and that $r = 3$.

Section 5.3

1. $$\sum_{i=1}^{n} f(x_i{}^*) \Delta x = \sum_{i=1}^{5} (i/5)^2 (1/5)$$

$$= \frac{1}{125} (5/6)(6)(11) = \frac{11}{25} .$$

4. 8.382332 (rounded)

10. 0.16

16. 4.092967 (rounded)

19. 6086/3465 ~ 1.756421

22. 35.9375

25. $\dfrac{5}{7} + \dfrac{5}{12} + \dfrac{5}{17} + \dfrac{5}{22} + \dfrac{5}{27} = \dfrac{259{,}775}{141{,}372} \sim 1.83752795.$

28. Choose $x_i = \dfrac{4i}{n}$, $\Delta x = \dfrac{4}{n}$, and $x_i{}^*$ in the interval
$[x_{i-1}, x_i]$ for $1 \leq i \leq n$. Then

$$(x_{i-1})^3 \leq (x_i{}^*)^3 \leq (x_i)^3$$

for all such i, and so

$$\sum (x_{i-1})^3 \Delta x \leq \sum (x_i{}^*)^3 \Delta x \leq \sum (x_i)^3 \Delta x.$$

103

Thus

$$\sum_{i=1}^{n-1} (4i/n)^3 (4/n) \;\leq\; \sum_{i=1}^{n} (x_i^*)^3 \,\Delta x \;\leq\; \sum_{i=1}^{n} (4i/n)^3 (4/n),$$

and so

$$\frac{256}{n^4} \left(\frac{(n-1)n}{2} \right)^2 \;\leq\; \sum_{i=1}^{n} (x_i^*)^3 \,\Delta x \;\leq\; \frac{256}{n^4} \left(\frac{n(n+1)}{2} \right)^2 .$$

That is,

$$64 \left(\frac{n-1}{n} \right)^2 \;\leq\; \sum_{i=1}^{n} (x_i^*)^3 \,\Delta x \;\leq\; 64 \left(\frac{n+1}{n} \right)^2 .$$

So

$$64 \;\leq\; \lim_{\Delta x \to 0} \sum_{i=1}^{n} (x_i^*)^3 \,\Delta x \;\leq\; 64;$$

therefore

$$\int_0^4 x^3 \, dx \;=\; 64.$$

31. With $x_i = \dfrac{3i}{n}$ and $\Delta x = \dfrac{3}{n}$, the integral is

$$\lim_{n \to \infty} \frac{27}{2} \left(2 + \frac{3}{n} + \frac{1}{n^2} \right) + 3 \;=\; 30.$$

34. Take $x_i = \dfrac{bi}{n}$ and $\Delta x = \dfrac{b}{n}$. The integral is equal to

$$\lim_{n \to \infty} \frac{n^2(n+1)^2}{4n^4} b^4 \;=\; \frac{1}{4} b^4.$$

1. An antiderivative: $G(x) = \frac{1}{10}(x^2 + 1)^5$. Value of the integral:

   $G(1) - G(-1) = 0$.

4. An antiderivative: $G(x) = -\frac{1}{3x^3}$. Value of the integral:

   $G(-1) - G(-2) = \frac{7}{24}$.

7. An antiderivative: $G(x) = \frac{1}{4}(x + 1)^4$.

10. An antiderivative: $G(x) = 2\sqrt{x}$. Value of the integral:
    $G(4) - G(1) = 2\sqrt{4} - 2\sqrt{1} = 2$.

13. An antiderivative: $G(x) = \frac{1}{100}x^{100}$. Value of the integral:

    $G(1) - G(-1) = 0$.

16. An antiderivative of $f(x) = (x^2 + 1)^3 = x^6 + 3x^4 + 3x^2 + 1$ is

    $$G(x) = \frac{1}{7}x^7 + \frac{3}{5}x^5 + x^3 + x.$$

    Value of the integral: $G(2) - G(1) = \frac{1566}{35} \sim 44.742857$.

19. An antiderivative: $G(x) = \frac{3}{5}x^{5/3}$. Value of the integral:

    $G(8) - G(1) = \frac{93}{5}$.

22. An antiderivative: $G(t) = \frac{2}{3}t^{3/2}\sqrt{3}$. Value of the integral:

    $G(4) - G(1) = \frac{14}{3}\sqrt{3}$.

25. An antiderivative of $f(x) = x^{3/2} - x^{-1/2}$ is

    $$G(x) = \frac{2}{5}x^{5/2} - 2x^{1/2}.$$

    So the value of the integral is $G(4) - G(1) = \frac{52}{5}$.

28. $\displaystyle\int_0^{\pi/2} \cos 2x \; dx = \left[\frac{1}{2}\sin 2x \right]_0^{\pi/2} = 0$.

31. Choose $x_i = \dfrac{i}{n}$, $\Delta x = \dfrac{1}{n}$, $x_0 = 0$, and $x_n = 1$. Then the limit in question is the limit of Riemann sums for the function $f(x) = 2x - 1$ on the interval $0 \leq x \leq 2$, and its value is therefore

$$\int_0^1 (2x - 1)\, dx = \left[x^2 - x \right]_0^1 = 1 - 1 = 0.$$

34. This limit is the integral of $f(x) = x^3$ on the interval $0 \leq x \leq 1$, and its value is thus $\dfrac{1}{4}$.

37. It is $\dfrac{25\pi}{4}$ because it is the area of a quarter-circle of radius 5; specifically, the first-quadrant portion of such a circle with center at the origin.

43. $\dfrac{0.2}{1.2} + \dfrac{0.2}{1.4} + \dfrac{0.2}{1.6} + \dfrac{0.2}{1.8} + \dfrac{0.2}{2.0}$

$$\leq \int_1^2 \frac{1}{x}\, dx$$

$$\leq \dfrac{0.2}{1.0} + \dfrac{0.2}{1.2} + \dfrac{0.2}{1.4} + \dfrac{0.2}{1.6} + \dfrac{0.2}{1.8}.$$

Therefore

$$\frac{1627}{2520} \leq \int_1^2 \frac{1}{x}\, dx \leq \frac{1879}{2520}.$$

In decimal form -- rounded down on the left, up on the right --

$$0.6456349 \leq \int_1^2 \frac{1}{x}\, dx \leq 0.7456350.$$

106

1. $\dfrac{1}{2} \displaystyle\int_0^2 x^3\, dx = 2.$

4. 16

10. $\dfrac{2}{\pi} \displaystyle\int_0^{\pi/2} \sin 2x\, dx = \dfrac{2}{\pi}.$

16. $\dfrac{58}{7}$

22. On the interval $-1 \leq x \leq 1$ of integration, the integrand is equal to $x - 2$, so the value of the integral is -4.

25. Split the integral into three integrals -- one on the interval from -2 to -1, one on the interval from -1 to 1, and one on the interval from 1 to 2.

28. An antiderivative: $2\sqrt{x - 1}$. Value of integral: 2.

31. $f'(x) = (x^2 + 1)^{17}$

34. $A'(x) = \dfrac{1}{x}$

37. $G'(x) = \sqrt{x + 4}$

40. First, $f(x) = g(u)$ where $g(u) = \displaystyle\int_0^u (1 + t^3)^{1/2}\, dt$

and $u = x^2$. Now $g'(u) = (1 + u^3)^{1/2}$, and therefore $f'(x) = g'(u)\dfrac{du}{dx} = 2x(1 + x^6)^{1/2}.$

46. $f'(x) = 5x^4(1 + x^{10})^{1/2}$

52. $P_{AV} = \dfrac{1}{10} \displaystyle\int_0^{10} \{100 + 10t + (0.5)t^2 + (0.02)t^3\}\, dt$

$$= \frac{1}{10} \left[100t + 5t^2 + \frac{1}{6} t^3 + (0.005)t^4 \right]_0^{10}$$

$$= \frac{1}{10} (1000 + 500 + \frac{1000}{6} + 50) = \frac{515}{3},$$

approximately 171.667.

Section 5.6

1. $du = 4x^3 \, du$, so $x^3 \, dx = \frac{1}{4} \, du$. Therefore

$$f(x) \, dx = \frac{1}{4} (1 + u)^{1/2} \, du.$$

4. $f(x) \, dx = \dfrac{2}{(1 + u)^2} \, du; \quad -\dfrac{2}{1 + u} + C = -\dfrac{2}{1 + x^{1/2}} + C.$

7. $du = 2x \, dx; \quad x \, dx = \frac{1}{2} u \, du;$

$$f(x) \, dx = \frac{1}{2} u^{14} \, du;$$

Antiderivative: $\dfrac{1}{30} u^{15} + C = \dfrac{1}{30} (x^2 + 1)^{15} + C.$

10. $du = (4x^3 + 2x) \, dx$, so $(x + 2x^3) \, dx = \frac{1}{2} \, du.$

$$f(x) \, dx = \frac{1}{2u^3} \, du;$$

Antiderivative: $-\dfrac{1}{4u^2} + C = -\dfrac{1}{4(x^4 + x^2)^2} + C.$

13. Let $u = 4x - 3$. Then

$$\int (4x - 3)^5 \, dx = \frac{1}{4} \int 4(4x - 3)^5 \, dx$$

108

$$= \frac{1}{4} \int u^5 \, du = \frac{1}{4} \left(\frac{1}{6} u^6 \right) + C$$

$$= \frac{1}{24} (4x - 3)^6 + C.$$

16. Let $u = 1 - 2t^2$; $du = -4t \, dt$. Then

$$\int 3t(1 - 2t^2)^{10} \, dt = -\frac{3}{4} \int u^{10} \, du$$

$$= -\frac{3}{44} u^{11} + C = -\frac{3}{44} (1 - 2t^2)^{11} + C.$$

19.
$$\int x^2 (2 - 4x^3)^{1/3} \, dx = -\frac{1}{12} \int -12x^2 (2 - 4x^3)^{1/3} \, dx$$

$$= -\frac{1}{12} \left\{ \frac{3}{4} (2 - 4x^3)^{4/3} \right\} + C = -\frac{1}{16} (2 - 4x^3)^{4/3} + C.$$

22. Let $u = x^{1/2}$, $du = \frac{1}{2} x^{-1/2} \, dx$. Then

$$\int \frac{\cos(x^{1/2})}{x^{1/2}} \, dx = \int 2 \cos u \, du$$

$$= 2 \sin u + C = 2 \sin \sqrt{x} + C.$$

25. Recommended substitution: $u = 2x + 1$, $du = 2 \, dx$.

28. Let $u = \sin x$, $du = \cos x \, dx$. (Alternative: Let $u = \cos x$, $du = -\sin x \, dx$.) We obtain

$$\int_0^{\pi/2} \sin x \cos x \, dx = \int_0^1 u \, du = \left[\frac{1}{2} u^2 \right]_0^1 = \frac{1}{2}.$$

31. Let $u = 1 + \sin t$.

34. Let $u = 1 + x^{-2}$; then $du = -2x^{-3} \, dx$. The resulting antiderivative is

$$-\frac{3}{16} u^{8/3} + C = -\frac{3}{16}(1 + x^{-2})^{8/3} + C.$$

43. We use the substitution $u = -x$, so that $du = -dx$. Then

$$\int_{-a}^{a} f(x)\,dx = \int_{-a}^{0} f(x)\,dx + \int_{0}^{a} f(x)\,dx$$

$$= \int_{a}^{0} f(-u)(-du) + \int_{0}^{a} f(x)\,dx$$

$$= \int_{0}^{a} f(-u)\,du + \int_{0}^{a} f(x)\,dx$$

$$= \int_{0}^{a} -f(u)\,du + \int_{0}^{a} f(x)\,dx = 0.$$

Section 5.7

1. $A = \displaystyle\int_{1}^{3} \frac{1}{x^2}\,dx = \left[-\frac{1}{x} \right]_{1}^{3} = 1 - \frac{1}{3} = \frac{2}{3}.$

4. A suitable antiderivative: $G(x) = -4(x^2 + 1)^{-1/2}$. The area

$$G(1) - G(0) = 4(1 - \frac{1}{\sqrt{2}}).$$

7. $A = \left[\frac{1}{4} \sin^4 x \right]_{0}^{\pi/2} = \frac{1}{4}.$

10. $A = \displaystyle\int_{0}^{2} \{x - (x^2 - x)\}\,dx = \left[x^2 - \frac{1}{3} x^3 \right]_{0}^{2} = \frac{4}{3}.$

110

16. $A = \displaystyle\int_0^4 (4x - x^2)\, dx = \left[2x^2 - \frac{1}{3} x^3 \right]_0^4 = \frac{32}{3}.$

22. $A = \displaystyle\int_{-2}^2 (4 - x^2)\, dx = \left[4x - \frac{1}{3} x^3 \right]_{-2}^2 = \frac{32}{3}.$

28. $\dfrac{1}{3}$

34. $\dfrac{32}{27}$

40. $4\sqrt{6}$

46. The graph of $y = 2x^3 - 2x^2 - 12x$ crosses the x-axis where $x = -2$, 0, and 3. The area of the region between the graph and the x-axis in the second quadrant is $\dfrac{32}{3}$ and the area between the graph and the x-axis in the fourth quadrant is $\dfrac{63}{2}$ (the value of the integral is $-\dfrac{63}{2}$). So the total area is $\dfrac{253}{6}.$

49. Given:

$$A(u) = \frac{2}{3} u^{3/2} = \int_0^u f(x)\, dx.$$

We differentiate with respect to u to find that

$$A'(u) = \sqrt{u} = f(u),$$

and therefore $f(x) = \sqrt{x}$.

Section 5.8

4. 0.72; 0.67

7. $M_{10} \sim 0.946208579.$

10. 21.4918; 21.3550

16. (a) 14.33 °C;   (b) 14.23 °C

19. The integral lies between the midpoint and trapezoidal approximations because the graph of the integrand is concave upward over the interval of integration.

22. Simpson's approximation with n = 10 gives

$$\int_{1}^{2.7} \frac{1}{x}\,dx \sim 0.993253452 \quad \text{and} \quad \int_{1}^{2.8} \frac{1}{x}\,dx \sim 1.029621528.$$

The error is in each case less than

$$\frac{(24)(1.8)^3}{(180)(10^4)} \sim 0.000077760,$$

so the first integral above is less than 0.993332 and the second is greater than 1.029543.   Therefore 2.7 < e < 2.8.

Chapter 5 Miscellaneous Problems

1.   1700

4.   1 + 0 - 1 + 0 + 1 + 0 - 1 + 0 + ... + 0 - 1 = 0.

7.   The antiderivative is $\frac{2}{3}\pi(1 + x^2)^{3/2}$, so the value of the integral and of the limit is $\frac{2}{3}\pi(2\sqrt{2} - 1)$.

10. Note that the limit of a nonnegative quantity cannot be negative.

13. Write the integrand in the form

$$(\sqrt{2})x^{1/2} - \frac{1}{\sqrt{3}}x^{-1/3}.$$

16. Use if necessary the substitution u = 3 - 2t.   The antiderivative is $\frac{1}{2u}$, and the value of the integral is $\frac{1}{3}$.

19. Use the substitution $u = \frac{1}{t}$, $du = -\frac{1}{t^2}\,dt$.

112

22. The substitution $u = \cos t$ yields $-2\sqrt{\cos t}$ for the antiderivative and $2 - 2^{3/4}$ for the value of the integral.

25. The substitution $u = (4x^2 - 1)^{1/2}$ will work.

28. The curves cross at $(3, -\sqrt{3})$ and at $(3, \sqrt{3})$. We take advantage of symmetry -- we double a simple integral to obtain the total area:

$$A = 2 \int_0^{\sqrt{3}} \{y^2 - (3y^2 - 6)\} \, dy$$

$$= 2 \left[6y - \frac{2}{3} y^3 \right]_0^{\sqrt{3}} = 8\sqrt{3}.$$

31. The curves cross at $(-3, 25)$ and at $(2, 0)$. The area is the integral of $10 - 5x - (x - 2)^2$ over the interval $-3 \le x \le 2$.

34. $y^2 = 6x - 5 - x^2$ can be written in the form

$$(x - 3)^2 + y^2 = 2^2.$$

This is the equation of a circle with radius 2 and center $(3, 0)$. When $x = 1$, $y = 0$; when $x = 5$, $y = 0$. So the given integral is the area of a semicircle of radius 2; its value is therefore 2π.

40. First,

$$(x_{i-1})^2 \le \frac{1}{3} \{(x_{i-1})^2 + x_{i-1}x_i + (x_i)^2\} \le (x_i)^2.$$

Therefore $x_{i-1} \le x_i^* \le x_i$. Then

$$(x_i^*)^2 (x_i - x_{i-1})$$

$$= \frac{1}{3} \{(x_{i-1})^2 + x_{i-1}x_i + (x_i)^2\}(x_i - x_{i-1})$$

$$= \frac{1}{3} \{(x_i)^3 - (x_{i-1})^3\},$$

and when such expressions are summed for $i = 1, 2, 3, \ldots, n$, the result is $\frac{1}{3}(b^3 - a^3)$.

Section 6.1

1. $\displaystyle\int_0^{10} -32t\,dt = -320$ is the net distance;

$\displaystyle\int_0^{10} 32t\,dt = 320$ is the total distance.

4. $\displaystyle\int_0^5 |2t - 5|\,dt = 2\int_0^{5/2}(5 - 2t) = \frac{25}{2}$

is the net distance and the total distance.

10. Net distance: 2.   Total distance: $2\sqrt{2}$.

13. $\displaystyle\int_0^1 \sin \pi x \, dx = \frac{2}{\pi}$.

16. $\displaystyle\int_2^4 x^2\,dx = \frac{56}{3}$.

19. $\displaystyle\int_{-3}^0 x(x^2 + 16)^{1/2}\,dx = -1$.

22. $\displaystyle\int_0^{10} (1 + \{f(x)\}^2)^{1/2}\,dx$

25. $\displaystyle\int_{10}^{20} (100 - 3t)\,dt = 550$ (gallons).

114

31. Let $f(x) = x^{1/3}$; on the interval $0 \leq x \leq 1$, let $x_i = x_i^* = i/n$ and $\Delta x = 1/n$. Then the limit given is

$$\int_0^1 x^{1/3}\,dx = \frac{3}{4}.$$

Section 6.2

1. $V = \displaystyle\int_0^1 \pi x^4\,dx = \frac{\pi}{5}.$

4. $V = \displaystyle\int_{0.1}^1 \frac{\pi}{x^2}\,dx = 9\pi.$

7. $V = \displaystyle\int_0^1 (\pi x - \pi x^4)\,dx = \frac{3}{10}\pi.$

10. $V = \displaystyle\int_{-2}^3 \pi\{(y+6)^2 - (y^2)^2\}\,dy = \frac{500}{3}\pi.$

13. $V = \displaystyle\int_0^1 \pi(\sqrt{1-y})^2\,dy = \frac{\pi}{2}.$

16. $V = \displaystyle\int_0^1 \pi\{(2+\sqrt{1-y})^2 - (2-\sqrt{1-y})^2\}\,dy$

$= \dfrac{16}{3}\pi.$

19. $V = \displaystyle\int_0^4 \pi(\sqrt{y})^2\,dy = 8\pi.$

22. First, $y^2 = b^2 - \dfrac{b^2}{a^2} x^2$. Therefore

$$V = 2 \int_0^a \pi(b^2 - \frac{b^2}{a^2} x^2)\, dx = \frac{4}{3} \pi ab^2.$$

25. We set up a coordinate system in which AB is the segment on the x-axis from $x = -a$ to $x = a$. Then

$$V = 2 \int_0^a 4(a^2 - x^2)\, dx = \frac{16}{3} a^3.$$

28. $V = \displaystyle\int_0^1 (\sqrt{x} - x^2)^2\, dx = \dfrac{9}{70}$.

34. $V = \displaystyle\int_{r-h}^r \pi(r^2 - y^2)\, dy.$

Section 6.3

1. $V = \displaystyle\int_0^2 (2\pi x)(x^2)\, dx = 8\pi.$

4. $V = \displaystyle\int_0^2 2\pi x(8 - 2x^2)\, dx = 16\pi.$

7. $V = \displaystyle\int_0^1 2\pi y(3 - 3y)\, dy = \pi.$

10. $V = \displaystyle\int_0^3 (2\pi x)(3x - x^2)\, dx = \dfrac{27\pi}{2}.$

116

13. $V = \displaystyle\int_0^1 2\pi x(x - x^3)\,dx = \dfrac{4}{15}\pi.$

16. $V = \displaystyle\int_0^2 (2\pi x)(x^3)\,dx = \dfrac{64}{5}\pi.$

19. $V = \displaystyle\int_{-1}^1 2\pi(2 - x)(x^2)\,dx = \dfrac{8}{3}\pi.$

This is one of many examples in which you do not obtain the correct answer by doubling the value of the integral from 0 to 1.

22. $V = \displaystyle\int_0^1 2\pi(2 - y)(\sqrt{y} - y)\,dy = \dfrac{8}{15}\pi.$

25. $V = \displaystyle\int_{-1}^1 2\pi(1 - y)(2 - 2y^2)\,dy = \dfrac{16}{3}\pi.$

28. $V = \displaystyle\int_0^1 2\pi(y + 1)(\sqrt{y} - y^2)\,dy = \dfrac{29}{30}\pi.$

31. $V = 2\displaystyle\int_0^a (2\pi x)\left(\dfrac{b}{a}\right)(a^2 - x^2)^{1/2}\,dx = \dfrac{4}{3}\pi a^2 b.$

34. (a) $V = \displaystyle\int_{-1}^2 2\pi(x + 2)(x + 2 - x^2)\,dx = \dfrac{45}{2}\pi.$

    (b) $V = \displaystyle\int_{-1}^2 2\pi(3 - x)(x + 2 - x^2)\,dx = \dfrac{45}{2}\pi.$

37. $a^2 + \dfrac{1}{4}h^2 = r^2$, so $r^2 - a^2 = \dfrac{1}{4}h^2$. Therefore

$$V = \frac{4}{3} \pi \left(\frac{1}{4} h^2 \right)^{3/2}.$$

So the answer to part (a) is $V = \frac{1}{6} \pi h^3$.

(b) The answer involves neither the radius r of the sphere nor the radius a of the hole; it depends only on the length of the hole.

Section 6.4

1. $\displaystyle\int_0^1 (1 + 4x^2)^{1/2} \, dx$

4. $\displaystyle\int_{-1}^1 \left(1 + \frac{8}{9} x^{2/3} \right)^{1/2} \, dx$

7. $\displaystyle\int_{-1}^2 (1 + 16y^6)^{1/2} \, dy$

10. $\displaystyle\int_0^2 \frac{2}{(4 - x^2)^{1/2}} \, dx$

13. $\displaystyle\int_0^1 2\pi (x - x^2)(4x^2 - 4x + 2)^{1/2} \, dx$

16. $\displaystyle\int_0^1 2\pi (x - x^3)(9x^4 - 6x^2 + 2)^{1/2} \, dx$

19. $\displaystyle\int_1^4 2\pi (x + 1) \left(1 + \frac{9}{4} x \right)^{1/2} \, dx$

22. $\dfrac{dx}{dy} = \sqrt{y - 1}.$ So

$$L = \int_1^5 (1 + \sqrt{y - 1})^{1/2}\, dy = \frac{2}{3}(5\sqrt{5} - 1).$$

25. $\dfrac{dy}{dx} = \dfrac{6x^4 - 8y}{4x}$.   But $8y = \dfrac{2x^6 + 1}{x^2}$,   so

$$\frac{dy}{dx} = x^3 - \frac{1}{4}x^{-3}.\quad \text{Therefore}$$

$$1 + \left(\frac{dy}{dx}\right)^2 = \left(x^3 + \frac{1}{4}x^{-3}\right)^2.$$

$$L = \int_1^2 \left(x^3 + \frac{1}{4}x^{-3}\right) dx = \frac{123}{32} = 3.84375.$$

28. $2(y - 3)\dfrac{dy}{dx} = 12(x + 2)^2$,   so $\dfrac{dy}{dx} = \dfrac{6(x + 2)^2}{y - 3}$.

Thus

$$1 + \left(\frac{dy}{dx}\right)^2 = 1 + \frac{36(x + 2)^4}{(y - 3)^2}$$

$$= 1 + \frac{36(x + 2)^4}{4(x + 2)^3} = 1 + 9(x + 2) = 9x + 19.$$

Therefore

$$L = \int_{-1}^2 (9x + 19)^{1/2}\, dx = \frac{2}{27}(37\sqrt{37} - 10\sqrt{10}).$$

31. $1 + \left(\dfrac{dy}{dx}\right)^2 = \left(x^4 + \dfrac{1}{4}x^{-4}\right)^2.$ Therefore

$$A = \int_1^2 2\pi x\left(x^4 + \frac{1}{4}x^{-4}\right) dx = \frac{339}{16}\pi.$$

34. $A = \displaystyle\int_1^2 2\pi x\sqrt{1 + x}\, dx.$

Let $u = 1 + x$; then $x = u - 1$ and $dx = du$. As x takes on values from 1 to 2, u takes on values from 2 to 3.   So

119

$$A = \int_2^3 2\pi(u - 1)u^{1/2}\, du = \frac{8}{15}\pi(6\sqrt{3} - \sqrt{2}).$$

40. Take $y = f(x) = (r^2 - x^2)^{1/2}$, $-r \leq x \leq r$. Then

$$\frac{dy}{dx} = -\frac{x}{(r^2 - x^2)^{1/2}}.$$

So

$$A = \int_{-r}^{r} 2\pi(r^2 - x^2)^{1/2}(1 + \frac{x^2}{r^2 - x^2})^{1/2}\, dx$$

$$= 2\pi \int_{-r}^{r} (r^2)^{1/2}\, dx = 4\pi r^2.$$

Section 6.5

1. $W = \displaystyle\int_{-2}^{1} 10\, dx = 30.$

4. $W = \displaystyle\int_{0}^{4} -3\sqrt{x}\, dx = -16.$

7. $W = \displaystyle\int_{0}^{1} 30x\, dx = 15$ (ft-lb).

10. $W = \displaystyle\int_{0}^{10} (62.4)(y)(25\pi)\, dy = 78{,}000\pi$ (ft-lb),

approximately 245,044.23 ft-lb.

13. Take $y = -10$ as ground level, so that the radius x of a thin horizontal cylinder of water at height y above ground level satisfies the equation $x^2 = 5y$. Therefore

120

$$W = \int_0^5 (y + 10)(50)(5\pi y)\,dy = \frac{125,000}{3}\,\pi,$$

approximately 130,900 ft-lb.

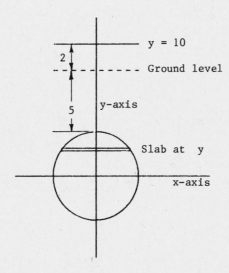

16. Set up a coordinate system as shown immediately above: The x-axis and y-axis cross at the center of one end of the tank, so that the equation of the circular (vertical) cross section of the tank is $x^2 + y^2 = 9$. Then the gasoline must be lifted to the level $y = 10$. A horizontal cross section of the tank at the level y is a rectangle of length 10 and width $2x$ where x and y satisfy the above equation, so that $x = (9 - y^2)^{1/2}$. So

$$W = \int_{-3}^3 (10 - y)(10)(2)(9 - y^2)^{1/2}(45)\,dy$$

$$= 900 \int_{-3}^3 10(9 - y^2)^{1/2}\,dy$$

$$- 900 \int_{-3}^3 y(9 - y^2)^{1/2}\,dy$$

$$= 40,500\pi,$$

approximately 127,234.5 ft-lb.

121

19. Take $y = 0$ at ground level. At time t, $0 \le t \le 50$, the
    bucket is at height $y = 2t$, and its weight is $F = 100 - \frac{1}{2} t$.
    So $t = \frac{1}{2} y$, and therefore the work is given by

$$W = \int_0^{100} (100 - \frac{1}{4} y) \, dy = 8750 \quad \text{(ft-lb)}.$$

22. $$W = \int_{x_1}^{x_2} Ap(Ax) \, dx.$$

    Let $V = Ax$; then $dV = A \, dx$.   Therefore

$$W = \int_{V_1}^{V_2} p(V) \, dV.$$

25. $$W = \int_0^1 60\pi (1 - y)\sqrt{y} \, dy = 16\pi \quad \text{(ft-lb)}.$$

28. There are a number of ways to work this problem. Here is a way to
    check your answer by using elementary physics and no calculus.
    Stage 1: Imagine the chain hanging in the shape of an "L" with
    40 feet vertical and 10 feet horizontal, the latter on the floor of
    the monkey's cage in a neat heap. Stage 2: Cut off this ten-foot
    length of chain and move it to its final position -- hanging from
    the top of the cage. It weighs 5 pounds and has moved an average
    distance of 45 feet, so the work to lift this segment of the
    chain is $W_1 = (5)(45) = 225$ ft-lb.   Stage 3: Return to
    the dangling chain. Cut off its bottom 15 feet and move it to
    its final position -- hanging from the 10-foot segment now hanging
    from the top of the cage. The top end of this segment is lifted
    $30 - 15 = 15$ feet and it weighs 7.5 pounds, so the work to
    lift the second segment is $W_2 = (15)(7.5) = 112.5$ ft-lb.
    The remaining 25 feet of the chain doesn't move at all. Finally,
    the monkey lifts her own 20 pounds a distance of 40 feet, so
    the work involved here is $W_3 = 800$ ft-lb.   So the total work
    in the process is $W = W_1 + W_2 + W_3 = 1137.5$ ft-lb.
    Of course, to gain the maximum benefit from this problem, you
    should work it using techniques of calculus.

4. $M_y = \displaystyle\int_0^3 x(3 - x)\,dx = \dfrac{9}{2}$;

The area of the region is the same, so $\bar{x} = 1$. By symmetry, $\bar{y} = 1$ as well. Answer: $(1,1)$.

10. By symmetry, $\bar{x} = 0$.

$$M_x = \frac{1}{2} \int_{-2}^{2} (x^2 + 1)^2\,dx = \frac{206}{15}.$$

The area of the region is $\dfrac{28}{3}$, so $\bar{y} = \dfrac{103}{70}$.

13. $M_y = \displaystyle\int_0^1 3x^3\,dx = \dfrac{3}{4}$.

$$M_x = \int_0^1 \frac{9}{4} x^4\,dx = \frac{9}{10}.$$

The area is $A = 1$, and therefore $(\bar{x}, \bar{y}) = (0.75, 0.9)$.

16. First note that $\bar{x} = \bar{y}$ by symmetry.

$$A = \int_0^1 (\sqrt{x} - x^2)\,dx = \frac{1}{3}.$$

$$M_y = \int_0^1 (x^{3/2} - x^3)\,dx = \frac{3}{20}.$$

Therefore $\bar{x} = \bar{y} = \dfrac{9}{20}$.

19. $M_y = \displaystyle\int_0^r x(r^2 - x^2)^{1/2}\,dx = \dfrac{1}{3} r^3$.

$A = \frac{1}{4} \pi r^2$, and so $\bar{x} = \frac{4r}{3\pi}$. By symmetry $\bar{y} = \bar{x}$, so the centroid is located at the point $(\frac{4r}{3\pi}, \frac{4r}{3\pi})$.

22. By Pappus's second theorem,

$$(\frac{1}{2} \pi r)(2\pi x) = 2\pi r^2,$$

so -- with the aid of symmetry -- $\bar{x} = \frac{2r}{\pi} = \bar{y}$.

25. $A = (2\frac{\pi r}{2})(r^2 + h^2)^{1/2} = \pi r(r^2 + h^2)^{1/2} = \pi r L$.

28. The lateral surface is generated by revolving around the axis of the cylinder a vertical line of length h. Its midpoint is at $(r, h/2)$ and the radius of the circle through which the midpoint moves is r, so the lateral surface area is $A = (2\pi r)h$.

    Alternatively, from Problem 27,

$$A = \pi(r_1 + r_2)L = \pi(2r)h.$$

Section 6.7

1. $V = \displaystyle\int_0^2 (\pi)(2x)\,dx = 4\pi$.

$M_{yz} = \displaystyle\int_0^2 (\pi)(2x^2)\,dx = \frac{16}{3}\pi$.

Therefore $(\bar{x}, \bar{y}, \bar{z}) = (4/3, 0, 0)$.

4. The curve meets the y-axis at $y = 0$ and at $y = 3$.

$$V = \int_0^3 \pi(3y - y^2)^2\,dy = \frac{81}{10}\pi.$$

$$M_{xz} = \int_0^3 \pi y(3y - y^2)^2 \, dy = \frac{243}{20}\pi.$$

Now $\bar{x} = 0 = \bar{z}$, so the centroid is located at the point $(\bar{x}, \bar{y}, \bar{z}) = (0, 3/2, 0)$.

7. $\quad V = \int_3^5 \pi(x^2 - 9)\, dx = \frac{44}{3}\pi.$

$$M_{yz} = \int_3^5 \pi(x^3 - 9x)\, dx = 64\pi.$$

10. Consider the plane region S in the first quadrant bounded by the coordinate axes and the graph of the equation $x^2 + y^2 = R^2$. We rotate S about the y-axis to generate a solid hemisphere of radius R. It is clear by symmetry that the centroid lies on the y-axis, the axis of symmetry of the hemisphere. Moreover,

$$V = \frac{2}{3}\pi R^3$$

and

$$M_{xz} = \int_0^R \pi y(R^2 - y^2)\, dy = \frac{\pi}{4} R^4.$$

Therefore $\bar{y} = \frac{1}{V}M_{xz} = \frac{3}{8}R.$

13. $\quad V = \int_0^h \pi y^{2/n}\, dy = \frac{n}{n+2}\pi h^{(n+2)/n}.$

$$M_{xz} = \int_0^h \pi y^{1 + (2/n)}\, dy = \frac{n}{2(n+1)}\pi h^{2(n+1)/n}.$$

Then the desired result follows.

16. The diagram to the right shows the end of the trough -- note that a narrow horizontal strip at height y has width

$$2x = \frac{2}{3} y\sqrt{3}.$$

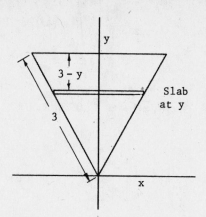

Therefore the total force on the end of the trough is given by

$$F = \int_0^{\frac{3}{2}\sqrt{3}} \rho\left(\frac{3}{2}\sqrt{3} - y\right)\left(\frac{2}{3} y\sqrt{3}\right) dy$$

$$= \rho \int_0^{\frac{3}{2}\sqrt{3}} \left(3y - \frac{2}{3} y^2\sqrt{3}\right) dy$$

$$= \frac{27}{8}\rho = 210.6 \quad \text{(pounds)}.$$

19. $$F = \int_{-15}^{-10} \rho(-y)(5)\,dy = \frac{625}{2}\rho \quad \text{(pounds)}.$$

22. The equation of the semicircle is $x^2 + y^2 = 16$, $y \leqq 0$. So

$$F = \int_{-4}^0 2\rho(10 - y)(16 - y^2)^{1/2}\,dy$$

$$= 20\rho \int_{-4}^0 (16 - y^2)^{1/2}\,dy - 2\rho \int_{-4}^0 y(16 - y^2)^{1/2}\,dy$$

$$= \frac{1}{3}\rho(240\pi + 128) \sim 18{,}345.23 \quad \text{(pounds)}.$$

25. (a) $F = \rho h A = (62.4)(12.5)(25) = 19{,}500 \quad \text{(pounds)}.$

(b) $F = (62.4)(13)(9\pi) = (7300.8)\pi \sim 22{,}936.14 \quad \text{(pounds)}.$

(c) $F = (52.4)(10 + \dfrac{4r}{3\pi})(\dfrac{1}{2}\pi r^2)$

$= (62.4)(10 + \dfrac{16}{3\pi})(8\pi) \sim 18,345.231$ (pounds).

Section 6.8

1. $\displaystyle\int_0^1 x^2\,dx = \dfrac{1}{3}$.

4. $\displaystyle\int_0^3 \dfrac{x}{(16 + x^2)^{1/2}}\,dx = 1$.

7. $\displaystyle\int_0^2 x^2(1 + x^3)^{1/2}\,dx = \dfrac{52}{9}$.

Chapter 6 Miscellaneous Problems

1.   Note that $t^2 - t - 2 = (t + 1)(t - 2)$ is negative on the interval $(-1, 2)$. Therefore the net distance traveled is

$$\int_0^3 (t^2 - t - 2)\,dt = -\dfrac{3}{2},$$

while the total distance traveled is

$$-\int_0^2 (t^2 - t - 2)\,dt + \int_2^3 (t^2 - t - 2)\,dt = \dfrac{31}{6}.$$

4. $\displaystyle\int_{-1}^2 (3x^2 + 2)\,dx = 15$.

7. $\displaystyle\int_1^2 \frac{x^3 - 1}{x^2}\,dx = 1.$

10. $V = \displaystyle\int_0^1 (2x - x^2 - x^3)^2\,dx = \dfrac{22}{105}.$

13. $M = \displaystyle\int_0^{20} \frac{\pi}{16}(8.5)\,dx = (10.625)\pi \sim 33.379 \quad (\text{grams}).$

16. Because $(a - h, r)$ lies on the ellipse,

$$\left(\frac{a - h}{a}\right)^2 + \left(\frac{r}{h}\right)^2 = 1.$$

Therefore

$$r^2 = \frac{2ah - h^2}{a^2}\,b^2.$$

And so

$$V = \int_{a-h}^{a} \pi y^2\,dx$$

$$= \int_{a-h}^{a} \pi b^2\left(1 - \frac{x^2}{a^2}\right)dx$$

$$= \pi\,\frac{b^2 h^2}{3a^2}(3a - h).$$

But

$$r^2 = \frac{b^2}{a^2}h(2a - h), \quad \text{so} \quad \frac{b^2}{a^2}h = \frac{r^2}{2a - h}.$$

Therefore

$$V = \frac{1}{3}\pi r^2 h\,\frac{3a - h}{2a - h}.$$

128

19. $V(t) = \displaystyle\int_1^t \pi\{f(x)\}^2\, dx = \dfrac{\pi}{6}\{(1 + 3t)^2 - 16\}.$

Thus

$$\pi\{f(x)\}^2 = \frac{\pi}{6}\{(2)(1 + 3x)(3)\} = \pi(1 + 3x).$$

Therefore $f(x) = \sqrt{1 + 3x}.$

22. With the aid of the figure to the right, we see that the vertical strip above x is rotated in a circle of radius $x + 2$. Therefore the volume generated is given by

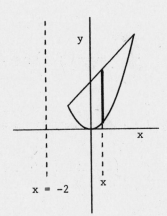

$$V = \int_{-1}^2 2\pi(x + 2)(x + 2 - x^2)\, dx = \frac{45}{2}\pi.$$

25. $\dfrac{dx}{dy} = \dfrac{3}{8}\left(\dfrac{4}{3}y^{1/3} - \dfrac{4}{3}y^{-1/3}\right).$ So -- after some algebra --

$$\{1 + \left(\frac{dx}{dy}\right)^2\}^{1/2} = \frac{1}{2}(y^{1/3} + y^{-1/3}).$$

Therefore

$$L = \frac{1}{2}\int_1^8 (y^{1/3} + y^{-1/3})\, dt = \frac{63}{8}.$$

28. $\dfrac{dy}{dx} = -\dfrac{x}{(r^2 - x^2)^{1/2}},$ so

$$1 + \left(\frac{dy}{dx}\right)^2 = \frac{r^2}{r^2 - x^2}.$$

Therefore

$$A = \int_a^b 2\pi(r^2 - x^2)^{1/2}\frac{r}{(r^2 - x^2)^{1/2}}\, dx = 2\pi r h.$$

31. $L = \int_1^2 \frac{1}{2}(y^3 + y^{-3})\,dy = \frac{33}{16}.$

$M_y = \int_1^2 (\frac{1}{8}y^4 + \frac{1}{4}y^{-2})(\frac{1}{2})(y^3 + y^{-3})\,dy = \frac{1179}{512}.$

$M_x = \int_1^2 \frac{1}{2}(y^4 + y^{-2})\,dy = \frac{67}{20}.$

Therefore $\bar{x} = \frac{393}{352}$ and $\bar{y} = \frac{268}{165}.$

34. The two curves meet at $(0,0)$ and at $(1,1)$.

$A = \int_0^1 (2x - x^2 - x^3)\,dx = \frac{5}{12}.$

$M_y = \int_0^1 (2x^2 - x^3 - x^4)\,dx = \frac{13}{60}.$

$M_x = \int_0^1 \frac{1}{2}(2x - x^2 - x^3)(2x - x^2 - x^3)\,dx = \frac{41}{210}.$

Therefore $\bar{x} = \frac{13}{25}$ and $\bar{y} = \frac{82}{175}.$

37. $2\pi\bar{y}\frac{\pi ab}{2} = \frac{4}{3}\pi ab^2$, and it follows that $\bar{y} = \frac{4b}{3\pi}.$

40. By Problem 16, the rotated volume is

$$V = \frac{\pi b^2 h^2}{3a^2}(3a - h).$$

Next,

$$M_{yz} = \int_{a-h}^a \pi x b^2 (1 - \frac{x^2}{a^2})\,dx.$$

After a large amount of algebra, we find that

$$M_{yz} = \frac{\pi b^2 h^2}{4a^2} (2a - h)^2.$$

Therefore

$$x = \frac{1}{V} M_{yz} = \frac{3(2a - h)^2}{4(3a - h)}.$$

43. Denote by K the spring constant. Then

$$\int_2^5 K(x - L)\,dx = 5\int_2^3 K(x - L)\,dx.$$

After applying the fundamental theorem of calculus, we find that

$$(5 - L)^2 - (2 - L)^2 = 5(3 - L)^2 - 5(2 - L)^2,$$

so that

$$(5 - L)^2 + 4(2 - L)^2 = 5(3 - L)^2.$$

Therefore

$$25 - 10L + L^2 + 16 - 16L + 4L^2 = 45 - 30L + 5L^2;$$

thus

$$-26L + 30L = 45 - 41.$$

Hence $4L = 4$, and therefore the natural length of the spring is 1 foot.

46. Set up a coordinate system with the axis of the cone lying on the y-axis and with a diameter of the cone lying on the x-axis. Now a horizontal slice of the cone at height y has radius given by $x = \frac{1}{2}(1 - y)$; the units here are in feet. Therefore the work done in building the anthill is

$$W = \int_0^1 \frac{1}{4}(150y)\pi(1 - y)^2\,dy = \frac{25}{8}\pi;$$

131

that is, approximately 9.82 ft-lb.

49. If the coordinate system is chosen with the origin at the midpoint
of the bottom of the dam and with the x-axis horizontal, then the
equation of the slanted edge of the dam is $y = 2x - 200$ (with
units in feet). Therefore the width of the dam at level y is
$2x = y + 200$. Thus the total force on the dam is

$$F = \int_0^{100} \rho(100 - y)(y + 200)\, dy.$$

52. The volume of the solid is

$$V = \int_0^c 2\pi\left(y + \frac{1}{c}\right)\frac{2}{c}\sqrt{y}\, dy$$

$$= 8\pi\left(\frac{1}{5}c^{3/2} + \frac{1}{3}c^{-1/2}\right).$$

It is clear that there is no maximum volume, because $V \to +\infty$ as
$c \to 0^+$. But $V \to +\infty$ as $c \to +\infty$ as well, so there is
a minimum volume; $dV/dc = 0$ when $c = \frac{1}{3}\sqrt{5}$, so this value
of c minimizes V.

Section 7.1

1. $(2^3)(2^4) = 2^{(3+4)} = 2^7 = 128.$

4. $2^{(2^3)} = 2^8 = 256.$

7. $(2^{12})^{1/3} = 2^{(12/3)} = 2^4 = 16.$

10. $(6^5)(3^{-5}) = (2^5)(3^5)(3^{-5}) = (2^5)(3^0) = 32.$

16. $\log_{12} 12^2 = 2\log_{12} 12 = 2.$

19. $\ln 6 = \ln(2\cdot 3) = (\ln 2) + (\ln 3).$

22. $\ln 200 = \ln(2^3 5^2) = (3\ln 2) + (2\ln 5)$.

28. $f'(x) = 3e^{3x}$.

34. $f'(x) = \dfrac{1}{2x}$.

37. $P(t) = (e^{\ln 2})^{-t} = e^{-t\ln 2}$, so

$$P'(t) = (-\ln 2)e^{-t\ln 2} = -2^{-t}\ln 2.$$

40. If $x = \log_{0.5} 16$, this means that $(0.5)^x = 16$. Take the reciprocal of each side in the last equation to obtain

$$2^x = \frac{1}{16} = \frac{1}{2^4} = 2^{-4},$$

then take the base 2 logarithm of the first and last terms above to conclude that $x = -4$. Finally verify this answer by substitution (because the method is predicated on the assumption that x <u>exists</u> -- that is, that the logarithm to the base $1/2$ of 16 exists).

43. $10^{-x} = 10^2$: $x = -2$.

46. $\log_x 16 = 2$ implies that $x^2 = 16$, so that $x = 4$ (only positive numbers other than 1 may be used as bases for logarithms).

49. Apply the natural logarithm after division of both sides by 3 to obtain $\ln(e^x) = \ln 1$, so that $x = 0$.

Section 7.2

4. $\dfrac{3(1 + x)^2}{(1 + x)^3} = \dfrac{3}{1 + x}$

10. $\dfrac{1}{\ln x} D_x(\ln x) = \dfrac{1}{x\ln x}$

13. Rewrite the given function as

$$f'(x) = \frac{1}{2}\left(\frac{-2x}{4 - x^2} - \frac{2x}{9 + x^2}\right) = -\frac{13x}{(4 - x^2)(9 + x^2)}.$$

16. $f'(x) = \dfrac{6x + 2}{3x^2 + 2x}$

19. Method 1: $g(t) = 2t\ln t$, so

$$g'(t) = \frac{2t}{t} + 2\ln t = 2(1 + \ln t).$$

Method 2: $g'(t) = (t)\left(\dfrac{2t}{t^2}\right) + \ln(t^2)$

$$= 2 + 2\ln t = 2(1 + \ln t).$$

22. $f'(x) = \dfrac{2\cos x}{2\sin x} = \cot x.$

28. $f(x) = \ln(\sin x) - \ln(\cos x)$, so

$$f'(x) = \frac{\cos x}{\sin x} + \frac{\sin x}{\cos x}$$

$$= \frac{1}{\sin x \cos x} = \sec x \csc x.$$

31. <u>Suggestion</u>: Write $g(t) = 2\ln t - \ln(t^2 + 1)$.

34. $\displaystyle\int \frac{dx}{3x + 5} = \frac{1}{3}\ln|3x + 5| + C.$

40. $\ln|\ln x| + C$

46. $\displaystyle\int \frac{\ln(x^3)}{x}\,dx = 3\int \frac{1}{x}(\ln x)\,dx = \frac{3}{2}(\ln x)^2 + C.$

49. The numerator is $\dfrac{1}{3}$ the derivative of the denominator.

134

52. $\dfrac{3 \ln x}{x^2} \to 0$ as $x \to +\infty$.

55. Suggestion: Make the substitution $x = \dfrac{1}{u^2}$.

58. $f^{(1)}(x) = x^{-1}$, $f^{(2)}(x) = (-1)x^{-2}$, $f^{(3)}(x) = (-2)(-1)x^{-3}$, $f^{(4)}(x) = (-3)(-2)(-1)x^{-4}$, ..., and in general, $f^{(n)}(x) = (-1)^{n-1}(n-1)! \, x^{-n}$ for $n \geq 1$. Proof: By induction on n.

64. Given: $y = f(x) = x \ln x$ for $x > 0$. Then

$$f'(x) = 1 + \ln x \quad \text{and} \quad f''(x) = \frac{1}{x}.$$

The critical point occurs where $\ln x = -1$, so $x = 1/e$ and

$$y = \frac{1}{e} \ln \frac{1}{e} = -\frac{1}{e}.$$

There are no possible points of inflection. The graph is decreasing on $(0, 1/e)$ and is increasing if $x > 1/e$. It is concave upward everywhere, and its only intercept is $(1, 0)$. As $x \to 0^{+}$, $y \to 0$; moreover, $dy/dx \to -\infty$. This helps sketch the graph near the point $(0, 0)$.

67. After simplifications, you will find that

$$\frac{dy}{dx} = \frac{2 - \ln x}{2x^{3/2}} \quad \text{and} \quad \frac{d^2 y}{dx^2} = \frac{3 \ln x - 8}{4x^{5/2}}.$$

70. $\dfrac{dy}{dx} = -\dfrac{1}{x^2}$;

$$\left\{ 1 + \left(\frac{dy}{dx} \right)^2 \right\}^{1/2} = (1 + x^{-4})^{1/2} = \frac{(x^4 + 1)^{1/2}}{x^2}.$$

The surface area of the part of the trumpet over the interval from $x = 1$ to $x = b$ (for $b > 1$) is then

$$A_b = \int_1^b \frac{2\pi}{x^3}(x^4 + 1)^{1/2}\, dx$$

$$\geq \int_1^b \frac{2\pi}{x^3} x^2\, dx = 2\pi \ln b.$$

Therefore the surface area of Gabriel's trumpet is infinite because $A_b \to +\infty$ as $b \to +\infty$. Next,

$$V_b = \int_1^b \frac{\pi}{x^2}\, dx = \pi\left(1 - \frac{1}{b}\right);$$

$V_b \to \pi$ as $b \to +\infty$. In summary, the volume is finite although the surface area is infinite.

71. The true value of the integral is approximately 872.5174045.

Section 7.3

1. $f'(x) = e^{2x} D_x(2x) = 2e^{2x}.$

4. $f'(x) = -3x^2 e^{4 - x^3}.$

10. $g'(t) = \frac{1}{2}(e^t - e^{-t})^{-1/2}(e^t + e^{-t}).$

16. $f'(x) = e^x \cos 2x - 2e^x \sin 2x.$

22. $g'(t) = \frac{2e^t}{(1 - e^t)^2}.$

28. $f'(x) = \frac{1}{2}x^{-1/2}(e^{\sqrt{x}} - e^{-\sqrt{x}}).$

34. $f'(x) = -(e^x - e^{-x})\sin(e^x + e^{-x}).$

40. $\frac{1}{3}e^{2x\sqrt{x}} + C$

46. $\dfrac{1}{2} e^{2x+3} + C$

49. Suggestion: Let $u = \sqrt{x}$.

52. Because $e^{a+b} = e^a e^b$, we have

$$\int \exp(x + e^x)\, dx = \int e^x \exp(e^x)\, dx = e^{e^x} + C.$$

Note that e^{e^x} means $e^{(e^x)}$, and is perhaps less likely to be misinterpreted if written in the form $\exp(e^x)$ or $\exp(\exp(x))$.

58. e^2

64. First, $\dfrac{dy}{dx} = 3x^2 e^{-x} - x^3 e^{-x} = x^2(3 - x)e^{-x}$

and

$$\dfrac{d^2 y}{dx^2} = x(x^2 - 6x + 6)e^{-x}.$$

Note that $y = 0$ when $x = 0$ and that this is the only intercept. Next, $dy/dx = 0$ when $x = 0$ and when $x = 3$, so there are horizontal tangents at $(0,0)$ and at $(3, 27/e^3)$ -- near the point $(3, 1.344)$. The second derivative vanishes when $x = 0$ and when $x^2 - 6x + 6 = 0$; the latter equation has the two solutions $x = 3 + \sqrt{3}$ and $x = 3 - \sqrt{3}$. Consequently there may be inflection points at $(0,0)$, near $(1.268, 0.574)$, and near $(4.732, 0.933)$. The graph is increasing if $x < 3$ and decreasing if $x > 3$. It is concave downward if $x < 0$ and if $|x - 3| < \sqrt{3}$, concave upward if both $|x - 3| > \sqrt{3}$ and $x > 0$. Because $x^3 e^{-x} \to 0$ as $x \to +\infty$, the x-axis is a horizontal asymptote. The graph is shown at the top of the next page.

67. $V = \displaystyle\int_0^1 \pi e^{2x}\, dx = \dfrac{\pi}{2}(e^2 - 1) \sim 10.0359.$

70. $A = \displaystyle\int_0^1 (2\pi)\{\dfrac{1}{2}(e^x + e^{-x})\}\{\dfrac{1}{2}(e^x + e^{-x})\}\, dx$

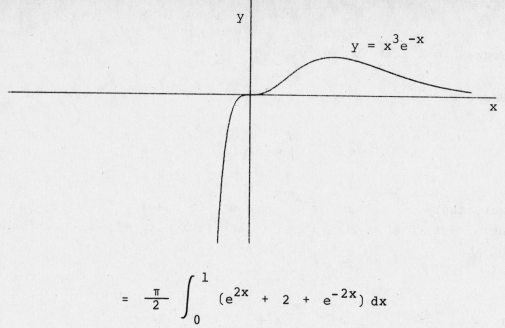

$y = x^3 e^{-x}$

$$= \frac{\pi}{2} \int_0^1 (e^{2x} + 2 + e^{-2x}) \, dx$$

$$= \frac{\pi}{2} (e^2 + 4 + e^{-2}) \sim 8.83865.$$

73. $f'(x) = (n - x)x^{n-1}e^{-x}$ and $f''(x) = \{(x - n)^2 - n\}x^{n-2}e^{-x}$. Because $f(x) \geq 0$ for $x \geq 0$, $f(0) = 0$, and $f(x) \to 0$ as $x \to +\infty$, $f(x)$ must have a maximum, and the critical point where $x = n$ is the sole candidate. Evaluate $f(n)$ to obtain the global maximum value of $f(x)$.

76. To avoid subscripts, write p for m_1, q for m_2, A for C_1, and B for C_2. Then with

$$y(x) = Ae^{px} + Be^{qx}, \quad \text{we obtain}$$

$$y'(x) = Ape^{px} + Bqe^{qx} \quad \text{and}$$

$$y''(x) = Ap^2e^{px} + Bq^2e^{qx}.$$

So

$$ay''(x) + by'(x) + cy(x)$$

$$= (aAp^2 + bAp + cA)e^{px} + (aBq^2 + bBq + cB)e^{qx}$$

$$= A(ap^2 + bp + c)e^{px} + B(aq^2 + bq + c)e^{qx}$$

$$= (A)(0)e^{px} + (B)(0)e^{qx} = 0.$$

138

1. $f'(x) = 10^x \ln 10.$

4. $f(x) = (\log_{10} e)(\ln \cos x) = \dfrac{1}{\ln 10} \ln(\cos x),$ so

$$f'(x) = \frac{1}{\ln 10} \cdot \frac{-\sin x}{\cos x}.$$

10. $f'(x) = 7^{(8^x)}(\ln 7)(8^x \ln 8).$

16. $f(x) = (\log_2 e)(\log_e x) = \dfrac{\ln x}{\ln 2},$ so

$$f'(x) = \frac{1}{x \ln 2}.$$

22. $f'(x) = \pi^x \ln \pi + \pi x^{\pi - 1}.$

28. The substitution $u = \dfrac{1}{x}$ yields

$$\int \frac{10^{1/x}}{x^2}\,dx = \int -10^u\,du$$

$$= -\frac{10^u}{\ln 10} + C = -\frac{10^{1/x}}{\ln 10} + C.$$

31. Write $\log_2 x$ as $(\ln x)(\ln 2)$. Then, if you wish, use the substitution $u = \ln x$.

34. $\ln y = \dfrac{1}{3} \ln(3 - x^2) - \dfrac{1}{4} \ln(x^4 + 1).$ So

$$\frac{dy}{dx} = (y)\left(\frac{-2x}{3(x^2 - 3)} - \frac{4x^3}{4(x^4 + 1)} \right)$$

$$= (y)\frac{2x^5 + 2x - 3x^5 + 9x^3}{3(x^2 - 3)(x^4 + 1)}$$

$$= \frac{x(x^4 - 9x^2 - 2)}{3(3 - x^2)^{2/3}(x^4 + 1)^{5/4}}.$$

37. $\ln y = (\ln x)^2.$ So

$$\frac{dy}{dx} = (y)\frac{2 \ln x}{x} = (x^{\ln x})\frac{2 \ln x}{x}.$$

139

40. $\dfrac{dy}{dx} = (y)\left(\dfrac{1}{2(x+1)} + \dfrac{1}{3(x+2)} + \dfrac{1}{4(x+3)} \right).$

46. $\ln y = x\ln\left(1 + \dfrac{1}{x}\right) = x\ln(x+1) - x\ln x.$

Therefore

$$\dfrac{dy}{dx} = \left(1 + \dfrac{1}{x}\right)^x \left\{ \ln(x+1) + \dfrac{x}{x+1} - (\ln x) - 1 \right\}.$$

52. $\ln y = x\ln(\cos x).$ Therefore

$$\dfrac{dy}{dx} = (\cos x)^x \left(\ln(\cos x) - \dfrac{x \sin x}{\cos x} \right).$$

55. If $y = \ln(a^{1/x})$ then $y = \dfrac{1}{x}\ln a.$ So

$$\lim_{x \to \infty} y = \lim_{x \to \infty} \dfrac{1}{x}(\ln a) = 0.$$

Therefore

$$\lim_{x \to \infty} \ln(a^{1/x}) = 0,$$

and consequently $\displaystyle\lim_{x \to \infty} a^{1/x} = e^0 = 1.$

58. (a)   Because $\ln x$ is an increasing function, the following two statements are equivalent:

$$2^x = x^{10} \qquad \text{and} \qquad x\ln 2 = 10\ln x.$$

The second of the two is equivalent to

$$\dfrac{\ln x}{x} = \dfrac{\ln 2}{10}$$

because $x = 0$ is a solution of neither.

(b) $\dfrac{\ln 2}{10} \sim 0.07$ is positive and less than $\dfrac{1}{3} \sim 0.37.$

So the graph of $y = \dfrac{1}{x}\ln x$ crosses the horizontal line

$y = \dfrac{\ln 2}{10}$ exactly twice.   Thus the equation

$$\dfrac{1}{x}\ln x = \dfrac{\ln 2}{10}$$

has exactly two solutions, and therefore so does the equation $2^x = x^{10}$.

(c)   Let $g(x) = \frac{1}{x} \ln x.$ Then

$$g(1) = 0 < \frac{\ln 2}{10} < \frac{\ln 2}{2} = g(2)$$

and

$$g(60) \sim 0.68 < \frac{\ln 2}{10} < 0.0078 \sim g(50).$$

So one solution lies in the interval $(1,2)$ and the other lies in $(50,60)$ because the function g has the intermediate value property of continuous functions.   Now let

$$h(x) = \frac{1}{x} \ln x - \frac{1}{10} \ln 2.$$

We use the Newton's method iteration

$$x \; \longleftarrow \; x - \frac{h(x)}{h'(x)},$$

which in this case can be written in the easily managed form

$$x \; \longleftarrow \; x - \frac{x \ln x - (0.1)x^2 \ln 2}{1 - \ln x}.$$

Results:

x_0	1.1	55.0
x_1	1.076820355	58.56671589
x_2	1.077549389	58.76951642
x_3	1.077550150	58.77010593
x_4	1.077550150	58.77010594

Therefore the two solutions of the equation $2^x = x^{10}$ are approximately 1.07755 and 58.77011.

Section 7.5

1.   The principal at time t is $P(t) = 1000e^{(0.08)t}.$ So

$$P'(t) = 80e^{(0.08)t}.$$

Answers: $P'(5) = \$119.35$ and $P'(20) = \$396.24.$

4. Suppose that the skull was formed at time $t = 0$ (in years). Then the amount of C^{14} it contains at time t will be

$$Q(t) = Q_0 e^{-kt}$$

where Q_0 is the initial amount and

$$k = \frac{\ln 2}{5700} \sim 0.0001216.$$

We find the value $t = T$ corresponding to "now" by solving

$$Q(t) = \frac{1}{6} Q_0:$$

$$\frac{1}{6} Q_0 = Q_0 e^{-kT}, \quad \text{so} \quad 6 = e^{kT};$$

therefore

$$T = \frac{1}{6} \ln 6 = 5700 \frac{\ln 6}{\ln 2} \sim 14{,}734.$$

Consequently the age of the skull is approximately 14,734 years.

7. $1 + r = (1 + \frac{0.09}{4})^4$ for quarterly compounding, and in this case we find that

(a) $r \sim 9.308\%.$

With the aid of similar formulas, we obtain the other four answers.

10. If $C(t)$ is the concentration of the drug at time t (hours), then

$$C(t) = C_0 e^{-kt}$$

where $k = \frac{1}{5} \ln 2$. We require C_0 so large that

$$C(1) = (45)(20) = 2250.$$

Thus $C_0 e^{-k} \geq 2250$; that is,

$$C_0 \geq 2250 e^k \sim 2584.57 \quad (mg).$$

13. Let $Q(t)$ denote the amount of radioactive cobalt remaining at time t (in years), with the occurrence of the accident set at time $t = 0$. Then

$$Q(t) = Q_0 \exp\left(-\frac{t \ln 2}{5.27}\right).$$

If T is the number of years until the level of radioactivity has dropped to a hundredth of its initial value, then

$$\frac{1}{100} = \exp\left(-\frac{T \ln 2}{5.27}\right),$$

and it follows that $T = (5.27)\dfrac{\ln 100}{\ln 2} \sim 35$ (years).

16. Let $T = T(t)$ denote the temperature at time t; by Newton's law of cooling, we have

$$\frac{dT}{dt} = k(T - A).$$

Here, $A = 0$, $T(0) = 25$, and $T(20) = 15$. Also $\dfrac{dT}{dt} = kT$, so $T(t) = T_0 e^{kt} = 25 e^{kt}$. Next,

$$15 = T(20) = 25 e^{20k},$$

so

$$k = \frac{1}{20} \ln\left(\frac{3}{5}\right).$$

Now $T(t) = 5$ when $5 = 25 e^{kt}$; that is, when

$$t = -\frac{20 \ln 5}{\ln(3/5)} \sim 63.01.$$

Answer: About one hour and three minutes after putting it on the porch.

19. We begin with the equation $p(x) = (29.92)e^{-x/5}$.

   (a) $p\left(\dfrac{10,000}{5280}\right) \sim 20.486$ (inches);

   $p\left(\dfrac{30,000}{5280}\right) \sim 9.406$ (inches).

(b) If x is the altitude in question, then we must solve

$$15 = (29.92)e^{-x/5}:$$

$$5\ln(\frac{29.92}{15}) = x \sim 3.4524 \quad (miles),$$

approximately 18,230 feet.

Section 7.6

1. Given: $\frac{dy}{dx} = y + 1; \quad y(0) = 1.$

$$\frac{1}{y + 1} \frac{dy}{dx} = 1;$$

$$\ln(y + 1) = x + C;$$

$$y + 1 = Ke^{x}.$$

When x = 0, y = 1. Therefore

$$2 = (K)(1) = K,$$

so the solution is $y(x) = -1 + 2e^{x}.$

4. $\frac{dy}{dx} = \frac{1}{4} - \frac{y}{16} = -\frac{1}{16}(y - 4); \quad y(0) = 20.$

$$\frac{1}{y - 4} \frac{dy}{dx} = -\frac{1}{16};$$

$$\ln(y - 4) = C_1 - \frac{x}{16};$$

$$y = 4 + \exp(-\frac{x}{16}).$$

We are given $20 = y(0) = 4 + C$, so C = 16. Answer:

$$y(x) = 4 + 16e^{-x/16}.$$

10. $v(t) = 10 - 20e^{5t}.$

16. Let $Q(t)$ be the number of pounds of salt in the tank at time t (in seconds). Now $Q(0) = 50$, and

$$\frac{dQ}{dt} = -\frac{5}{1000} Q(t) = -\frac{1}{200} Q(t).$$

Therefore

$$Q(t) = 50e^{-t/200}.$$

Next, $Q(t) = 10$ when $e^{-t/200} = \frac{1}{5}$, so that $t = 200 \ln 5$. So 10 pounds of salt will remain in the tank after approximately 5 minutes and 22 seconds.

19. In the notation of Problem 18, we have $v = v_0 e^{-kt}$ where we are given $v_0 = 40$. Here, also, $v(10) = 20$, so that $20 = 40e^{-10k}$. It follows that $k = (0.1) \ln 2$, so by Part (b) of Problem 18 the total distance traveled will be $\frac{1}{k} v_0 = \frac{(40)(10)}{\ln 2}$ -- that is, approximately 577 feet.

22. $\frac{dx}{dt} + ax = be^{ct}$, $x(0) = x_0$, $a + c \neq 0$.

$$e^{at} \frac{dx}{dt} + axe^{at} = be^{(a+c)t}.$$

$$D_t \{e^{at} x(t)\} = be^{(a+c)t}.$$

$$e^{at} x(t) = C + \frac{b}{a+c} e^{(a+c)t} \qquad (a + c \neq 0).$$

So

$$x(t) = Ce^{-at} + \frac{b}{a+c} e^{ct}.$$

Also

$$x_0 = x(0) = C + \frac{b}{a+c},$$

and hence

$$C = x_0 - \frac{b}{a+c}.$$

Therefore

$$x(t) = (x_0 - \frac{b}{a + c})e^{-at} + \frac{b}{a + c}e^{ct}$$

$$= x_0 e^{-at} + \frac{b}{a + c}(e^{ct} - e^{-at}).$$

25. $\frac{dv}{dt} = -\rho v - g, \quad \rho = \frac{k}{m} > 0.$

$$v(t) = (v_0 + \frac{g}{\rho})e^{-\rho t} - \frac{g}{\rho}.$$

So the limiting velocity is $v_\tau = \frac{g}{\rho}.$

$$y(t) = y_0 - v_\tau t + \frac{1}{\rho}(v_0 + v_\tau)(1 - e^{-\rho t}).$$

With $\rho = 0.1$ and $v_0 = 160,$ we find that

$$v(t) = (160 + 320)e^{-t/10} - 320.$$

The velocity of the ball is zero when $480e^{-t/10} = 320,$ and it follows that this occurs when $t = 10\ln(1.5) \sim 4.05465$ (seconds). Next,

$$Y_{max} = -320t + (10)(160 + 320)(1 - \frac{2}{3})$$

$$= -(320)\{10\ln(1.5)\} + 1600 \sim 302.51165 \quad (feet).$$

So here are the answers to Part (a): The maximum height attained by the ball is approximately 302.5 feet, and the time required for the ball to reach that height is about 4.055 seconds.

Now we turn to the downward part of the ball's flight. Note that $v_0 = 0,$ that $v_\tau = 320,$ and therefore that

$$v(t) = 320e^{-t/10} - 320;$$

$$y(t) = y_{max} - 320t + (10)(320)(1 - e^{-t/10}).$$

We solve the equation $y(t) = 0$:

$$1600 - 3200\ln(1.5) - 320t + 32000(1 - e^{-t/10}) = 0;$$

146

$$3200e^{-t/10} + 320t + 3200\ln(1.5) - 4800 = 0;$$

$$10e^{-t/10} + t + 10\ln(1.5) - 15 = 0.$$

The iteration

$$t \longleftarrow 15 - 10\ln(1.5) - 10e^{-t/10}$$

leads to the solution $t \sim 4.6875$ (seconds). The total time in air is therefore about 8.7422 seconds. The impact velocity is the value of v evaluated at $t \sim 4.6875$, and that's

$$v_{imp} = 320(e^{-t/10} - 1) \sim -119.75 \quad (\text{ft/sec}).$$

Section 7.7

1. Consumption rate: $C(t) = C_0 e^{(0.05)t}$; $C_0 = 3 \times 10^{14}$.

$$1.2 \times 10^{16} = \int_0^T (3 \times 10^{14}) e^{(0.05)t} \, dt;$$

$$\frac{120}{3} = \left[\frac{1}{0.05} e^{(0.05)t} \right]_0^T ,$$

so $e^{T/20} = 3$. Therefore the time T that the known reserves will last is $T = 20\ln 3 \sim 22$ years.

4. We require

$$\int_0^{60} (3 \times 10^{14}) e^{rt} \, dt = 1.2 \times 10^{16}.$$

This leads to the equation $e^{60r} - 1 = 40r$. The iteration

$$r \longleftarrow r - \frac{e^{60r} - 40r - 1}{60e^{60r} - 40}$$

of Newton's method gives these results (rounded, of course):

$$r_0 = -0.01,$$
$$r_1 = -0.0172,$$
$$r_2 = -0.0148,$$
$$r_3 = -0.0146,$$
$$r_4 = -0.0146.$$

Answer: Consumption would have to be decreased at an annual rate of about 1.5%.

7. Let R denote the annual rate in question. We require

$$100,000 = \int_5^{15} Re^{-(0.08)t} \, dt,$$

so that

$$\frac{100,000}{R} = \left[\frac{e^{-(0.08)t}}{0.08} \right]_{15}^{5};$$

$$\frac{8000}{R} = e^{-0.4} - e^{-1.2};$$

$$R = \frac{8000}{e^{-0.4} - e^{-1.2}} \sim \$21,672.83.$$

Section 7.8

1. Given: $\frac{dx}{dt} = 2t - 1$; $x(0) = 3$.

$$\int 1 \, dx = \int (2t - 1) \, dt,$$

so that $x = t^2 - t + C$. Because $x(0) = 3$, we find that $C = 3$. Therefore $x(t) = t^2 - t + 3$.

4. Given: $\frac{dx}{dt} = e^{t-x}$; $x(0) = \ln 2$.

$$\int e^x \, dx \; = \; \int e^t \, dt;$$

$e^x \; = \; e^t + C.$ But $e^{\ln 2} \; = \; 2 \; = \; 1 + C,$ so $C = 1:$

$e^x \; = \; 1 + e^t,$ and therefore $x(t) \; = \; \ln(1 + e^t).$

7. $\displaystyle \int \frac{1}{x^2} \, dx \; = \; \int \sin t \, dt;$

$$-\frac{1}{x} \; = \; -\cos t \; + \; C;$$

$$-1 \; = \; -1 \; + \; C: \quad C = 0. \quad \text{So}$$

$$x(t) \; = \; \frac{1}{\cos t} \; = \; \sec t.$$

10.   Given: $\displaystyle \frac{dP}{dt} \; = \; kP^2; \quad P(0) \; = \; P_0 \; > \; 0.$

$$\int \frac{1}{P^2} \, dP \; = \; \int k \, dt;$$

$$-\frac{1}{P} \; = \; C \; + \; kt;$$

$$P(t) \; = \; -\frac{1}{C + kt} \, .$$

$$P_0 \; = \; P(0) \; = \; -\frac{1}{P}: \quad C \; = \; -\frac{1}{P_0} \, .$$

(a) $\displaystyle P(t) \; = \; \frac{P_0}{1 - P_0 kt} \, .$

(b)   Given $P_0 = 2$ and $P(3) = 4,$

$$4 \; = \; P(3) \; = \; \frac{2}{1 - (2)(k)(3)} \; = \; \frac{2}{1 - 6k} \, .$$

It now follows that $k = \dfrac{1}{12}$,   so "doomsday" occurs at

$$t \; = \; \frac{1}{kP_0} \; = \; 6 \quad \text{(months)}.$$

13. Given: $\dfrac{dx}{dt} = x^2 + 3x + 2; \quad x(0) = 0.$

$$\int \frac{dx}{(x+2)(x+1)} = \int 1 \, dt;$$

$$\int \left(\frac{1}{x+1} - \frac{1}{x+2} \right) dx = t + C;$$

$$\ln \frac{x+1}{x+2} = t + C.$$

Because $x(0) = 0$, $C = \ln \dfrac{1}{2}$. So

$$\frac{x+1}{x+2} = \frac{1}{2} e^t;$$

$$x + 1 = \frac{1}{2} x e^t + e^t.$$

Therefore

$$\left(1 - \frac{1}{2} e^t \right) x = e^t - 1;$$

$$x(t) = (-2) \frac{e^t - 1}{e^t - 2}.$$

16. $\dfrac{dx}{dt} = 3k(a - x)^2:$

$$\int \frac{dx}{(a-x)^2} = \int 3k \, dt;$$

$$\frac{1}{a-x} = C + 3kt;$$

$$x - a = - \frac{1}{C + 3kt};$$

$$x(t) = a - \frac{1}{C + 3kt}.$$

Now $0 = x(0) = a - \dfrac{1}{C}$, so $C = \dfrac{1}{a}$. Hence

150

$$x(t) = a(1 - \frac{1}{3akt + 1}).$$

It is now clear that $x(t) \to a$ as $t \to +\infty$. Because $b = 3a$ initially and during the reaction, all of substances A and B are used.

Chapter 7 Miscellaneous Problems

1. $\ln 2\sqrt{x} = \ln 2 + \frac{1}{2} \ln x$, so $f'(x) = \frac{1}{2x}$.

4. $f'(x) = \frac{1}{2}(x^{-1/2})10^{(x^{1/2})} \ln 10$

7. $f'(x) = 3x^2 e^{-1/x^2} + x^3 e^{-1/x^2}(2x^{-3})$

$$= (2 + 3x^2)e^{-1/x^2}.$$

10. $f'(x) = \{\exp(10^x)\}\{10^x\}\{\ln 10\}$

13. $f'(x) = \frac{(x - 1) - (x + 1)}{(x - 1)^2} \exp(\frac{x + 1}{x - 1})$

$$= -\frac{2}{(x - 1)^2} \exp(\frac{x + 1}{x - 1})$$

16. $f'(x) = \frac{1}{x} \cos(\ln x)$

19. $f'(x) = \frac{3^x \cos x + (3^x \ln 3) \sin x}{3^x \sin x}$

$$= \frac{\cos x + (\ln 3) \sin x}{\sin x} = \cot x + \ln 3.$$

22. If $y = x^{\sin x}$ then $\ln y = (\sin x)(\ln x)$. So

$$\frac{dy}{dx} = y\{\frac{1}{x} \sin x + (\cos x)(\ln x)\}$$

$$= (x^{\sin x})\{\frac{1}{x} \sin x + (\cos x)(\ln x)\}.$$

28. $\displaystyle\int \frac{e^x - e^{-x}}{e^x + e^{-x}}\, dx \;=\; \ln(e^x + e^{-x}) \;+\; C.$

31. Let $u = \sqrt{x}$.

34. Let $u = \ln x$. Then $du = \dfrac{1}{x}\, dx$, and so

$$\int \frac{1}{x}\,(1 + \ln x)^{1/2}\, dx \;=\; \int (1 + u)^{1/2}\, du$$

$$=\; \frac{2}{3}\,(1 + u)^{3/2} + C \;=\; \frac{2}{3}\,(1 + \ln x)^{3/2} + C.$$

37. First, $dx = 2t\, dt$, and so $x = t^2 + C$. But $x(0) = 17$, and so $x(t) = t^2 + 17$.

40. $e^{-x}\, dx = dt$, so $-e^{-x} = C + t$. Now $e^{-2} = C + 0$, and so

$$-e^{-x} \;=\; -e^{-2} + t;$$

$$e^{-x} \;=\; e^{-2} + t;$$

$$-x \;=\; \ln(e^{-2} - t);$$

$$x(t) \;=\; -\ln(e^{-2} - t).$$

43. $\dfrac{dx}{x} = \cos t\, dt$, so $\ln|x| = C_1 + \sin t$. Consequently $x(t) = Ce^{\sin t}$. Because $x(0) = \sqrt{2}$, $C = \sqrt{2}$. So

$$x(t) \;=\; \sqrt{2}\, e^{\sin t}.$$

46. $\dfrac{dy}{dx} = 1 - \dfrac{1}{x}$ and $\dfrac{d^2 y}{dx^2} = \dfrac{1}{x^2}$.

The graph is concave upward for all x, and there is a horizontal tangent at $(1,1)$. The function is decreasing on $(0,1)$ and increasing for $x > 1$. Note that as $x \to 0^{+}$, $y(x) \to +\infty$ while $dy/dx \to -\infty$. The graph is shown next.

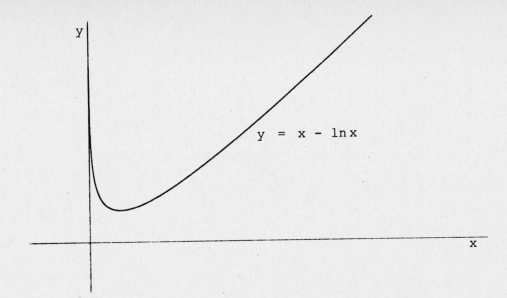

$$y = x - \ln x$$

49. $\dfrac{dy}{dx} = \dfrac{1}{x^2} e^{-1/x}$ and $\dfrac{d^2y}{dx^2} = \dfrac{1 - 2x}{x^4} e^{-1/x}$.

The graph is shown in the answer section of the text.

52. At time t (in years), the amount to be repaid will be

$$1000\, e^{(0.1)t}.$$

So the profit on selling would be

$$P(t) = 800 \exp\left(\frac{1}{2}\sqrt{t}\right) - 1000 \exp\left(\frac{t}{10}\right).$$

$$P'(t) = 200 t^{-1/2} \exp\left(\frac{1}{2} t^{1/2}\right) - 100 \exp\left(\frac{t}{10}\right).$$

$$P'(t) = 0 \quad \text{when} \quad 2 \exp\left(\frac{1}{2} t^{1/2}\right) = t^{1/2} \exp\left(\frac{t}{10}\right).$$

The iteration

$$t \quad \longleftarrow \quad \left\{ 2 \exp\left(\frac{1}{2} t^{1/2}\right) \exp\left(-\frac{t}{10}\right) \right\}^2$$

yields $t \sim 11.7519$ years as the optimal time to cut and sell. The resulting profit would be $1202.37.

153

58. Let $v = v(t)$ denote its velocity at time t and $x = x(t)$ its position (distance traveled) at time t. We choose $t = 0$ for the beginning of the slide, so that

$$\frac{dv}{dt} = -kv, \quad v(0) = v_0, \quad x(0) = 0,$$

where k is a positive constant. Now

$$\frac{dv}{v} = -k\,dt, \quad \text{so} \quad \ln v = C_1 - kt;$$

$$v(t) = Ce^{-kt}.$$

But $v_0 = v(0) = C$, so $v(t) = v_0 e^{-kt}$. Also

$$\frac{dx}{dt} = v(t), \quad \text{so} \quad x(t) = C_2 - \frac{1}{k}v_0 e^{-kt}.$$

But $0 = x(0) = C_2 - \frac{1}{k}v_0$, so $C_2 = \frac{1}{k}v_0$. So

$$x(t) = \frac{1}{k}v_0(1 - e^{-kt}).$$

Finally, $v'(0) = -kv_0 = -2$, so $k = \frac{2}{v_0}$. Thus

$$v(t) = v_0 \exp(-\frac{2t}{v_0})$$

and

$$x(t) = \frac{1}{2}(v_0)^2\{1 - \exp(-\frac{2t}{v_0})\}.$$

We are given $x = 1800$ when $v = 0$. Therefore

$$\lim_{t \to \infty} x(t) = 1800 = \lim_{t \to \infty} \frac{1}{2}(v_0)^2\{1 - \exp(-\frac{2t}{v_0})\}.$$

Therefore $(v_0)^2 = 3600$. Answer: $v_0 = 60$ meters per second, approximately 134.22 miles per hour.

61. Let $Q(t)$ denote the temperature at time t, with t in hours and $t = 0$ corresponding to 11:00 P.M., the time of the power failure. Let $A = 20$ be the room temperature. By Newton's law of cooling,

$$\frac{dQ}{dt} = k(A - Q), \quad \text{so that} \quad \frac{1}{A - Q} dQ = k \, dt$$

where k is a positive constant. Next,

$$\ln(A - Q) = C_1 - kt,$$

so that $Q(t) = A - Ce^{-kt}$. Now $Q_0 = Q(0) = A - C$, so $C = A - Q_0$. Thus

$$Q(t) = A + (T_0 - A)e^{-kt}.$$

We are given $Q_0 = -16$, $A = 20$, and $Q(7) = -10$. We must find the value $t = T$ at which $Q(T) = 0$. Now

$$Q(t) = 20 - 36e^{-kt};$$

$$Q(7) = -10 = 20 - 36e^{-7k};$$

$$30 = 36e^{-7k};$$

$$k = \frac{1}{7} \ln(1.2).$$

Next,

$$0 = Q(T) = 20 - 36e^{-kT};$$

$$20 = 36e^{-kT}:$$

Therefore $e^{kT} = 1.8$, and thus

$$T = \frac{1}{k} \ln(1.8) = \frac{7 \ln(1.8)}{\ln(1.2)} \sim 22.5673.$$

Answer: The critical temperature will be reached about 22 hours and 34 minutes after the power goes off; that is, at about 9:34 P.M. on the following day. (The data used in this problem are those obtained during an actual incident of the sort described.)

64. Let $x(t)$ denote the distance traveled after t seconds and let $v(t) = dx/dt$ denote the velocity of the car then. We are given $x(0) = 0$, $v(0) = 0$, and

$$\frac{dv}{dt} = a - \rho v.$$

Part (a): $\dfrac{dv}{a - \rho v} = dt,$ so $\dfrac{-\rho\, dv}{a - \rho v} = -\rho\, dt.$

Thus

$$\ln(a - \rho v) = C_1 - \rho t,$$

and so

$$a - \rho v = Ce^{-\rho t}.$$

But $v(0) = 0,$ so $C = a.$ Moreover,

$$a - \rho v = ae^{-\rho t},$$

so

$$v(t) = \frac{a}{\rho}(1 - e^{-\rho t}).$$

Part (b): Given $a = 17.6$ and $\rho = 0.1,$ we are to find $v(10)$ and the limiting velocity $v_{lim}.$

$$v_{lim} = \lim_{t \to \infty} \frac{a}{\rho}(1 - e^{-\rho t}) = \frac{a}{\rho} = 176$$

feet per second, exactly 120 miles per hour. And

$$v(10) = \frac{a}{\rho}(1 - e^{-10\rho}) = 176(1 - e^{-1}) \sim 111.2532$$

feet per second, approximately 75.85 miles per hour.

Section 8.2

1. $f'(x) = \{\cos(2x + 3)\} D_x(2x + 3) = 2\cos(2x + 3).$

4. $-\dfrac{\csc^2(x^{1/2})}{2x^{1/2}}$

10. $-2e^{\cot 2x}\csc^2 2x$

16. $\dfrac{\cos^2 x}{1 - \sin x} = 1 + \sin x,$ so $f'(x) = \cos x.$

22. $\dfrac{1}{2}(1 + \sec^3 x)^{-1/2}(3\sec^3 x \tan x)$

28. $\dfrac{7}{x}\sec(7\ln x)\tan(7\ln x)$

34. Let $u = \sqrt{x}$. Then $du = \dfrac{1}{2}x^{-1/2}\,dx$, so that $\dfrac{dx}{\sqrt{x}} = 2\,du$. So

$$\int \frac{\tan^2(x^{1/2})}{x^{1/2}}\,dx = \int 2\tan^2 u\,du$$

$$= 2\int(\sec^2 u - 1)\,du$$

$$= 2\tan u - 2u + C = 2\tan\sqrt{x} - 2\sqrt{x} + C.$$

40. $$\int \frac{\tan^2 x}{\sec x}\,dx = \int \frac{\sec^2 x - 1}{\sec x}\,dx$$

$$= \int(\sec x - \cos x)\,dx$$

$$= \ln|\sec x + \tan x| - \sin x + C.$$

43. $\dfrac{\sin x}{\cos^2 x} = (\cos x)^{-2}\sin x = \sec x \tan x.$

46. $\cos^2 2x = \dfrac{1}{2}(1 + \cos 4x)$, so the answer is

$$\frac{x}{2} + \frac{\sin 4x}{8} + C.$$

52. $e^{\tan x} + C$

58. $\dfrac{1}{5}\tan 5x + C$

61. $f'(x) = \sec^2 x$ is never zero. $f''(x) = 2\sec^2 x \tan x$ is zero at $(0,0)$, $(\pi,0)$, $(2\pi,0)$, $(-\pi,0)$, and so forth. These are not only all the intercepts, they are each inflection points as well. There are vertical asymptotes at $x = \pi/2$, $x = -\pi/2$, $x = 3\pi/3$, and so on. The function is increasing on each interval between consecutive asymptotes.

64. $f'(x) = -e^{-x}(\sin x + \cos x)$; $f''(x) = 2e^{-x}\sin x$.

$f'(x) = 0$ when $\tan x = -1$:

$$x = \frac{3\pi}{4}, \quad \frac{7\pi}{4}, \quad \frac{11\pi}{4}, \quad \ldots$$

Thus there are local maxima at $\pi/4$, $7\pi/4$, $15\pi/4$, $23\pi/4$, ..., and local minima at $3\pi/4$, $11\pi/4$, $19\pi/4$, ... The graph is shown below.

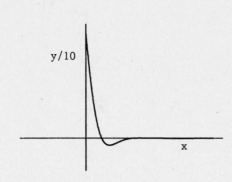

The actual graph for
Problem 64

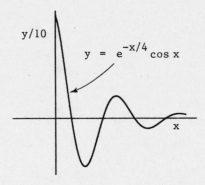

A "distortion" of the
graph for Problem 64

67. By the method of cylindrical shells:

$$V = \int_0^1 2\pi x \tan(\pi x^2/4)\, dx$$

$$= 4\left[\ln\{\sec(\pi x^2/4)\}\right]_0^1$$

$$= 4\ln\left(\frac{\sec(\pi/4)}{\sec(0)}\right) = 4\ln\sqrt{2} = \ln 4.$$

70. $\frac{1}{2}\sin^2 x + \frac{1}{2}\cos^2 x = C_1 - C_2 = \frac{1}{2}$.

Section 8.3

4. (a) 0; (b) π; (c) $\pi/3$; $3\pi/4$

158

10. $\dfrac{x}{1 + x^2} + \arctan x$

16. $\dfrac{1}{2x\sqrt{x - 1}}$

22. $\dfrac{\exp(\arcsin x)}{(1 - x^2)^{1/2}}$

28. $\dfrac{1}{(a^2 - x^2)^{1/2}}$, provided that $a > 0$.

34. $\operatorname{arcsec}|-2/\sqrt{3}| - \operatorname{arcsec}|-2| = \dfrac{\pi}{6} - \dfrac{\pi}{3} = -\dfrac{\pi}{6}$

37. Suggestion: Let $u = 2x$.

40. Let $u = \dfrac{2}{3}x$, so that $2x = 3u$ and $dx = \dfrac{3}{2}du$. Then

$$\int \frac{1}{x(4x^2 - 9)^{1/2}}\,dx = \int \frac{(3/2)\,du}{(3/2)u(9u^2 - 9)^{1/2}}$$

$$= \int \frac{1}{3u(u^2 - 1)^{1/2}}\,du = \frac{1}{3}\sec^{-1}|u| + C$$

$$= \frac{1}{3}\sec^{-1}\left|\frac{2}{3}x\right| + C.$$

43. Suggestion: Let $u = \dfrac{1}{5}x^3$.

46. Suggestion: Let $u = \sec x$.

49. Suggestion: Let $u = \ln x$.

52. $\displaystyle\int_0^1 \frac{x^3}{1 + x^4}\,dx = \left[\frac{1}{4}\ln(1 + x^4)\right]_0^1 = \frac{1}{4}\ln 2.$

58. Part (a): We begin with the identity

$$\tan(A + B) = \frac{\tan A + \tan B}{1 - \tan A \tan B}.$$

Let $x = \tan A$ and $y = \tan B$, and suppose that $xy < 1$. We will treat only the case in which x and y are both positive; the other cases are similar. In this case, the formula above shows that $0 < A + B < \pi/2$, so it is valid to apply the inverse tangent function to each side of the above identity to obtain

$$A + B = \arctan \frac{x + y}{1 - xy},$$

and therefore

$$\arctan x + \arctan y = \arctan \frac{x + y}{1 - xy}.$$

Part (b/i): $\arctan \dfrac{(1/2) + (1/3)}{1 - (1/6)} = \arctan(1) = \dfrac{\pi}{4}$.

(b/ii): $\arctan \dfrac{(1/3) + (1/3)}{1 - (1/9)} + \arctan(1/7)$

$= \arctan(3/4) + \arctan(1/7)$

$= \arctan \dfrac{(3/4) + (1/7)}{1 - (3/28)} = \arctan \dfrac{25}{25} = \dfrac{\pi}{4}$.

(b/iii): $\arctan \dfrac{(120/119) - (1/239)}{1 + (120/119)(1/239)}$

$= \arctan \dfrac{28561/28441}{28561/28441} = \dfrac{\pi}{4}$.

(b/iv): $2 \arctan \dfrac{1}{5} = \arctan \dfrac{2/5}{1 - (1/25)}$

$= \arctan \dfrac{10}{24} = \arctan \dfrac{5}{12}$;

$4 \arctan \dfrac{1}{5} = \arctan \dfrac{10/12}{1 - (25/144)}$

$= \arctan \dfrac{120}{119}$;

the rest of Part (b/iv) follows from Part (b/iii).

64. See the diagram at the top of the next page for the meanings of the variables. We are to maximize $d\xi/dt$ given $dy/dt = -25$. Now

160

$$\tan \xi = \frac{y - 100}{50},$$

so

$$\xi = \tan^{-1}\left(\frac{y - 100}{50}\right).$$

Therefore

$$\frac{d\xi}{dt} = \frac{d\xi}{dy}\frac{dy}{dt}$$

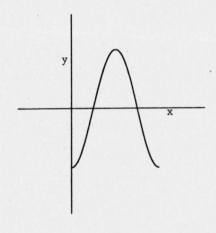

$$= -25 \frac{1/50}{1 + \{(y - 100)/50\}^2} = \frac{(-25)(50)}{2500 + (y - 100)^2}.$$

To find the value of y that maximizes $f(y) = d\xi/dt$, we need only minimize the last denominator above: $y = 100$. Answer: The elevator has maximum apparent speed when it's at eye level.

Section 8.4

4. The maximum value 2 occurs at odd multiples of $\pi/2$; the minimum value -2 occurs at multiples of π. One cycle of the graph is shown at the right.

10. Frequency: $2/\pi$. Period: $\pi/2 = 2\pi/k$, so $k = 4$. So

$$x(t) = 0\cos 4t - \frac{4}{4}\sin 4t = -\sin 4t.$$

Answer: The amplitude of the motion is 1.

13. Given: $x(t) = 5\cos \pi t$. Then $v = dx/dt = -5\pi \sin \pi t$. When $t = 1$, we have $v = v_{max} = 5\pi$.

16. Recall that we write ξ for the Greek lower-case letter theta throughout. Now $\xi = \pi$ when $t = 0$; $\xi = 11\pi$ when $t = 1$. So $\xi = \pi + 10\pi t = \pi(10t + 1)$. And

$$y = 3\sin\xi = 3\sin(\pi\{10t + 1\}).$$

Displacement: $f(t) = 5 + 3\sin(\pi\{10t + 1\})$.

Velocity: $v(t) = 30\pi\cos(\pi\{10t + 1\})$.

$$v'(t) = -300\pi^2\sin(\pi\{10t + 1\});$$

$v'(t) = 0$ when t is an integral multiple of 0.1, so $v_{max} = v(-0.1) = 30\pi\cos 0 = 30\pi$ (ft/sec).

19. We use the formula

$$p_1/p_2 = (R_1/R_2)(L_1/L_2)^{1/2}$$

derived in the solution of Problem 17. Thus

$$(3960)(100.10)^{1/2} = R_2(100)^{1/2};$$

$$R_2 = \frac{(3960)(100.10)^{1/2}}{10} \sim 3961.9795.$$

Therefore the height of the mountain is about 1.9795 miles -- that is, approximately $10{,}452$ feet.

22. If $y(t) = x(t) - \dfrac{a}{k^2}$, then

$$y'(t) = x'(t) \quad \text{and} \quad y''(t) = x''(t).$$

Thus

$$y(t) = A\cos kt + B\sin kt,$$

and therefore

$$x(t) = \frac{a}{k^2} + y(t)$$

$$= \frac{a}{k^2} + A\cos kt + B\sin kt.$$

4. $-2e^{2x} \operatorname{sech} e^{2x} \tanh e^{2x}$

10. $\dfrac{\operatorname{sech}^2 x}{1 + \tanh^2 x}$

16. $\displaystyle \int \cosh^2 3u \, du = \int \frac{1}{2}(1 + \cosh 6u) \, du$

$$= \frac{1}{2}\left(u + \frac{1}{6}\sinh 6u\right) + C$$

$$= \frac{1}{2}u + \frac{1}{6}\sinh 3u \cosh 3u + C$$

19. If necessary, let $u = 2x$.

22. $\displaystyle \int \sinh^4 x \, dx = \int (\sinh^2 x)^2 \, dx$

$$= \int \frac{1}{4}(\cosh 2x - 1)^2 \, dx$$

$$= \frac{1}{4}\int (\cosh^2 2x - 2\cosh 2x + 1) \, dx$$

$$= \frac{1}{4}\int \left\{ \frac{1}{2}(\cosh 4x + 1) - 2\cosh 2x + 1 \right\} dx$$

$$= \frac{1}{32}\sinh 4x - \frac{1}{4}\sinh 2x + \frac{3}{8}x + C$$

28. $\displaystyle \int \frac{e^x + e^{-x}}{e^x + e^{-x}} \, dx = \ln|e^x - e^{-x}| + C_1$

$$= -\ln 2 + \ln|e^x - e^{-x}| + C = \ln|\sinh x| + C$$

31. By (8), $\cosh(x + y) = \cosh x \cosh y + \sinh x \sinh y$. Therefore

$$\cosh 2x = \cosh^2 x + \sinh^2 x, \qquad (10)$$

and so

$$\cosh 2x = \cosh^2 x + \cosh^2 x - 1$$

$$= 2\cosh^2 x - 1.$$

Consequently

$$\cosh^2 x = \frac{1}{2}(1 + \cosh 2x). \qquad (11)$$

34. By the "slab" method, we find that

$$V = \int_0^\pi \pi \sinh^2 x \, dx$$

$$= \frac{\pi}{2} \int_0^\pi (\cosh 2x - 1) \, dx$$

$$= \frac{\pi}{2} \left[\frac{1}{2} \sinh 2x - x \right]_0^\pi$$

$$= \frac{\pi}{2} \left(\frac{1}{2} \sinh 2\pi - \pi \right)$$

$$= \frac{\pi}{8} (e^{2\pi} - e^{-2\pi}) - \frac{1}{2} \pi^2 \sim 205.3515.$$

Section 8.6

4. $\dfrac{1}{1 - (x^2 + 1)} \cdot \dfrac{x}{(x^2 + 1)^{1/2}} = -\dfrac{1}{x(x^2 + 1)^{1/2}}$

10. $D_x (\tanh^{-1} 3x)^{-1} = -(\tanh^{-1} 3x)^{-2} D_x \tanh^{-1} 3x$

$$= -\frac{1}{(\tanh^{-1} 3x)^2} \cdot \frac{3}{1 - 9x^2}$$

164

13. Let $x = 2u$; then $dx = 2\,du$, and so

$$\int_{1/2}^{1} \frac{dx}{4 - x^2} = \int_{1/4}^{1/2} \frac{2}{4(1 - u^2)}\,du$$

$$= \left[\frac{1}{4} \ln \frac{1 + u}{1 - u} \right]_{1/4}^{1/2}$$

$$= \frac{1}{4}\left(\ln 3 - \ln \frac{5}{3} \right) = \frac{1}{4} \ln \frac{9}{5} \sim 0.14695.$$

16. Let $x = 5u$; then $dx = 5\,du$, and so

$$\int \frac{1}{x(x^2 + 25)^{1/2}}\,dx = \int \frac{5}{5u(25u^2 + 25)^{1/2}}\,du$$

$$= \frac{1}{5} \int \frac{1}{u(u^2 + 1)^{1/2}}\,du = -\frac{1}{5} \operatorname{csch}^{-1}|u| + C$$

$$= -\frac{1}{5} \operatorname{csch}^{-1}\left| \frac{x}{5} \right| + C.$$

19. $$\int \frac{dx}{(1 - e^{2x})^{1/2}} = \int \frac{e^x}{e^x(1 - e^{2x})^{1/2}}\,dx = -\operatorname{sech}^{-1}(e^x) + C$$

28. $y = y_0 - \dfrac{1}{\rho} \ln(\cosh t\sqrt{\rho g})$, $\rho = 0.001$, $g = 32$, and $y_0 = 500$. So

$$v = \frac{dy}{dt} = -\frac{1}{\rho} \frac{(\rho g)^{1/2} \sinh(t\{\rho g\}^{1/2})}{\cosh(t\{\rho g\}^{1/2})}.$$

Let T be the time of impact. Then

$$0 = 500 - 1000 \ln(\cosh t\sqrt{32/1000});$$

$$\frac{1}{2} = \ln(\cosh T\sqrt{32/1000});$$

$$e^{1/2} = \cosh(2T\sqrt{5}/25).$$

So

$$T = \frac{5}{2}\sqrt{5}\,\cosh^{-1}(\sqrt{e}\,)$$

$$= \frac{5}{2}\sqrt{5}\,\ln(\sqrt{e} + \sqrt{e-1}) \sim 6.0655$$

seconds. The impact speed is

$$v = \sqrt{g/\rho}\,\tanh(T\sqrt{g\rho}\,).$$

Now $\cosh(T\sqrt{\rho g}\,) = \sqrt{e}$, so

$$\sinh(T\sqrt{\rho g}\,) = \sqrt{e-1}.$$

Therefore

$$v = \sqrt{g/\rho}\,\sqrt{(e-1)/e}$$

$$= 80\sqrt{5}\,\sqrt{(e-1)/e}$$

feet per second; that is, about 142.22 feet per second.

31. $y = a\cosh(x/a)$ where $a = T_0/w$.

$$s = \int_0^x \{1 + (dy/dx)^2\}^{1/2}\,dx.$$

Now $dy/dx = \sinh(x/a)$, so

$$s = \int_0^x \{1 + \sinh^2(x/a)\}^{1/2}\,dx$$

$$= \int_0^x \cosh(x/a)\,dx = a\sinh(x/a);$$

$$s = \frac{T_0}{w}\sinh\left(\frac{wx}{T_0}\right).$$

34. $T^2 = (T_0)^2 + w^2 s^2$

$$= (T_0)^2 + w^2\{(T_0)^2/w^2\}\sinh^2\left(\frac{wx}{T_0}\right)$$

$$= (T_0)^2\{1 + \sinh^2\left(\frac{wx}{T_0}\right)\}$$

$$= (T_0)^2\cosh^2\left(\frac{wx}{T_0}\right);$$

$$T = T_0\cosh\left(\frac{wx}{T_0}\right).$$

But $y = (T_0/w)\cosh(wx/T_0)$. Therefore

$$wy = T = T_0\cosh(wx/T_0).$$

Chapter 8 Miscellaneous Problems

4. $6\sec^2(3x + 1)\tan(3x + 1)$

10. $\dfrac{1}{(\sin^{-1}x)(1 - x^2)^{1/2}}$

16. $\dfrac{\sinh x}{\cosh x} = \tanh x$

22. $\sec(e^x) + C$

25. If you wish, let $u = \dfrac{1}{x}$.

28. $-2(1 - e^x)^{1/2} + C$

31. Let $u = \dfrac{2}{3}x$; $x = \dfrac{3}{2}u$, $dx = \dfrac{3}{2}du$, and
$9 - 4x^2 = 9 - 9u^2$, so that

$$\int\frac{dx}{(9 - 4x^2)^{1/2}} = \frac{3}{2}\int\frac{du}{3(1 - u^2)^{1/2}}$$

$$= \frac{1}{2}\arcsin\left(\frac{2x}{3}\right) + C.$$

34. Let $u = \sin x$; $du = \cos x\, dx$. Then

$$\int \frac{\cos x}{1 + \sin^2 x}\, dx = \int \frac{du}{1 + u^2} = \arctan(\sin x) + C.$$

37. Note that $|e^x| = e^x$. Therefore

$$\int \frac{dx}{(e^{2x} - 1)^{1/2}} = \int \frac{e^x}{e^x(e^{2x} - 1)^{1/2}}\, dx = \sec^{-1}(e^x) + C.$$

40. $\dfrac{1}{3} \tanh(3x - 2) + C$

43. Let $x = \dfrac{3}{2} u$; then $dx = \dfrac{3}{2}\, du$, $u = \dfrac{2}{3} x$, and

$$\int \frac{dx}{(4x^2 + 9)^{1/2}} = \frac{3}{2} \int \frac{du}{3(u^2 + 1)^{1/2}}$$

$$= \frac{1}{2} \sinh^{-1}\left(\frac{2x}{3}\right) + C.$$

46. By the method of cylindrical shells,

$$V = \int_0^1 2\pi x \frac{1}{(x^4 + 1)^{1/2}}\, dx.$$

Let $u = x^2$. Then $du = 2x\, dx$, and we obtain

$$V = \int_0^1 \pi \frac{1}{(u^2 + 1)^{1/2}}\, du$$

$$= \pi\{\sinh^{-1}(1) - \sinh^{-1}(0)\} = \pi \sinh^{-1}(1)$$

$$= \pi \ln(1 + \sqrt{2}) \sim 2.7689.$$

53. By Problem 31 in Section 8.6 and with the notation used there, the length of the cable is

$$S = \frac{2T_0}{w} \sinh\left(\frac{wL}{T_0}\right).$$

So

$$\sinh\left(\frac{wL}{T_0}\right) = \frac{wS}{2T_0}.$$

From Problem 32 in Section 8.6 we obtain

$$\cosh\left(\frac{wL}{T_0}\right) = \frac{wH}{T_0} + 1.$$

Now

$$\cosh^2\left(\frac{wL}{T_0}\right) - \sinh^2\left(\frac{wL}{T_0}\right) = 1;$$

$$\frac{w^2 H^2}{(T_0)^2} + \frac{2wH}{T_0} + 1 - \frac{w^2 S^2}{4(T_0)^2} = 1;$$

$$4w^2 H^2 + 8wHT_0 - w^2 S^2 = 0;$$

and therefore

$$4wH^2 - w^2 S^2 + 8HT_0 = 0.$$

55. We begin with the equation

$$T_0 = \frac{wS^2 - 4wH^2}{8H} = \frac{2S^2 - 8H^2}{8H} = \frac{S^2 - 4H^2}{4H}.$$

Now $S = 400$, so

$$T_0 = \frac{160,000 - 4H^2}{4H} = \frac{40,000 - H^2}{H}.$$

$$T^2 = (T_0)^2 + w^2 S^2; \quad s = 200 = \frac{S}{2}; \quad w = 2:$$

$$T^2 = (T_0)^2 + (2s)^2 = (T_0)^2 + S^2;$$

$$T^2 = (T_0)^2 + 160,000;$$

$$(T_0)^2 = T^2 - 160,000.$$

With $T = 5000$:

$$(T_0)^2 = 25,000,000 - 160,000 = 24,840,000,$$

169

and therefore $T_0 = 200\sqrt{621}$.

$$40,000 - H^2 = 200H\sqrt{621};$$

consequently

$$H^2 + 200H\sqrt{621} - 40,000 = 0.$$

From the quadratic formula, we find that

$$H = \pm 2500 - 100\sqrt{621}.$$

Now $H > 0$, so we must take the plus sign above. Therefore the minimum sag that can be allowed is $H = 2500 - 100\sqrt{621} \sim 8.0128$ -- just a little over eight feet.

Section 9.2

1. Let $u = 2 - 3x$ and apply Formula (1) of Fig. 9.1.

4. With $u = 5 + 2t^2$ and Formula (2) of Fig. 9.1, we obtain

$$\frac{5}{4} \ln|u| + C = \frac{5}{4} \ln(5 + 2t^2) + C.$$

7. Let $u = \sqrt{y}$ and apply Formula (9) of Fig. 9.1.

10. Let $u = 4 + \cos 2x$. Then Formula (2) of Fig. 9.1 yields

$$-\frac{1}{2} \ln|u| + C = -\frac{1}{2} \ln(4 + \cos 2x) + C.$$

13. Let $u = \ln t$ and apply Formula (1) of Fig. 9.1.

16. With $u = 1 + e^{2x}$, $du = 2e^{2x}\,dx$, $e^{2x}\,dx = \frac{1}{2}\,du$, and Formula (2) of Fig. 9.1, we obtain

$$\int \frac{e^{2x}}{1 + e^{2x}}\,dx = \frac{1}{2} \int \frac{1}{u}\,du$$

$$= \frac{1}{2} \ln|u| + C = \frac{1}{2} \ln(1 + e^{2x}) + C.$$

19. Let $u = x^2$ and apply Formula (10) of Fig. 9.1.

22. Let $u = 2t$. Then $du = 2\,dt$, and therefore

$$\int \frac{1}{1 + 4t^2}\,dt = \frac{1}{2} \int \frac{1}{1 + u^2}\,du$$

$$= \frac{1}{2}\tan^{-1}u + C = \frac{1}{2}\tan^{-1}(2t) + C.$$

25. Let $v = 1 + \sqrt{x}$. Then $dv = \frac{1}{2}x^{-1/2}\,dx$, so

$$\int \frac{(1 + x^{1/2})^4}{x^{1/2}}\,dx = 2 \int v^4\,dv$$

$$= \frac{2}{5}v^5 + C = \frac{2}{5}(1 + \sqrt{x})^5 + C.$$

28. Let $u = 1 + \sec x$; $du = 2\sec 2x \tan 2x\,dx$, and we get

$$\int \frac{1}{2}u^{-3/2}\,du = -u^{-1/2} + C = -\frac{1}{(1 + \sec 2x)^{1/2}} + C.$$

31. With $u = x - 2$ we have $du = dx$, and the result is

$$\int (u + 2)^2 u^{1/2}\,du = \int (u^{5/2} + 4u^{3/2} + 4u^{1/2})\,du$$

$$= \frac{2}{7}u^{7/2} + \frac{8}{5}u^{5/2} + \frac{8}{3}u^{3/2} + C$$

$$= \frac{2}{7}(x - 2)^{7/2} + \frac{8}{5}(x - 2)^{5/2} + \frac{8}{3}(x - 2)^{3/2} + C$$

$$= (x - 2)^{3/2}\{\frac{2}{7}(x - 2)^2 + \frac{8}{5}(x - 2) + \frac{8}{3}\} + C$$

$$= \frac{1}{105}(x - 2)^{3/2}\{30(x^2 - 4x + 4) + 168(x - 2) + 280\} + C$$

$$= \frac{2}{105}(x - 2)^{3/2}(15x^2 + 24x + 32) + C.$$

34. With $u = x + 1$, $x = u + 1$, $dx = du$:

$$\int x(x - 1)^{1/3}\, dx = \int (u + 1)u^{1/3}\, du$$

$$= \int (u^{3/2} + u^{1/3})\, du = \frac{3}{7} u^{7/3} + \frac{3}{4} u^{4/3} + C$$

$$= (3u^{4/3})\frac{4u + 7}{28} + C = \frac{3(x - 1)^{4/3}}{28}(4x + 3) + C$$

$$= \frac{3}{28}(x - 1)^{1/3}(4x^2 - x - 3) + C.$$

37. Let $u = \frac{1}{3} e^x$. Then

$$\int e^x(9 + e^{2x})^{1/2}\, dx = 9\int (1 + u^2)^{1/2}\, du$$

$$= \frac{u}{2}(u^2 + 1)^{1/2} + \frac{1}{2}\ln|u + (u^2 + 1)^{1/2}| + C$$

(by Formula 44 of the endpapers)

$$= \frac{1}{6} e^x(\frac{1}{9} e^{2x} + 1)^{1/2}$$

$$+ \frac{1}{2}\ln\left|\frac{1}{3} e^x + (\frac{1}{9} e^{2x} + 1)^{1/2}\right| + C.$$

40. Let $u = 4e^x$. Then $u^2 = 16e^{2x}$, $du = 4e^x\, dx$, $e^x\, dx = \frac{1}{4}\, du$, $e^{2x} = \frac{1}{16} u^2$, and $e^{3x}\, dx = \frac{1}{64} u^2\, du$. Take $a = 5$. The integral becomes

$$\frac{1}{64}\int \frac{u^2}{(a^2 + u^2)^{1/2}}\, du.$$

Now apply Formula 49 of the endpapers. The final answer may be written in the form

$$\frac{1}{128}\{4e^x(25 + 16e^{2x})^{1/2} - 25\ln|4e^x + (25 + 16e^{2x})^{1/2}|\} + C.$$

172

43. As x "goes from -1 to 1," does u "go from 1 to 1?"

Section 9.3

1. $\displaystyle\int \sin^3 x \, dx = \int (\sin x)(1 - \cos^2 x) \, dx$

$\displaystyle = \int (\sin x - \cos^2 x \sin x) \, dx = \frac{1}{3} \cos^3 x - \cos x + C.$

4. $\displaystyle\int \sin^3 t \cos^3 t \, dt = \int (\sin^3 t)(1 - \sin^2 t)(\cos t) \, dt$

$\displaystyle = \int (\sin^3 t \cos t - \sin^5 t \cos t) \, dt$

$\displaystyle = \frac{1}{4} \sin^4 t - \frac{1}{6} \sin^6 t + C.$

7. $\displaystyle\int (\sin^3 x)(\cos x)^{-1/2} \, dx = \int (\sin x)(1 - \cos^2 x)(\cos x)^{-1/2} \, dx$

$\displaystyle = \int \{(\cos x)^{-1/2} \sin x - (\cos x)^{3/2} \sin x\} \, dx$

$\displaystyle = \frac{2}{5} (\cos x)^{5/2} - 2(\cos x)^{1/2} + C.$

10. $\displaystyle\int \sin^{3/2} x \cos^3 x \, dx = \int (\sin^{3/2} x)(1 - \sin^2 x)(\cos x) \, dx$

$\displaystyle = \int (\sin^{3/2} x \cos x - \sin^{7/2} x \cos x) \, dx$

$\displaystyle = \frac{2}{5} \sin^{5/2} x - \frac{2}{9} \sin^{9/2} x + C.$

13. $\displaystyle\int \sec^4 t \; dt \;=\; \int (1 \,+\, \tan^2 t)\sec^2 t \; dt$

$$= \; \frac{1}{3}\tan^3 t \;+\; \tan t \;+\; C.$$

16. $\tan \xi \, \sec^4 \xi \;=\; (\sec^3 \xi)(\sec \xi \, \tan \xi).$

19. $\csc^6 v \;=\; (\csc v)^2 (1 \,+\, \cot^2 v)^2$

$$= \; \cot^4 v \csc^2 v \;+\; 2\cot^2 v \csc^2 v \;+\; \csc^2 v.$$

22. $\displaystyle\int \frac{\cot^3 x}{\csc^2 x} \; dx \;=\; \int \frac{\cos^3 x}{\sin^3 x}\sin^2 x \; dx \;=\; \int \frac{\cos^3 x}{\sin x} \; dx$

$$= \; \int \frac{(1 - \sin^2 x)(\cos x)}{\sin x} \; dx \;=\; \int \left(\frac{\cos x}{\sin x} \,-\, \sin x \cos x\right) dx$$

$$= \; \ln|\sin x| \;+\; \frac{1}{2}\cos^2 x \;+\; C.$$

25. $\displaystyle\int \frac{\cos \xi}{\sin \xi}\sin^3 \xi \; d\xi \;=\; \frac{1}{3}\sin^3 \xi \;+\; C.$

28. $\tan^4 x \;=\; (\sec^2 x \,-\, 1)\tan^2 x \;=\; \tan^2 x \sec^2 x \,-\, (\sec^2 x \,-\, 1).$
Therefore the desired antiderivative is

$$\frac{1}{3}\tan^3 x \;-\; \tan x \;+\; x \;+\; C.$$

31. $\sin^5 2t \cos^{3/2} 2t \;=\; (1 \,-\, \cos^2 2t)^2 \cos^{3/2} 2t \sin 2t$

$$= \; \cos^{3/2} 2t \sin 2t \;-\; 2\cos^{7/2} 2t \sin 2t \;+\; \cos^{11/2} 2t \sin 2t.$$

34. $\displaystyle\frac{\cot x}{\sin x} \;=\; \csc x \cot x \quad \text{and} \quad \frac{\csc x}{\sin x} \;=\; \csc^2 x,$

so the antiderivative is $-\csc x \,-\, \cot x \,+\, C.$

37. $\tan x \sec^4 x \;=\; (\sec x)^3 D_x(\sec x)$

$$= (\tan x \sec^2 x)(\tan^2 x + 1)$$

$$= (\tan x)^3 D_x (\tan x) + (\tan x)^1 D_x (\tan x).$$

40. $\sin 2x \sin 4x = \dfrac{1}{2}(\cos 2x - \cos 6x).$

So the required antiderivative is

$$\frac{1}{2} \sin 2x - \frac{1}{12} \sin 6x + C.$$

Section 9.4

1. Choose $u = x$ and $dv = e^{2x} dx$. Then $v = \dfrac{1}{2} e^{2x}$ and $du = dx$. Therefore

$$\int x e^{2x} dx = \frac{1}{2} x e^{2x} - \int \frac{1}{2} e^{2x} dx$$

$$= \frac{1}{2} x e^{2x} - \frac{1}{4} e^{2x} + C.$$

4. Choose $u = t^2$, $dv = \sin t\, dt$. Then $du = 2t\, dt$ and $v = -\cos t$. Thus

$$\int t^2 \sin t\, dt = -t^2 \cos t + 2 \int t \cos t\, dt.$$

7. Choose $u = \ln x$, $dv = x^3 dx$. Then $du = \dfrac{1}{x} dx$ and $v = \dfrac{1}{4} x^4$;

$$\int x^3 \ln x\, dx = \frac{1}{4} x^4 \ln x - \frac{1}{16} x^4 + C.$$

10. Choose $u = \tan^{-1} x$, $dv = x\, dx$. Then $du = \dfrac{dx}{1 + x^2}$; we choose $v = \dfrac{1}{2} x^2 + \dfrac{1}{2} = \dfrac{1}{2}(x^2 + 1)$ for the purpose of providing a fortuitous cancellation:

$$\int x\tan^{-1}x\,dx = \frac{1}{2}(x^2 + 1)\tan^{-1}x - \frac{1}{2}\int \frac{x^2 + 1}{1 + x^2}\,dx$$

$$= \frac{1}{2}(x^2 + 1)\tan^{-1}x - \frac{x}{2} + C.$$

13. Choose $u = (\ln t)^2$ and $dv = dt$. The necessity of integrating $\ln t$ then arises; a second integration by parts is necessary, and works well with the choices $u = \ln t$, $dv = dt$.

16. Choose $u = x^2$ and $dv = x(1 - x^2)^{1/2}\,dx$. The answer is

$$-\frac{1}{3}x^2(1 - x^2)^{3/2} - \frac{2}{15}(1 - x^2)^{5/2} + C.$$

19. Choose $u = \csc\xi$, $dv = \csc^2\xi\,d\xi$. Replace $\cot^2\xi$ by $\csc^2\xi - 1$ in the resulting integral to obtain

$$I = -\csc\xi\cot\xi + \int \csc\xi\,d\xi - I$$

where I is the original integral. Solve for I and use Formula 15 of the endpapers to obtain the answer.

22. Choose $u = \ln(1 + x^2)$, $dv = dx$. Then

$$\int \ln(1 + x^2)\,dx = x\ln(1 + x^2) - 2\int \frac{x^2}{x^2 + 1}\,dx$$

$$= x\ln(1 + x^2) - 2\int \frac{x^2 + 1}{x^2 + 1}\,dx - 2\int \frac{dx}{x^2 + 1}$$

$$= x\ln(1 + x^2) - 2x + 2\tan^{-1}x + C.$$

25. Choose $u = \tan^{-1}\sqrt{x}$ and $dv = dx$. To simplify the resulting computations, choose $v = x + 1$.

28. Let $u = \csc x$ and $dv = \csc^2 x\,dx$. Then

$$I \;=\; \int \csc^3 x \, dx \;=\; -\csc x \cot x \;-\; \int \csc x \cot^2 x \, dx$$

$$=\; -\csc x \cot x \;+\; \int (\csc x)(1 - \csc^2 x) \, dx$$

$$=\; -\csc x \cot x \;-\; \ln|\csc x + \cot x| \;-\; I;$$

therefore

$$I \;=\; -\frac{1}{2} \csc x \cot x \;-\; \frac{1}{2} \ln|\csc x + \cot x| \;+\; C.$$

31. Choose $u = \ln x$ and $dv = x^{-3/2} dx$. Then

$$\int \frac{\ln x}{x^{3/2}} \, dx \;=\; -2x^{-1/2} \ln x \;+\; 2 \int x^{-3/2} \, dx$$

$$=\; -2x^{-1/2} \ln x \;-\; 4x^{-1/2} \;+\; C$$

$$=\; -\frac{2}{\sqrt{x}} (2 + \ln x) \;+\; C.$$

34. First method:

$$\int e^x \cosh x \, dx \;=\; \frac{1}{2} \int (e^{2x} + 1) \, dx$$

$$=\; \frac{1}{4} e^{2x} \;+\; \frac{1}{2} x \;+\; C_1$$

$$=\; \frac{1}{4} (e^{2x} + 1) \;-\; \frac{1}{4} \;+\; \frac{1}{2} x \;+\; C_1$$

$$=\; \frac{1}{4} e^x (e^x + e^{-x}) \;+\; \frac{1}{2} x \;+\; C$$

$$=\; \frac{1}{2} e^x \cosh x \;+\; \frac{1}{2} x \;+\; C.$$

Second method: Presented because no integration by parts is used in the first method, although what follows is somewhat artificial.

Let $u = e^x$ and $dv = \cosh x\, dx$. Then

$$J = \int e^x \cosh x\, dx = e^x \sinh x - \int e^x \sinh x\, dx.$$

Now

$$e^x \sinh x = \frac{1}{2}(e^{2x} - 1) = \frac{1}{2}(e^{2x} + 1) - 1$$

$$= e^x \cosh x - 1.$$

Therefore

$$J = e^x \sinh x - J + \int 1\, dx;$$

it follows that

$$\int e^x \cosh x\, dx = \frac{1}{2} e^x \sinh x + \frac{1}{2} x + C.$$

37. $V = \displaystyle\int_1^e \pi (\ln x)^2\, dx.$ Now apply the solution of Problem 13.

40. The substitution $u = \sqrt{x}$, $u^2 = x$, $dx = 2u\, du$ leads to area

$$A = \int_0^1 \exp(\sqrt{x}\,)\, dx = \int_0^1 2u e^u\, du = 2.$$

The antiderivative can be obtained by any of several methods; see the solution to Problem 1, or use Formula 63 of the endpapers.

$$M_y = \int_0^1 x \exp(\sqrt{x}\,)\, dx = \int_0^1 2u^3 e^u\, du$$

$$= 4(3 - e) \sim 1.1269.$$

Use Formula 64 of the endpapers or derive the result of Problem 41 in advance to get the antiderivative.

$$M_x = \int_0^1 \frac{1}{2} \{\exp(\sqrt{x})\}^2 \, dx = \frac{1}{2} \int_0^1 \exp(2\sqrt{x}) \, dx.$$

Now use the substitution

$$u = 2\sqrt{x}, \quad u^2 = 4x; \quad x = \frac{1}{4} u^2, \quad dx = \frac{1}{2} u \, du.$$

This yields

$$M_x = \frac{1}{4} \int_0^2 u e^u \, du = \frac{1}{4}(e^2 + 1) \sim 2.09726.$$

You can obtain the antiderivative as in the computation of the area A above. Thus we find that

$$\overline{x} = 6 - 2e \sim 0.563436, \qquad \overline{y} = \frac{1}{8}(e^2 + 1) \sim 1.048632.$$

43. Let $u = (\ln x)^n$, $dv = dx$.

46. Let $u = \cos^{n-1} x$ and $dv = \sin x \, dx$.

49.
$$\int (\ln x)^3 \, dx = x(\ln x)^3$$

$$- 3\left(x(\ln x)^2 - 2\left[x \ln x - \int 1 \, dx \right] \right).$$

So

$$\int_1^e (\ln x)^3 \, dx = \left[x(\ln x)^3 - 3x(\ln x)^2 + 6x(\ln x) - 6x \right]_1^e$$

$$= e - 3e + 6e - 6e + 6 = 6 - 2e \sim 0.563436.$$

Section 9.5

1. Let $x = \sin u$; then $dx = \cos u \, du$ and (the motive for the substitution) $(1 - x^2)^{1/2} = \cos u$. Therefore

$$\int \frac{(1 - x^2)^{1/2}}{x^2} \, dx \;=\; \int \frac{\cos^2 u}{\sin^2 u} \, du$$

$$=\; \int \cot^2 u \, du \;=\; \int (\csc^2 u - 1) \, du$$

$$=\; -\cot u - u + C \;=\; -\frac{(1 - x^2)^{1/2}}{x} - \arcsin x + C.$$

4. Let $x = 2 \sin u$; $dx = 2 \cos u \, du$, $(4 - x^2)^{1/2} = 2 \cos u$. Then

$$\int x^3 (4 - x^2)^{1/2} \, dx \;=\; \int 32 \sin^3 u \cos^2 u \, du$$

$$=\; 32 \int (\sin u)(\cos^2 u - \cos^4 u) \, du$$

$$=\; 32 \left(\frac{1}{5} \cos^5 u - \frac{1}{3} \cos^3 u \right) + C$$

-- which, after some tedious algebra, can be written in the form

$$-\frac{1}{15} (4 - x^2)^{3/2} (3x^2 + 8) + C.$$

Use the triangle shown at the right to express $\cos u$ in terms of x.

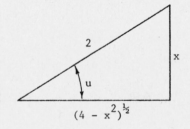

7. Let $x = \frac{1}{2} \sin \xi$. Then $1 - 4x^2 = \cos^2 \xi$, and the integrand becomes $\csc \xi - \sin \xi$.

10. Let $x = \frac{1}{2} \tan z$; $2x = \tan z$, $dx = \frac{1}{2} \sec^2 z \, dz$, and $1 + 4x^2 = \sec^2 z$. Therefore

$$\int (1 + 4x^2)^{1/2}\, dx \;=\; \int \frac{1}{2} (\sec z)(\sec^2 z)\, dz \;=\; \frac{1}{2} \int \sec^3 z\, dz.$$

Now do a moderately difficult integration by parts, or apply Formula 28 of the endpapers, to obtain

$$\frac{1}{4}(\sec z \tan z \;+\; \ln|\sec z \;+\; \tan z|) \;+\; C$$

$$= \;\frac{1}{4}\{2x(1 + 4x^2)^{1/2} \;+\; \ln|2x \;+\; (1 + 4x^2)^{1/2}|\} \;+\; C.$$

13. Use the substitution $x = \tan u$ to transform the integrand into

$$\tan^2 u \sec u \;=\; \sec^3 u \;-\; \sec u,$$

then apply Formulas 14 and 28 of the endpapers.

16. Let $x = \sin z$; $dx = \cos z\, dz$, $(1 - x^2)^{1/2} = \cos z$. Then

$$\int (1 - x^2)^{3/2}\, dx \;=\; \int \cos^4 z\, dz \;=\; \frac{1}{4} \int (1 + \cos 2x)^2\, dz$$

$$= \;\frac{1}{4} \int \left(1 \;+\; 2\cos 2z \;+\; \frac{1 + \cos 4z}{2}\right) dz$$

$$= \;\frac{1}{4}\left(\frac{3}{2} z \;+\; \sin 2z \;+\; \frac{1}{8}\sin 4z\right) \;+\; C$$

$$= \;\frac{3}{8} z \;+\; \frac{1}{2}\sin z \cos z \;+\; \frac{1}{16}\sin 2z \cos 2z \;+\; C$$

$$= \;\frac{3}{8} z \;+\; \frac{1}{2}\sin z \cos z \;+\; \frac{1}{8}(\sin z \cos z)(\cos^2 z \;-\; \sin^2 z) \;+\; C$$

$$= \;\frac{3}{8} z \;+\; \frac{1}{2}\sin z \cos z \;+\; \frac{1}{8}\sin z \cos^3 z \;-\; \frac{1}{8}\sin^3 z \cos z \;+\; C$$

$$= \;\frac{3}{8}\arcsin x \;+\; \frac{1}{2} x(1 - x^2)^{1/2}$$

$$+ \;\frac{1}{8} x(1 - x^2)^{3/2} \;-\; \frac{1}{8} x^3(1 - x^2)^{1/2} \;+\; C$$

$$= \;\frac{1}{8}\{3\arcsin x \;+\; x(5 \;-\; 2x^2)(1 \;-\; x^2)^{1/2}\} \;+\; C.$$

19. The substitution $x = 2 \sin u$ transforms the integral into

$$\frac{1}{32} \int \sec^5 u \, du.$$

Application of Formula 37 of the endpapers transforms this integral into

$$\frac{1}{32} \left(\frac{1}{4} \sec^3 u \tan u \; + \; \frac{3}{4} \int \sec^3 u \, du \right).$$

Then Formula 28 from the endpapers yields the antiderivative

$$\frac{1}{128} \sec^3 u \tan u \; + \; \frac{3}{256} \sec u \tan u$$

$$+ \; \frac{3}{256} \ln|\sec u \; + \; \tan u| \; + \; C.$$

Finally make the replacements

$$\sec u \; = \; \frac{2}{(4 - x^2)^{1/2}} \qquad \text{and} \qquad \tan u \; = \; \frac{x}{(4 - x^2)^{1/2}}$$

to obtain the final answer.

22. Use the substitution $4x = 3 \tan u$ to obtain

$$\frac{81}{4} \int \sec^5 u \, du.$$

With the aid of Formula 37 of the endpapers, we next obtain

$$\frac{81}{4} \left(\frac{1}{4} \sec^3 u \tan u \; + \; \frac{3}{8} \sec u \tan u \right.$$

$$+ \; \frac{3}{8} \ln|\sec u \; + \; \tan u| \left) \right. \; + \; C$$

$$= \; \frac{1}{4} x(9 + 16x^2)^{3/2} \; + \; \frac{27}{8} x(9 + 16x^2)^{1/2}$$

$$+ \; \frac{243}{32} \ln|4x \; + \; (9 + 16x^2)^{1/2}| \; + \; C$$

182

(we have allowed the constant $-\dfrac{243}{32}\ln 3$ to be "absorbed" by the constant C).

25. Let $x = \sec u$. Then $dx = \sec u \tan u \, du$, and the integral takes the form

$$\int \sec^3 u \tan^2 u \, du = \int (\sec^5 u - \sec^3 u) \, du$$

$$= \frac{1}{4}\sec^3 u \tan u - \frac{1}{8}\sec u \tan u - \frac{1}{8}\ln|\sec u + \tan u| + C$$

-- with the aid of Formula 37 of the endpapers. Then replace $\tan u$ by $(x^2 - 1)^{1/2}$ and $\sec u$ by x to obtain the final version of the answer.

28. Let $x = \dfrac{3}{2}\sec u$, so that $dx = \dfrac{3}{2}\sec u \tan u \, du$ and

$$(4x^2 - 9)^{1/2} = (9\sec^2 u - 9)^{1/2} = 3 \tan u.$$

The integral is thereby transformed into

$$\frac{2}{9}\int \cos u \, du = \frac{2}{9}\sin u + C$$

$$= \frac{(4x^2 - 9)^{1/2}}{9x} + C.$$

31. The substitution $x = 5 \sinh u$ yields

$$\int \frac{dx}{(25 + x^2)^{1/2}} = \int \frac{5 \cosh u}{5 \cosh u} \, du = \int 1 \, du$$

$$= u + C = \sinh^{-1}\left(\frac{x}{5}\right) + C.$$

34. Let $x = \dfrac{1}{3}\sinh u$. Then $9x^2 = \sinh^2 u$,

$$(1 + 9x^2)^{1/2} = \cosh u, \quad \text{and} \quad dx = \frac{1}{3}\cosh u \, du.$$

$$\int \frac{dx}{(1 + 9x^2)^{1/2}} = \frac{1}{3} \int \frac{\cosh u}{\cosh u} \, du$$

$$= \frac{1}{3} u + C = \frac{1}{3} \sinh^{-1}(3x) + C.$$

37. $A = \displaystyle\int_0^1 2\pi x^2 (1 + 4x^2)^{1/2} \, dx.$

Let $x = \frac{1}{2} \tan u;$ this yields the transformation

$$I = \int x^2 (1 + 4x^2)^{1/2} \, dx = \frac{1}{8} \int \sec^3 u \, \tan^2 u \, du$$

$$= \frac{1}{8} \int (\sec^5 u - \sec^3 u) \, du.$$

Apply Formula 37 of the endpapers with $n = 5,$ then Formula 28:

$$I = \frac{1}{32} \{ \sec^3 u \, \tan u - \frac{1}{2} \sec u \, \tan u$$

$$- \frac{1}{2} \ln | \sec u + \tan u | \} + C$$

$$= \frac{1}{64} \{ 4x(1 + 4x^2)^{3/2} - 2x(1 + 4x^2)^{1/2}$$

$$- \ln | 2x + (1 + 4x^2)^{1/2} | \} + C.$$

Now to obtain A, substitute $x = 1,$ subtract the value when $x = 0,$ and finally multiply by $2\pi;$ the result is that

$$A = \frac{\pi}{32} \{ 18\sqrt{5} - \ln(2 + \sqrt{5}) \} \sim 3.80973.$$

40. $A = \displaystyle\int_1^2 2\pi x \frac{(x^2 + 1)^{1/2}}{x} \, dx = 2\pi \int_1^2 (x^2 + 1)^{1/2} \, dx.$

The substitution $x = \tan u$ transforms the antidifferentiation problem into

184

$$2\pi \int \sec^3 z \, dz = \pi(\sec z \tan z + \ln|\sec z + \tan z|) + C$$

$$= \pi\{x(x^2 + 1)^{1/2} + \ln|x + (x^2 + 1)^{1/2}|\} + C.$$

Substitution of the limits $x = 1$ and $x = 2$ yields the answer:

$$A = \pi\{2\sqrt{5} - \sqrt{2} + \ln(2 + \sqrt{5}) - \ln(1 + \sqrt{2})\} \sim 11.37314434.$$

43. $A = 4\pi \displaystyle\int_0^{\pi/2} (\sin x)(1 + \cos^2 x)^{1/2} \, dx.$

With $u = \cos x$ and $du = -\sin x \, dx$, we obtain

$$A = 4\pi \int_0^1 (1 + u^2)^{1/2} \, du.$$

To find the antiderivative, we let $u = \sinh z$, $du = \cosh z \, dz$. Then we obtain

$$4\pi \int \cosh^2 z \, dz = 2\pi(z + \sinh z \cosh z) + C.$$

Therefore

$$A = 2\pi \left[\sinh^{-1} u + u(1 + u^2)^{1/2} \right]_0^1$$

$$= 2\pi\{\sinh^{-1}(1) + \sqrt{2}\}$$

$$= 2\pi\{\sqrt{2} + \ln(1 + \sqrt{2})\} \sim 14.4236.$$

46. You should find that the arc length element is

$$ds = \frac{x^{1/2}}{(x - 1)^{1/2}} \, dx.$$

After using the suggested substitution, it turns out that the antiderivative is

$$\{\sqrt{x}\,\sqrt{x-1}\ +\ \ln(\sqrt{x}\ +\ \sqrt{x-1})\}\ +\ C,$$

and that the value of the definite integral is approximately equal to 3.620184.

Section 9.6

1. First, $x^2 + 4x + 5 = (x+1)^2 + 1 = u^2 + 1$ where $u = x + 2$ and $dx = du$. So the integral becomes

$$\int \frac{du}{u^2 + 1}\ =\ \arctan u\ +\ C\ =\ \arctan(x+2)\ +\ C.$$

4. Let $u = x + 2$: $x = u - 2$ and $dx = du$. Thus

$$I\ =\ \int \frac{x+1}{(x^2 + 4x + 5)^2}\ dx\ =\ \int \frac{u-1}{(u^2 + 1)^2}\ du.$$

Next let $u = \tan \xi$. Then $du = \sec^2 \xi\, d\xi$, and

$$I\ =\ \int \frac{\tan \xi\ -\ 1}{\sec^2 \xi}\ d\xi\ =\ \int (\sin \xi \cos \xi\ -\ \cos^2 \xi)\, d\xi$$

$$=\ \frac{1}{2}\sin^2 \xi\ -\ \frac{1}{2}\xi\ -\ \frac{1}{2}\sin \xi \cos \xi\ +\ C$$

$$=\ \frac{u^2}{2(1+u^2)}\ -\ \frac{1}{2}\arctan u\ -\ \frac{u}{2(1+u^2)}\ +\ C$$

$$=\ \frac{x^2 + 3x + 2}{2(x^2 + 4x + 5)}\ -\ \frac{1}{2}\arctan(x+2)\ +\ C.$$

7. First, $3 - 2x - x^2 = 4 - (x+1)^2$, so we let

$$x\ =\ -1 + 2\sin u:\quad x + 1\ =\ 2\sin u,\quad dx\ =\ 2\cos u\, du.$$

Then $4 - (x+1)^2 = 4 - 4\sin^2 u = 4\cos^2 u$, so

$$\int x(3 - 2x - x^2)^{1/2}\, dx\ =\ \int (-1 + 2\sin u)(2\cos u)(2\cos u)\, du$$

$$= \int (-4\cos^2 u + 8\cos^2 u \sin u)\,du$$

$$= \int (-2 - 2\cos 2u + 8\cos^2 u \sin u)\,du$$

$$= -2u - 2\sin u \cos u - \frac{8}{3}\cos^3 u + C$$

$$= -2\arcsin\left(\frac{x+1}{2}\right) - \frac{1}{2}(x+1)(3 - 2x - x^2)^{1/2}$$

$$- \frac{1}{3}(3 - 2x - x^2)^{3/2} + C.$$

10. Because $4x^2 + 4x - 3 = (2x+1)^2 - 4$, we let

$$x = -\frac{1}{2} + \sec u: \quad dx = \sec u \tan u\,du,$$

$$2x + 1 = 2\sec u, \quad (2x+1)^2 - 4 = 4\tan^2 u.$$

So the integral is transformed into

$$\int 2\sec u \tan^2 u\,du = 2\int (\sec^3 u - \sec u)\,du$$

$$= \sec u \tan u - \ln|\sec u + \tan u| + C$$

$$= \frac{1}{4}(2x+1)(4x^2 + 4x - 3)^{1/2}$$

$$- \ln|2x + 1 + (4x^2 + 4x - 3)^{1/2}| + C$$

(the constant $\ln 2$ has been "absorbed" by C).

13. $3 + 2x - x^2 = 4 - (x-1)^2 = 4 - 4\sin^2 u$ if we let
$x = 1 + 2\sin u.$ Then $dx = 2\cos u\,du$, and therefore

$$\int \frac{1}{3 + 2x - x^2}\,dx = \int \frac{2\cos u}{4\cos^2 u}\,du$$

$$= \frac{1}{2}\int \sec u\,du = \frac{1}{2}\ln|\sec u + \tan u| + C$$

$$= \frac{1}{2} \ln \left| \frac{x + 1}{(3 + 2x - x^2)^{1/2}} \right| + C.$$

16. $4x^2 + 4x - 15 = (2x + 1)^2 - 16$, so we let $2x + 1 = 4 \sec z$. That is,

$$x = \frac{1}{2}(-1 + 4 \sec z), \qquad dx = 2 \sec z \tan z \, dz.$$

Therefore

$$\int \frac{2x - 1}{4x^2 + 4x - 15} \, dx = \int \frac{4 \sec z - 2}{16 \tan^2 z} (2 \sec z \tan z) \, dz$$

$$= \frac{1}{4} \int \frac{(2 \sec z - 1) \sec z}{\tan z} \, dz$$

$$= \frac{1}{4} \int \frac{\sec^2 z}{\tan z} \, dz - \frac{1}{4} \int \csc z \, dz$$

$$= \frac{1}{2} \ln |\tan z| - \frac{1}{4} \ln |\csc z - \cot z| + C_1.$$

With the aid of the reference triangle to the right, we can "translate" the expression above into a function of the original variable x. Thus we find the antiderivative to be

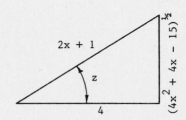

$$\frac{1}{2} \ln \frac{(4x^2 + 4x - 15)^{1/2}}{4} - \frac{1}{4} \ln \frac{2x + 1 - 4}{(4x^2 + 4x - 15)^{1/2}} + C_1,$$

which can be simplified to

$$\frac{3}{8} \ln |4x^2 + 4x - 15| - \frac{1}{4} \ln |2x - 3| + C.$$

19. First, $9 + 16x - 4x^2 = 25 - (2x - 4)^2$. Then use the trigonometric substitution

$$x = 2 + \frac{5}{2} \sin u.$$

The resulting integral is

$$\int \left(\frac{75}{2} \cos^2 u - \frac{125}{2} \cos^2 u \sin u\right) du$$

$$= \frac{25}{12} (9u + 9 \sin u \cos u + 10 \cos^3 u) + C.$$

22. Let $x = \tan u$. The integral becomes

$$\int \frac{\tan u - 1}{\sec^4 u} \sec^2 u \, du = \int \left(\frac{\tan u}{\sec^2 u} - \frac{1}{\sec^2 u}\right) du$$

$$= \int (\cos u \sin u - \cos^2 u) \, du$$

$$= \frac{1}{2} \sin^2 u - \frac{1}{2} u - \frac{1}{2} \sin u \cos u + C$$

$$= \frac{x^2}{2(x^2 + 1)} - \frac{1}{2} \tan^{-1} x - \frac{x}{2(x^2 + 1)} + C$$

$$= \frac{x(x - 1)}{2(x^2 + 1)} - \frac{1}{2} \tan^{-1} x + C.$$

25. We note that

$$x^2 + x + 1 = \frac{3}{4} \left\{\frac{4}{3} \left(x + \frac{1}{2}\right)^2 + 1\right\}.$$

This suggests that we attempt to obtain

$$\frac{4}{3} \left(x + \frac{1}{2}\right)^2 = \tan^2 u,$$

which we accomplish by using the substitution

$$x = \frac{1}{2} (-1 + \sqrt{3} \tan u).$$

This leads to

$$\int \left(3 \tan u - \frac{5}{3} \sqrt{3}\right) du,$$

and only the final answer is complicated.

189

28. Because $x - x^2 = \frac{1}{4}\{1 - (2x - 1)^2\}$, we want

$$2x - 1 = \sin u: \quad \text{We let} \quad x = \frac{1}{2}(1 + \sin u).$$

This yields

$$\frac{1}{4} \int \cos^4 u \, du.$$

Then we apply Formula 34 of the endpapers to obtain

$$\frac{1}{128}(3u + 4\sin u \cos u + \sin u \cos^3 u - \sin^3 u \cos u) + C$$

$$= \frac{3}{128}\sin^{-1}(2x - 1) - \frac{1}{64}(16x^3 - 24x^2 + 3)(x - x^2)^{1/2} + C.$$

31. First,

$$y = \frac{19}{4} + \{R^2 - (x + 1)^2\}^{1/2}$$

where $R = \sqrt{377/16}$. It follows that

$$\frac{dy}{dx} = \frac{R}{\{R^2 - (1 + x)^2\}^{1/2}} \, dx,$$

and hence the length of the road is given by

$$S = \int_0^3 R\{R^2 - (1 + x)^2\}^{-1/2} \, dx$$

$$= R\left[\sin^{-1}\left(\frac{1 + x}{R}\right)\right]_0^3 \sim 3.6940487.$$

Thus the length of the road is just over 3.69 miles.

Section 9.7

1. $\frac{x^2}{x + 1} = x - 1 + \frac{1}{x + 1}$, so the antiderivative is

$$\frac{1}{2}x^2 - x + \ln|x + 1| + C.$$

4. $\dfrac{x}{x^2 + 4x} = \dfrac{1}{x + 4}$, so the antiderivative is $\ln|x + 4| + C$.

7. $\dfrac{1}{x(x^2 + 4)} = \dfrac{A}{x} + \dfrac{Bx + C}{x^2 + 4}$ yields

$$A = \dfrac{1}{4}, \qquad B = -\dfrac{1}{4}, \qquad \text{and} \qquad C = 0.$$

So the antiderivative is

$$\dfrac{1}{4}\ln|x| - \dfrac{1}{8}\ln(x^2 + 4) + C.$$

10. $\dfrac{1}{(x^2 + 1)(x^2 + 4)} = \dfrac{Ax + B}{x^2 + 1} + \dfrac{Cx + D}{x^2 + 4}$ yields

$$A = C = 0, \qquad B = \dfrac{1}{3}, \qquad \text{and} \qquad D = -\dfrac{1}{3}.$$

Thus the antiderivative is

$$\dfrac{1}{3}\arctan x - \dfrac{1}{6}\arctan\left(\dfrac{x}{2}\right) + C.$$

13. Rewrite the integrand as

$$1 - \dfrac{1}{(x + 1)^2}.$$

16. After division, the problem becomes

$$\int \left(x^2 - 4x + 12 - (16)\dfrac{2x + 3}{(x + 2)^2} \right)\ dx$$

$$= \dfrac{1}{3}x^3 - 2x^2 + 12x - 16 \int \dfrac{2x + 4 - 1}{(x + 2)^2}\ dx$$

$$= \dfrac{1}{3}x^3 - 2x^2 + 12x - 16 \int \left(\dfrac{2}{x + 2} - \dfrac{1}{(x + 2)^2} \right)\ dx$$

$$= \dfrac{1}{3}x^3 - 2x^2 + 12x - \dfrac{16}{x + 2} - 32\ln|x + 2| + C.$$

19. $\dfrac{x^2 + 1}{x^3 + 2x^2 + x} = \dfrac{1}{x} + \dfrac{0}{x + 1} - \dfrac{2}{(x + 1)^2}.$

22. $\dfrac{2x^2 + 3}{x^4 - 2x^2 + 1} = \dfrac{A}{x - 1} + \dfrac{B}{(x - 1)^2} + \dfrac{C}{x + 1} + \dfrac{D}{(x + 1)^2}$

leads to $A = -\dfrac{1}{4}$, $B = \dfrac{5}{4}$, $C = \dfrac{1}{4}$, and $D = \dfrac{5}{4}$, and thereby to the antiderivative

$$\frac{1}{4} \ln \left| \frac{x + 1}{x - 1} \right| - \frac{5x}{2(x^2 - 1)} + C.$$

25. $\dfrac{1}{x^3 + x} = \dfrac{A}{x} + \dfrac{Bx + C}{x^2 + 1}$ leads to $A = 1$, $B = -1$, $C = 0$.

28. $\dfrac{x^2 + 1}{x^3 + x^2 + x} = \dfrac{A}{x} + \dfrac{Bx + C}{x^2 + x + 1}$ leads to $A = 1$, $B = 0$, and $C = -1$, and the antiderivative is

$$\ln |x| - \frac{2}{3} \sqrt{3} \tan^{-1} \left(\frac{1}{3} \sqrt{3} \{2x + 1\} \right) + C.$$

31. $\dfrac{x^2 - 10}{2x^4 + 9x^2 + 4} = \dfrac{Ax + B}{2x^2 + 1} + \dfrac{Cx + D}{x^2 + 4}$

yields $A = C = 0$, $B = -3$, and $D = 2$.

34. $\dfrac{x^2 + 4}{(x^2 + 1)^2 (x^2 + 2)} = \dfrac{Ax + B}{x^2 + 1} + \dfrac{Cx + D}{(x^2 + 1)^2} + \dfrac{Ex + F}{x^2 + 2}$

leads to $A = C = E = 0$, $B = -2$, $D = 3$, and $F = 2$. So we must perform the integration indicated below:

$$\int \left(- \frac{2}{x^2 + 1} + \frac{3}{(x^2 + 1)^2} + \frac{2}{x^2 + 2} \right) dx.$$

The first expression in the integrand presents no problem, and by Formula 17 of the endpapers the third yields

$$\sqrt{2} \arctan \left(\frac{1}{2} x \sqrt{2} \right) + C_3.$$

For the second expression, we use the substitution $x = \tan z$.

Then

$$\int \frac{3}{(x^2 + 1)^2} \, dx = 3 \int \frac{\sec^2 z}{\sec^4 z} \, dz$$

$$= 3 \int \frac{1}{2} (1 + \cos 2z) \, dz = \frac{3}{2} (z + \sin z \cos z) + C_2$$

$$= \frac{3}{2} (\tan^{-1} x + \frac{x}{1 + x^2}) + C_2.$$

When we assemble all this information, we find the answer to the original problem to be

$$\frac{3x}{2(1 + x^2)} - \frac{1}{2} \tan^{-1} x + \sqrt{2} \tan^{-1}(\frac{1}{2} x \sqrt{2}) + C.$$

37. Let $x = e^{2t}$. Then $dx = 2e^{2t} dt$; $e^{4t} dt = \frac{1}{2} x \, dx$.

This substitution transforms the given integral into

$$I = \frac{1}{2} \int \frac{x}{(x - 1)^3} \, dx.$$

Now

$$\frac{x}{(x - 1)^3} = \frac{A}{x - 1} + \frac{B}{(x - 1)^2} + \frac{C}{(x - 1)^3}$$

yields $A = 0$ and $B = C = 1$, so that

$$I = \frac{1}{2} \int \left(\frac{1}{(x - 1)^2} + \frac{1}{(x - 1)^3} \right) dx$$

$$= -\frac{1}{4} \left(\frac{2}{x - 1} + \frac{1}{(x - 1)^2} \right) + C$$

$$= -\frac{2x + 1}{4(x - 1)^2} + C = \frac{1 - 2e^{2t}}{4(e^{2t} - 1)^2} + C.$$

40. $\dfrac{1}{x^3 + 8} = \dfrac{A}{x + 2} + \dfrac{Bx + C}{x^2 - 2x + 4}$

193

leads to $A = \frac{1}{12}$, $B = -\frac{1}{12}$, and $C = \frac{1}{3}$. Thus

$$\int \frac{1}{x^3 + 8} \, dx = \frac{1}{12} \int \left(\frac{1}{x + 2} + \frac{4 - x}{x^2 - 2x + 4} \right) dx$$

$$= \frac{1}{12} \int \left(\frac{1}{x + 2} - \frac{1}{2} \left(\frac{2x - 2}{x^2 - 2x + 4} \right) + \frac{3}{x^2 - 2x + 4} \right) dx.$$

Note that $x^2 - 2x + 4 = (x - 1)^2 + 3$, and with the aid of Formula 17 of the endpapers we obtain the final answer; after simplifications, it's

$$\frac{1}{12} \ln \left| \frac{x^2 + 4x + 4}{x^2 - 2x + 4} \right| + \frac{1}{12} \sqrt{3} \arctan\left(\frac{1}{3} \sqrt{3} \{x - 1\} \right) + C.$$

43. First, $x^4 + x^2 + 1 = (x^2 + x + 1)(x^2 - x + 1)$. (It follows that $10^{12} + 10^6 + 1 = 1{,}000{,}001{,}000{,}001$ is composite.) And

$$\frac{x^3 + 2x}{x^4 + x^2 + 1} = \frac{Ax + B}{x^2 + x + 1} + \frac{Cx + D}{x^2 - x + 1}$$

yields the values $A = C = D = \frac{1}{2}$, $B = -\frac{1}{2}$.

Complete the solution by the method shown for Problem 41.

Section 9.8

1. The substitution $u = 3x - 2$ yields

$$\frac{1}{81} \int (u + 2)^3 u^{1/2} \, du$$

$$= \frac{1}{81} \int (u^{7/2} + 6u^{5/2} + 12u^{3/2} + 8u^{1/2}) \, du.$$

4. Let $u = x^{1/4}$; then $x^{1/2} = u^2$, $x = u^4$, and $dx = 4u^3 \, du$. These substitutions transform the given integral into

$$\int \frac{4u^3}{u^2 - u} \, du \;=\; \int \frac{4u^2}{u - 1} \, du$$

$$= \; 4 \int \left(u \,+\, 1 \,+\, \frac{1}{u - 1} \right) du$$

$$= \; 2u^2 \,+\, 4u \,+\, 4\ln|u - 1| \,+\, C$$

$$= \; 2x^{1/2} \,+\, 4x^{1/4} \,+\, 4\ln|x^{1/4} - 1| \,+\, C.$$

7. Let $u = x^4$. Then $dx = 4u^3 \, du$, and so

$$\int \frac{1 - x^{1/2}}{1 + x^{1/4}} \, dx \;=\; \int \frac{1 - u^2}{1 + u} \, 4u^3 \, du$$

$$= \; \int (4u^3 \,-\, 4u^4) \, du \;=\; u^4 \,-\, \frac{4}{5} u^5 \,+\, C$$

$$= \; x \,-\, \frac{4}{5} x^{5/4} \,+\, C.$$

10. Let $u = x^4 + 1$. Then $x^4 = u - 1$, $du = 4x^3 \, du$, and

$$\frac{1}{4} (u - 1) \, du \;=\; x^7 \, dx.$$

Therefore

$$\int x^7 (x^4 + 1)^{1/3} \, dx \;=\; \frac{1}{4} \int (u - 1) u^{1/3} \, du$$

$$= \; \frac{1}{4} \left(\frac{3}{7} u^{7/3} \,-\, \frac{3}{4} u^{4/3} \right) \,+\, C$$

$$= \; \frac{3}{4} u^{1/3} \left(\frac{1}{7} u^2 \,-\, \frac{1}{4} u \right) \,+\, C$$

$$= \; \frac{3}{112} (x^4 + 1)^{1/3} \{ 4(x^4 + 1)^2 \,-\, 7(x^4 + 1) \} \,+\, C$$

$$= \; \frac{3}{112} (x^4 + 1)^{1/3} (4x^8 + x^4 - 3) \,+\, C.$$

13. Let $u = \sqrt{x + 4}$; that is, $x = u^2 - 4$, $dx = 2u\,du$. This transforms the given integral into

$$\int \frac{2u}{1 + u}\,du = \int \left(2 - \frac{2}{1 + u}\right) du$$

$$= 2u - 2\ln|1 + u| + C$$

$$= 2\sqrt{x + 4} - 2\ln(1 + \sqrt{x + 4}) + C.$$

16. Let $u = \tan\frac{\xi}{2}$. Then formulas from the text yield

$$1 - \cos\xi = \frac{2u^2}{1 + u^2}.$$

so the given integral becomes (after simplifications)

$$\frac{1}{2} \int (u^{-4} + u^{-2})\,du$$

$$= \frac{1}{2}\left(-\frac{1}{3u^3} - \frac{1}{u}\right) + C.$$

Now because $u = \tan\frac{\xi}{2}$, it follows that

$$u^2 = \frac{\sin^2(\xi/2)}{\cos^2(\xi/2)}$$

$$= \frac{1 - \cos\xi}{1 + \cos\xi} = \frac{(1 - \cos\xi)^2}{\sin^2\xi},$$

so

$$u = \frac{1 - \cos\xi}{\sin\xi} = \frac{\sin\xi}{1 + \cos\xi},$$

at least for $0 < \xi < \pi$. This means that the antiderivative we seek may be written in the form

$$-\frac{1}{6}\left(\frac{1 + \cos\xi}{\sin\xi}\right)^3 - \frac{1 + \cos\xi}{2\sin\xi} + C.$$

An immensely patient person may wish to simplify this to

$$\frac{1}{3}\cot^3\xi - \csc^2\xi\cot\xi - \frac{2}{3}\csc^3\xi + C$$

$$= \frac{\cos^3 \xi - 3 \cos \xi - 2}{3 \sin^3 \xi} + C.$$

19. If you use the substitution $u = \tan \frac{\xi}{2}$, you'll need to evaluate

$$\int \frac{4u}{(u^2 + 1)(u^2 + 3)} \, du$$

by a particularly nasty partial fractions computation. It's much more efficient to notice that the numerator is very nearly the derivative of the denominator.

22. Let $y = c \sin^2 \xi$. Then $dy = 2c \sin \xi \cos \xi \, d\xi$, $c - y = c \cos^2 \xi$, $\sqrt{y} = \sqrt{c} \sin \xi$, and $\sqrt{c - y} = \sqrt{c} \cos \xi$. Therefore

$$\int \frac{y^{1/2}}{(c - y)^{1/2}} \, dy = \int \frac{c^{1/2} \sin \xi}{c^{1/2} \cos \xi} \, 2c \sin \xi \cos \xi \, d\xi$$

$$= 2c \int \sin^2 \xi \, d\xi = c \int (1 - \cos 2\xi) \, d\xi$$

$$= c(\xi - \sin \xi \cos \xi) + C.$$

Now $\xi = \sin^{-1} \sqrt{y/c}$ and $\sqrt{y} \sqrt{c - y} = c \sin \xi \cos \xi$. Hence

$$\int \frac{y^{1/2}}{(c - y)^{1/2}} \, dy = c \sin^{-1} \sqrt{y/c} - y^{1/2}(c - y)^{1/2} + C.$$

25. Here we have $dy/dx = x^{-1/2}$, so

$$ds = \{1 + (dy/dx)^2\}^{1/2} \, dx = \{1 + (1/x)\}^{1/2} \, dx.$$

So the arc length L is given by

$$L = \int_0^1 (1 + \frac{1}{x})^{1/2} \, dx.$$

Let $x = \tan^2 \xi$. Then $dx = 2 \sec^2 \xi \tan \xi \, d\xi$. Therefore

$$L = \int_0^{\pi/4} 2 \csc \xi \tan \xi \sec^2 \xi \, d\xi$$

$$= \int_0^{\pi/4} 2 \sec^3 \xi \, d\xi.$$

Apply Formula 28 from the endpapers to obtain the antiderivative

$$\sec \xi \tan \xi \ + \ \ln|\sec \xi \ + \ \tan \xi| \ + \ C$$

and thereby conclude that

$$L = \sqrt{2} \ + \ \ln(1 + \sqrt{2}) \ \sim \ 2.295587.$$

Chapter 9 Miscellaneous Problems

1. Let $x = u^2$.

4. $- \tan^{-1}(\csc x) + C$, using $u = \csc x$ if you wish.

7. Let $u = x$, $dv = \tan^2 x \, dx = (\sec^2 x - 1) \, dx$; then $du = dx$ and $v = -x + \tan x$.

10. Let $x = 2 \tan u$. The integrand becomes $\sec u$, and the antiderivative is

$$\ln|\sec u \ + \ \tan u| \ + \ C = \ln|\frac{1}{2}(x^2 + 4)^{1/2} \ + \ \frac{1}{2} x| \ + \ C_1$$

$$= \ln|x \ + \ (x^2 + 4)^{1/2}| \ + \ C.$$

13. Write $x^2 - x + 1 = (x - \frac{1}{2})^2 + \frac{3}{4}$, then apply Formula 17 from the endpapers.

16. The integrand is equal to

$$x^2 \; - \; 2 \; + \; \frac{5}{x^2 + 2} \; .$$

The antiderivative is

$$\frac{1}{3} x^3 \; - \; 2x \; + \; \frac{5}{2} \sqrt{2} \, \tan^{-1} \left(\frac{1}{2} x \sqrt{2} \right) \; + \; C.$$

19. Use the substitution $u = \sin x$.

22. Let $x^2 = \sin u$. The integrand becomes $\frac{1}{2} \sin^3 u$, and the antiderivative is

$$\frac{1}{6} (\cos u)(\cos^2 u \; - \; 3) \; + \; C$$

$$= \; - \frac{1}{6} (x^4 + 2)(1 - x^4)^{1/2} \; + \; C.$$

25. Let $x = 3 \tan u$.

28. $\dfrac{4x - 2}{x^3 - x} = \dfrac{2}{x} - \dfrac{3}{x + 1} + \dfrac{1}{x - 1}$,

so the antiderivative is

$$2 \ln|x| \; - \; 3 \ln|x + 1| \; + \; \ln|x - 1| \; + \; C$$

$$= \; \ln \left| \frac{x^2(x - 1)}{(x + 1)^3} \right| \; + \; C.$$

31. Let $x = -1 + \tan u$. The integral becomes

$$\int \frac{-1 + \tan u}{\sec^2 u} \, du \; = \; \int (-\cos^2 u + \sin u \cos u) \, du,$$

and the rest is routine.

34. $\displaystyle \int \frac{\sec x}{\tan x} \, dx = \int \csc x \, dx = \ln|\csc x - \cot x| \; + \; C.$

37. <u>Suggestion</u>: Develop a reduction formula for

$$\int x(\ln x)^n \, dx$$

by parts; take $u = (\ln x)^n$ and $dv = x \, dx$. Then apply your formula iteratively to evaluate the given antiderivative. You should find that

$$\int x(\ln x)^n \, dx = \frac{1}{2}x^2(\ln x)^n - \frac{n}{2}\int x(\ln x)^{n-1} \, dx.$$

40. Note that $4x - x^2 = 4 - (x - 2)^2$; let $x = 2 + 2\sin u$. This substitution transforms the integral into

$$\int 2(1 + \sin u) \, du = 2(u - \cos u) + C$$

$$= 2\arcsin\frac{x - 2}{2} - (4x - x^2)^{1/2} + C.$$

43. Use the method of partial fractions.

46. Here is a quick way to obtain the partial fractions decomposition that you need:

$$\frac{x^2 + 2x + 2}{(x + 1)^3} = \frac{(x + 1)^2 + 1}{(x + 1)^3}.$$

49. The partial fractions decomposition of the integrand is

$$\frac{1}{9}\left(-\frac{2}{x - 1} + \frac{1}{(x - 1)^2} + \frac{2x + 3}{x^2 + x + 1} + \frac{3x + 3}{(x^2 + x + 1)^2} \right).$$

Earlier techniques take care of most of these; the difficult one is

$$\frac{3}{2}\int \frac{1}{(x^2 + x + 1)^2} \, dx.$$

First let $u = \frac{1}{3}\sqrt{3}\,(2x + 1)$. The integral above becomes

$$\frac{4}{3}\sqrt{3}\int \frac{1}{(u^2 + 1)^2}\,du.$$

The substitution $u = \tan\xi$ will then suffice.

52. Let $u = x^3$ to transform the given integral into

$$3\int u(1 + u^2)^{3/2}\,du = \frac{3}{5}(1 + u^2)^{5/2} + C$$

$$= \frac{3}{5}(1 + x^{2/3})^{5/2} + C.$$

55. $(\tan z)(\sec^2 z - 1) = (\sec z)(\sec z \tan z) - \tan z.$

58. Note that

$$\frac{\cos^3 x}{(\sin x)^{1/2}} = \frac{(1 - \sin^2 x)(\cos x)}{(\sin x)^{1/2}}$$

$$= (\sin x)^{-1/2}\cos x - (\sin x)^{3/2}\cos x.$$

So the antiderivative is

$$\frac{2}{5}(\sin x)^{1/2}(5 - \sin^2 x) + C.$$

61. Use integration by parts with

$$u = \arcsin x \quad\text{and}\quad dv = \frac{1}{x^2}\,dx.$$

Then apply Formula 60 of the endpapers, or use the trigonometric substitution $x = \sin u$.

64. Because $2x - x^2 = 1 - (x - 1)^2$, let $x = 1 + \sin u$. Then

$$\int x(2x - x^2)^{1/2}\, dx = \int (1 + \sin u)(\cos^2 u)\, du$$

$$= \int \left(\frac{1 + \cos 2u}{2} + \cos^2 u \sin u \right) du$$

$$= \frac{1}{2}u + \frac{1}{2}\sin u \cos u - \frac{1}{3}\cos^3 u + C$$

$$= \frac{1}{2}\sin^{-1}(x - 1) + \frac{1}{2}(x - 1)(2x - x^2)^{1/2}$$

$$- \frac{1}{3}(2x - x^2)^{3/2} + C.$$

The answer can be further simplified to

$$\frac{1}{2}\sin^{-1}(x - 1) + \frac{1}{6}(2x - x^2)^{1/2}(2x^2 - x - 3) + C.$$

70. The substitution $u = \tan x$ yields

$$\int \frac{1}{u^2 + 2x + 2}\, du = \int \frac{1}{1 + (u + 1)^2}\, du$$

$$= \tan^{-1}(u + 1) + C = \tan^{-1}(1 + \tan x) + C.$$

73. Let $u = x^3 - 1$; the rest is routine.

76. Let $x = \tan^3 z$. The integral becomes

$$\int \frac{3 \tan^2 z \sec^2 z}{\sec^2 z \tan^2 z}\, dz = 3z + C = 3 \tan^{-1}(x^{1/3}) + C.$$

79. Multiply numerator and denominator of the integrand by

$$\sqrt{1 - \sin t}.$$

82. Let $u = e^x$. The integral becomes

$$I = \int \sin^{-1} u \, du.$$

Now do an integration by parts with $p = \sin^{-1} u$, $dq = du$:

$$I = u \sin^{-1} u - \int u(1 - u^2)^{-1/2} \, du$$

$$= u \sin^{-1} u + (1 - u^2)^{1/2} + C$$

$$= e^x \sin^{-1}(e^x) + (1 - e^{2x})^{1/2} + C.$$

85. The partial fractions decomposition of the integrand is

$$\frac{x}{x^2 + 1} - \frac{x}{(x^2 + 1)^2},$$

and integration of these terms presents no difficulties.

88. Use integration by parts with $u = \ln x$, $dv = x^{3/2} \, dx$. The antiderivative is

$$\frac{2}{25} x^{5/2} (-2 + 5 \ln x) + C.$$

91. By parts: A good choice is to let $u = x$ and $dv = e^x \sin x \, dx$. It turns out that one must antidifferentiate both $e^x \sin x$ and $e^x \cos x$, but here Formulas 67 and 68 of the endpapers may be used, or integration by parts will suffice for each.

94. Use integration by parts, with $u = \ln(1 + \sqrt{x})$ and $dv = dx$. If you choose $v = x - 1$, certain difficulties are skirted, and the resulting antiderivative is

$$(x - 1) \ln(1 + \sqrt{x}) - \frac{1}{27} x + \sqrt{x} + C.$$

97. Multiply numerator and denominator by $\cos \xi - 1$. Because $\cos^2 \xi - 1 = -\sin^2 \xi$, the integral becomes

$$\int (-\sin \xi \cos \xi - \sin \xi) \, d\xi$$

$$= \frac{1}{2} \cos^2 \xi \; + \; \cos \xi \; + \; C.$$

100. Let $u = x^2$. The integral becomes

$$\frac{1}{2} \int \left(\frac{1 - u}{1 + u} \right)^{1/2} du.$$

Now let $v^2 = \dfrac{1 - u}{1 + u}$; then $u = \dfrac{1 - v^2}{1 + v^2}$ and

$$du \; = \; - \; \frac{4v}{(1 + v^2)^2} \; dv.$$

The integral is thereby converted into

$$- \; \frac{1}{2} \int \frac{4v^2}{(1 + v^2)^2} \; dv.$$

Finally let $v = \tan z$. Then we obtain

$$- 2 \int \sin^2 z \; dz \; = \; \sin z \cos z \; - \; z \; + \; C.$$

Subsequent resubstitutions and simplifications lead to the answer:

$$\frac{1}{2} (1 - x^4)^{1/2} \; - \; \tan^{-1}(\{1 - x^2\}/\{1 + x^2\})^{1/2} \; + \; C.$$

103. $A_b = \displaystyle\int_0^b 2\pi e^{-x}(1 + e^{-2x})^{1/2} \, dx.$

Use the substitution $u = e^{-x}$. It follows that

$$A_b \; = \; \int_1^{e^{-b}} 2\pi u(1 + u^2)^{1/2} \left(- \frac{1}{u} \right) du$$

$$= \; \int_p^1 2\pi(1 + u^2)^{1/2} \, du \quad (\text{where } p = e^{-b}).$$

204

Let $u = \tan z$. Then

$$A_b = \int_p^1 2\pi(1 + \tan^2 z)^{1/2} \sec^2 z \, dx$$

$$= \pi\left[\sec z \tan z + \ln|\sec z + \tan z|\right]_p^1$$

$$= \pi\{\sqrt{2} + \ln(1 + \sqrt{2}) \, e^{-b}(1 + e^{-2b})^{1/2}$$

$$- \ln|e^{-b} + (1 + e^{-2b})^{1/2}|\}.$$

The limit as $b \to \infty$ is

$$A_\infty = \pi\{\sqrt{2} + \ln(1 + \sqrt{2})\} \sim 7.2118.$$

106. Part (a): Use integration by parts with $u = (\ln x)^n$ and $dv = x^m \, dx$.

Part (b): Application of the formula and simplification of the result yields

$$\frac{17e^4 + 3}{128} \sim 7.2747543.$$

109. The area is

$$A = 2\int_0^2 x^{5/2}(2 - x)^{1/2} \, dx.$$

The suggested substitution $x = 2\sin^2\xi$ yields

$$A = 64\int_0^{\pi/2} \sin^6\xi \cos^2\xi \, d\xi.$$

Then the formula of Problem 108 gives the answer $\frac{5}{4}\pi$.

112. Because $\{1 + (dy/dx)^2\}^{1/2} = (1 + \sqrt{x})^{1/2}$, the length of the curve is

$$L = \int_0^1 (1 + \sqrt{x})^{1/2} \, dx.$$

Let $x = \tan^4 u$. We obtain

$$L = \int_0^{\pi/4} 4(1 + \tan^2 u)^{1/2} \tan^3 u \sec^2 u \, du$$

$$= 4 \int_0^{\pi/4} \sec^3 u \tan^3 u \, du$$

$$= 4 \int_0^{\pi/4} (\sec^3 u)(\sec^2 u - 1) \tan u \, du$$

$$= 4 \int_0^{\pi/4} (\sec^4 u - \sec^2 u)(\sec u \tan u) \, du$$

$$= \left[\frac{4}{5} \sec^5 u - \frac{4}{3} \sec^3 u \right]_0^{\pi/4}$$

$$= \frac{4}{5}(4\sqrt{2} - 1) - \frac{4}{3}(2\sqrt{2} - 1)$$

$$= \frac{8}{15}(1 + \sqrt{2}) \sim 1.28758.$$

115. Use the substitution $u = e^x$. The integral then becomes

$$\int \frac{1}{u^2 + u + 1} \, du,$$

and we use now-familiar techniques to obtain the answer.

118. With the recommended substitution, the numerator is $\frac{1}{2} \, du$, so the integral becomes

$$\frac{1}{2} \int u^{-3} \, du = -\frac{1}{4} u^{-2} + C$$

$$= - \frac{1}{4(x^4 + x^2)^2} + C.$$

Section 10.1

1. The given line has slope $-\frac{1}{2}$.

4. By implicit differentiation, $\frac{dy}{dx} = \frac{1}{2y}$; in particular, the slope of the tangent at $(6,-3)$ is $-\frac{1}{6}$.   So the answer is

$$y + 3 = - \frac{1}{6}(x - 6);$$

that is, $x + 6y + 12 = 0$.

7. Write the equation in the form $x^2 + 2x + 1 + y^2 = 5$.

10. Write $x^2 + 8x + 16 + y^2 - 6y + 9 = 25$ to conclude that the center is at $(-4,3)$ and the radius is 5 .

13. Given $2x^2 + 2y^2 - 2x + 6y = 13$, write

$$x^2 + y^2 - x + 3y = \frac{13}{2} ;$$

$$x^2 - x + \frac{1}{4} + y^2 + 3y + \frac{9}{4} = \frac{36}{4} ;$$

$$(x - \frac{1}{2})^2 + (y + \frac{3}{2})^2 = 3^2 .$$

Thus the center is at $(\frac{1}{2}, -\frac{3}{2})$ and the radius is 3 .

16. Center: $(\frac{2}{3}, \frac{3}{2})$; radius: 2 .

19. Given: $x^2 + y^2 - 6x - 10y + 84 = 0$:

$$x^2 - 6x + 9 + y^2 - 10y + 25 + 50 = 0;$$

$$(x - 3)^2 + (y - 5)^2 = -50 .$$

It follows that there are no points on the graph.

22. The line has slope 1, so the radius to the point of tangency has slope -1. The radius is a segment of the line with equation

$$y + 2 = -(x - 2); \quad \text{that is,} \quad x + y = 0.$$

The point of tangency is the simultaneous solution of the equations of the two lines: $x = -2$, $y = 2$ -- therefore they meet at $(-2,2)$. The length of the radius is the distance from $(2,-2)$ to $(-2,2)$, which is $4\sqrt{2}$. Therefore the equation of the circle is $(x - 2)^2 + (y + 2)^2 = 32$.

25. The squares of the distances are equal, so $P(x,y)$ satisfies

$$(x - 2)^2 + (y - 2)^2 = (x - 7)^2 + (y - 4)^2.$$

Expand and simplify to obtain the answer.

28. The point $P(x,y)$ satisfies the equation

$$x + 3 = \{(x - 3)^2 + y^2\}^{1/2}.$$

Expand and simplify to obtain $y^2 = 12x$: The locus is a parabola, opening to the right, with its vertex at the origin, and symmetric about the x-axis.

31. If $P(a,b)$ is the point of tangency, then $b = a^2$, and the slope of the tangent line can be measured in two different ways. They are equal, and we thereby obtain

$$\frac{1 - a^2}{2 - a} = 2a.$$

We find two solutions: $a = 2 - \sqrt{3}$ and $a = 2 + \sqrt{3}$. But $b = a^2$, so $b = 7 - 4\sqrt{3}$ or $b = 7 + 4\sqrt{3}$. Thus we obtain the two answers given in the text.

34. The second condition means that all such lines have slope 3. If such a line is tangent to the graph of $y = x^3$ at the point (a, a^3), its slope must also be $3a^2 = 3$. Thus $a = 1$ or $a = -1$. Thus there are two such lines:

$$y - 1 = 3(x - 1) \quad \text{(through } (1,1) \text{ with slope 3)}$$

and

$$y + 1 = 3(x + 1) \qquad \text{(through } (-1,-1) \text{ with slope } 3).$$

Section 10.2

4. Answer: $r \sin \xi = 6$; better,

$$r = 6 \csc \xi, \quad 0 < \xi < \pi.$$

10. Answer: $r = \dfrac{4}{\sin \xi + \cos \xi}$. It would be best to restrict the values of ξ to the range $-\pi/4 < \xi < 3\pi/4$.

13. Begin by multiplying each side of the equation by r.

16. First, $r^2 = 2r + r \sin \xi$, so

$$x^2 + y^2 = 2(x^2 + y^2)^{1/2} + y.$$

Hence

$$(x^2 + y^2 - y)^2 = \{2(x^2 + y^2)^{1/2}\}^2 = 4x^2 + 4y^2;$$

$$x^4 + 2x^2 y^2 + y^4 - 2x^2 y - 2y^3 + y^2 = 4x^2 + 4y^2;$$

$$x^4 + 2x^2 y^2 + y^4 - 2x^2 y - 2y^3 - 4x^2 - 3y^2 = 0.$$

22. $y = x - 2$; $r(\cos \xi - \sin \xi) = 2$, $-5\pi/4 < \xi < \pi/4$

28. $(x - 5)^2 + (y + 2)^2 = 25$; $r^2 - 10r \cos \xi + 4r \sin \xi + 4 = 0$

34. Given:

$$r = 4 + 2 \cos \xi.$$

This graph is symmetric about the x-axis. It is shown at the right.

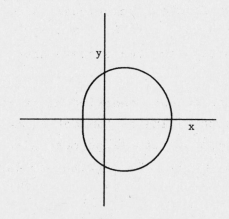

40. Given: $r = 3\xi$. There are no symmetries. The correct answer is an equally spaced spiral, similar to the one shown next, on the left.

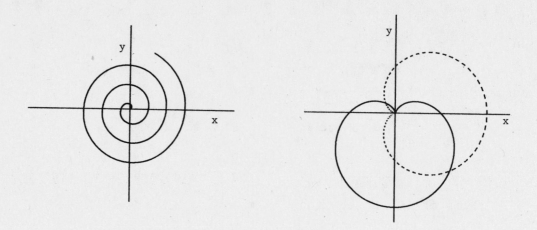

46. The graph of $r = 1 + \cos\xi$ is shown as a dashed line in the figure (above, right), while the graph of $r = 1 - \sin\xi$ is shown as a solid line. The graphs meet at three points:

$$\left(\frac{1}{2}\{2 - \sqrt{2}\}, 3\pi/4\right),$$

$$\left(\frac{1}{2}\{2 + \sqrt{2}\}, -\pi/4\right),$$

and $(0,0)$.

Section 10.3

1. $A = 2\displaystyle\int_0^{\pi/2} \frac{1}{2}(4\cos^2\xi)\, d\xi.$

4. $A = \displaystyle\int_0^{2\pi} \frac{1}{2}(4)(1 - \sin\xi)^2\, d\xi$

$\qquad = 2 \displaystyle\int_0^{2\pi} \{1 - 2\sin\xi + \frac{1}{2}(1 - \cos 2\xi)\}\, d\xi$

$\qquad = \left[2\xi + 4\cos\xi + \xi - \frac{1}{2}\sin 2\xi\right]_0^{2\pi} = 6\pi.$

210

7. $A = \dfrac{1}{2} \displaystyle\int_0^\pi 16 \cos^2 \xi \; d\xi$

$= 4 \displaystyle\int_0^\pi (1 + \cos 2\xi) \; d\xi$

$= 4 \left[\xi + \dfrac{1}{2} \sin 2\xi \right]_0^\pi = 4\pi.$

10. $A = \dfrac{1}{2} \displaystyle\int_0^{2\pi} (10 + 6 \sin \xi + 6 \cos \xi + 2 \sin \xi \cos \xi) \; d\xi$

$= \dfrac{1}{2} \left[10\xi - 6 \cos \xi + 6 \sin \xi + \sin^2 \xi \right]_0^{2\pi} = 10\pi.$

13. The graph of the given curve is shown at the left, below. The area within each of the eight loops is

$$A = 2 \int_0^{\pi/8} \dfrac{1}{2} (4 \cos^2 4\xi) \; d\xi.$$

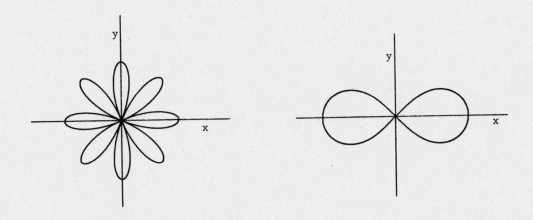

16. The graph of $r^2 = 4 \cos 2\xi$ is above at the right. The area within each of the loops is

$$A = \dfrac{1}{2} \int_{-\pi/4}^{\pi/4} 4 \cos 2\xi \; d\xi = \left[\sin 2\xi \right]_{-\pi/4}^{\pi/4} = 2.$$

19. The two curves are shown at the left, below. The region in question has area

$$A = \frac{1}{2} \int_{\pi/6}^{5\pi/6} (4 \sin^2 \xi - 1) \, d\xi.$$

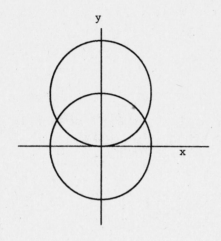
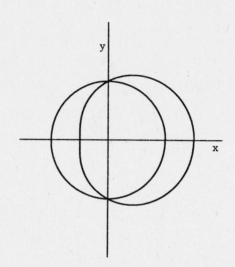

22. We are to find the area outside the circle $r = 2$ and within the curve $r = 2 + \cos \xi$; these curves are shown at the right, above. The curves meet where $\xi = \pi/2$ and where $\xi = -\pi/2$, so the area in question is

$$A = \frac{1}{2} \int_{-\pi/2}^{\pi/2} \{(2 + \cos \xi)^2 - 2^2\} \, d\xi$$

$$= \int_0^{\pi/2} \{4 \cos \xi + \frac{1}{2} (1 + \cos 2\xi)\} \, d\xi$$

$$= \left[4 \sin \xi + \frac{1}{2} \xi + \frac{1}{4} \sin 2\xi \right]_0^{\pi/2} = \frac{\pi + 16}{4}.$$

25. The curves intersect where $\xi = \pi/8$. By symmetry, the area between them is

$$A = 4 \int_0^{\pi/8} \frac{1}{2} \sin 2\xi \, d\xi.$$

212

28. The two curves meet at the origin, at the point with Cartesian coordinates $(-2,0)$, and at the two points where

$$\cos \xi = 3 - 2\sqrt{2}.$$

Let the least positive value of ξ that satisfies the latter equation be denoted by ω. Then the area within the figure-8 curve but outside the cardioid is given by

$$A = \int_0^\omega \{4 \cos \xi - (1 - \cos \xi)^2\}\, d\xi$$

$$= \int_0^\omega \{6 \cos \xi - 1 - \frac{1}{2}(1 + \cos 2\xi)\}\, d\xi$$

$$= \left[6 \sin \xi - \frac{3}{2}\xi - \frac{1}{4}\sin 2\xi \right]_0^\omega$$

$$= 12(3\sqrt{2} - 4)^{1/2} - \frac{3}{2}\omega - (3 - 2\sqrt{2})(3\sqrt{2} - 4)^{1/2}$$

$$\sim 3.7289587.$$

Section 10.4

1. The value of p is 3, so the parabola has equation $y^2 = 12x$.

4. The value of p is 2, so this parabola has equation

$$(y + 1)^2 = -8(x + 1).$$

The graph is at the right.

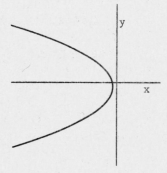

7. Here, we have $p = \dfrac{3}{2}$, so this parabola has equation

$$x^2 = -6(y + \dfrac{3}{2}).$$

10. Here we have $p = 1$, so this parabola has equation

$$(y - 1)^2 = 4(x + 3)$$

and its graph is shown at the right.

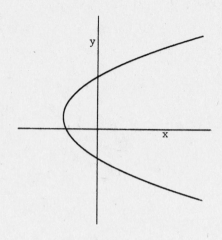

16. The given equation may be written in the form

$$y^2 + 6y + 9 = 2x - 6;$$

$$(y + 3)^2 = (4)(\dfrac{1}{2})(x - 3).$$

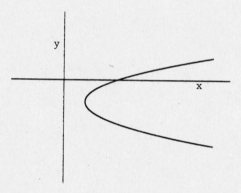

So $p = 1/2$; vertex $(3, -3)$; directrix $x = 5/2$; focus at $(7/2, -3)$; axis the horizontal line $y = -3$. The graph is at the right.

19. Note that this is a maximum-minimum problem, and recall that a distance is minimized when its square is minimized.

22. Set up coordinates so that the parabola has vertex $V(-p, 0)$. Then the equation of the comet's orbit is

$$y^2 = 4p(x + p).$$

The line $y = x$ meets the orbit of the comet at the point (a, b) (say), which is $100\sqrt{2}$ million miles from the origin (which is also where both the sun and the focus of the parabola are located). Therefore

$$a^2 = 4p(a + p)$$

and

$$(a^2 + a^2)^{1/2} = (100\sqrt{2})(10^6) = 10^8\sqrt{2}.$$

It follows that $a = 10^8$. Next, $a^2 = 4p(a + p)$. We apply the quadratic formula to find that

$$p = \frac{1}{2}(\sqrt{2} - 1)(10^8).$$

The vertex is at distance p from the focus; therefore, by the result of Problem 19, the closest approach is approximately 20.71 million miles.

28. For simplicity, we write v in place of v_0. Here we are given $v = 160$ and $g = 32$.

(a) If $\alpha = \pi/6$:

$$R = \frac{v^2 \sin 2a}{g} = 400\sqrt{3} \sim 692.82 \quad \text{(feet)}.$$

Now by Equation (8), $y = 0$ when $gt^2 = 2v(\sin\alpha)t$; and because $t > 0$, the time of impact is

$$t = \frac{2v \sin\alpha}{g}. \qquad (*)$$

In this case, then, the time in air is 5 seconds.

(b) If $\alpha = \pi/3$: Similar computations show that the range is again $400\sqrt{3} \sim 692.82$ (feet), and with the aid of Equation (*) above, the time in air can be evaluated; it is exactly $5\sqrt{3}$ seconds -- about 8.86 seconds.

Section 10.5

1. The location of the vertices makes it clear that the center of the ellipse is at $(0,0)$. Therefore its equation may be written in the standard form

$$(\frac{x}{4})^2 + (\frac{y}{5})^2 = 1.$$

4. We immediately have a = 6 and b = 4, so the equation is

$$\left(\frac{x}{4}\right)^2 + \left(\frac{y}{6}\right)^2 = 1.$$

7. First, a = 10 and e = 1/2. So c = ae = 5 and thus b^2 = 100 - 25 = 75.

So the equation is

$$\frac{x^2}{100} + \frac{y^2}{75} = 1.$$

10. First, c = 4 and 9 = c/e^2; therefore e = 2/3. So a = c/e = 6; b^2 = a^2 - c^2 = 20. Equation:

$$\frac{x^2}{20} + \frac{y^2}{36} = 1.$$

13. "Move" the center first to the origin to obtain the equation

$$\frac{x^2}{25} + \frac{y^2}{16} = 1.$$

Then apply the translation principle to obtain the answer.

16. In standard form, the equation of this ellipse is

$$\frac{x^2}{4} + \frac{y^2}{16} = 1.$$

So the major axis is vertical,
b = 2, a = 4, the minor axis
is of length 4, and the major
axis is of length 8. The
center is at the origin. Foci:
$(0,-2\sqrt{3})$ and $(0,2\sqrt{3})$.
Its graph is at the right.

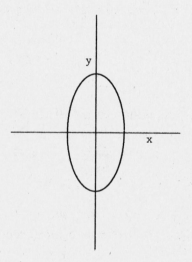

19. The equation can be put in the standard form

$$\left(\frac{x}{2}\right)^2 + \left(\frac{y-4}{3}\right)^2 = 1.$$

The rest is routine.

22. In the usual notation, we have 2a = 0.467 + 0.307 = 0.774.   So
a = 0.387, e = 0.206.   Therefore c = ae = 0.079722, and

$$b = (a^2 - c^2)^{1/2} \sim 0.378699621;$$

we'll use b = 0.3787.   Therefore the ellipse has major axis
0.774, minor axis 0.7574; in terms of percentages, a is about
2.2 % greater than b.   Is this a nearly circular orbit? Decide
for yourself: Compare the circle (on the left) below, with radius
0.7657, with the ellipse (on the right) below of the shape of the
orbit of the planet.

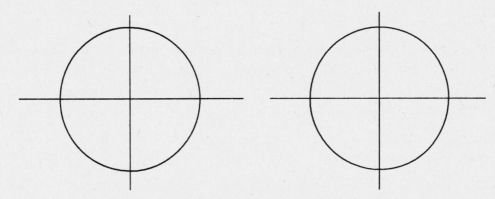

28. Begin with the equation

$$\{(x - 3)^2 + (y + 3)^2\}^{1/2} + \{(x + 3)^2 + (y - 3)^2\}^{1/2} = 10.$$

This leads to the equation $16x^2 + 18xy + 16y^2 = 175$.

Section 10.6

1. It follows that c = 4, a = 1, and $b^2 = 15$.   So the standard
equation is

$$x^2 - \frac{1}{15} y^2 = 1.$$

4. First, a = 3, and ba = 3/4 = b/3, so b = 9/4.   So the
equation of the hyperbola is

$$\frac{1}{9} x^2 - \frac{16}{81} y^2 = 1.$$

7. Let us interchange x and y in the data given in the problem,
then restore their meanings with a second interchange at the last
step.   That is, we assume the foci to be at (-6,0) and (6,0),
and that the eccentricity is e = 2.   It follows that c = 6,

and thus that $a = c/e = 3$. Thus $b^2 = c^2 - a^2 = 27$, and this hyperbola would have equation $x^2/9 - y^2/27 = 1$. Now we interchange x and y to obtain the correct answer.

10. We have $c = 9$; also, $4 = c/e^2$, so $e = 3/2$. Next, $a = c/e = 6$, so $b^2 = c^2 - a^2 = 45$. Hence the equation is

$$\frac{y^2}{36} - \frac{x^2}{45} = 1.$$

13. We "move" the data so that the center is at $(0,0)$: Replace x by $x - 1$ and y by $y + 2$. The translated hyperbola has vertices at $(0,3)$ and $(0,-3)$ and asymptotes $3x = 2y$ and $3x = -2y$. Now let's interchange x and y. One asymptote then has equation $y = 2x/3$, so $b/a = 2/3$. But $a = 3$, so $b = 2$. The equation of this hyperbola is $x^2/9 - y^2/4 = 1$. But we must interchange x and y again and then replace y by $y + 2$ and x by $x - 1$; this gives the answer.

16. Write

$$(x + 2)^2 - 2y^2 = 4,$$

thus

$$\frac{(x + 2)^2}{4} - \frac{y^2}{2} = 1.$$

So $a = 2$, $b = \sqrt{2}$, and

$$c^2 = a^2 + b^2 = 6.$$

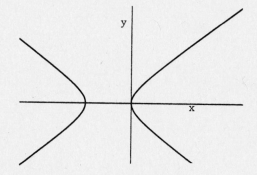

Therefore the center is at the point $(-2,0)$, the foci are at $(-2 + \sqrt{6},)$ and $(-2 - \sqrt{6},0)$, and the asymptotes have the equations

$$y = \left| \frac{1}{2} \sqrt{2} (x + 2) \right|.$$

22. First show that the equation of the tangent at $P_0(x_0 y_0)$ is

$$y - y_0 = (b^2 x_0 / a^2 y_0)(x - x_0).$$

If $y_0 = 0$, use dx/dy rather than dy/dx to get the result.

25. Note that $a^2 = (9/2) + (9/2)$, so that $a = 3$; therefore $2a = 6$. Then

$$\{(x - 5)^2 + (y - 5)^2\}^{1/2} + 6 = \{(x + 5)^2 + (y + 5)^2\}^{1/2}.$$

Now apply either the technique or the formula of the solution of Problem 24.

Section 10.7

Note: The following BASIC program was used to verify the solutions of most of the problems of this section. It follows exactly the discussion of rotation of axes given in the text.

```
10   DEFDBL A - Z
15       REM   All variable are double precision.
20   Z = 1.0D-10
25       REM   Criterion for being near zero.
30   P = 3.14159265358979324
35       REM   Value for pi.
40   PRINT " Enter coefficients  A, B, C, D, E, and F"
50   PRINT "      for the equation"
60   PRINT " A*X*X + B*X*Y + C*Y*Y + D*X + E*Y + F  =  0."
70   PRINT
80   INPUT " A, B, C, D, E, F: "; A, B, C, D, E, F
90   IF  A <> C  GOTO 140
95       REM   Go to 140 if the rotation angle is not 45°.
100  L = P/4.0D0
105      REM   This is the case in which the angle is 45°.
110  M = 0.5D0*1.414213562D0
115      REM   Half the square root of 2.
120  N = M
130  GOTO 220
135      REM   Computations will be done directly at 220.
140  L = 0.5D0*ATN(B/(A - C))
145      REM   Rotation angle in general case.
150  IF L >= 0.0D0  GOTO 170
155      REM   Jump to 170 if the angle is nonnegative.
160  L = L + 0.5D0*P
165      REM   Correction of negative angle.
```

219

```
170  O = ABS(A - C)
180  Y = O/SQR(O*O + B*B)
190  Y = Y*SGN((A - C)/B)
195       REM   Note assumption:  B  is nonzero.
200  M = SQR(0.5D0*(1.0D0 - Y))
210  N = SQR(0.5D0*(1.0D0 + Y))
215       REM   Equations from the text appear next.
220  G = A*N*N + B*N*M + C*M*M
230  H = B*(N*N - M*M) + 2.0D0*(C - A)*N*M
240  I = A*M*M - B*M*N + C*N*N
250  J = D*N + E*M
260  K = E*N - D*M
270  Q = B*B - 4.0D0*A*C
275       REM   Note the discriminant in line 270.
280  IF Q < Z GOTO 310
285       REM   Otherwise  Q  is surely positive.
290  PRINT "       Hyperbola:"
300  GOTO 360
305       REM   Line 360 is where we print the parameters.
310  IF Q > -Z GOTO 340
315       REM   Go to line 340 because  Q  is probably nonnegative.
320  PRINT "      Ellipse:"
325       REM   Because  Q  is definitely negative.
330  GOTO 360
335       REM   To print parameters.
340  PRINT "      Parabola"
350  PRINT "            ... probably.   Discriminant:   "; Q
355       REM   Because  Q  is zero or nearly zero.
360  PRINT " Rotation angle:  Alpha = "; L
370  R = 180.0D0*L/P
375       REM   Conversion to degrees.
380  PRINT " In degrees, that's "; R
390  PRINT "    Its sine is "; M
395       REM   To help identify the rotation angle.
400  PRINT "  Its cosine is "; N
410  S = M/N
420  PRINT " Its tangent is "; S
430  PRINT " In the appropriately rotated uv-coordinate system,"
440  PRINT "    the equation of the conic takes the form"
450  PRINT
460  PRINT "   "; G; "*U*U + "; H; "*U*V"
```

```
470  PRINT "        + "; I; "*V*V + "; J; "*U"
480  PRINT "        + "; K; "*V + "; F; "  =  0."
490  PRINT
500  END
```

---

4. $B^2 - 4AC = 36 - 100 = -64 < 0$: An ellipse. The transformed
equation is $2u^2 + 8v^2 = 8$, which has the standard form

$$\frac{1}{4} u^2 + v^2 = 1.$$

The graph is an ellipse, rotated 45°. The major axis has length
4 and the minor axis has length 2. The graph is shown on the
left, below.

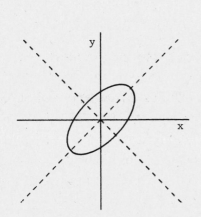
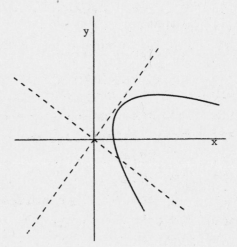

10. $B^2 - 4AC = 0$: The graph is a parabola. The transformed equation
is $25u^2 - 150u + 100v + 245 = 0$. The angle of rotation of
the uv-coordinate system is arctan(4/3). The equation can be
written in the standard form

$$(u - 3)^2 = -4 \left(v + \frac{1}{5} \right).$$

The vertex in the uv-system is at (3, -1/5). The graph of the
parabola is shown at the right, above.

16. Given: $x^2 + y^2 = r^2$. We have $A = 1 = C$, $B = D = E = 0$, and
$F = -r^2$. So

$$A' = \cos^2\alpha + \sin^2\alpha = 1,$$

$$B' = 0,$$

$$C' = \sin^2\alpha + \cos^2\alpha = 1,$$

$$D' = 0,$$

$$E' = 0, \quad \text{and}$$

$$F' = -r^2.$$

Consequently the equation $A'u^2 + B'v^2 + F' = 0$ becomes $u^2 + v^2 = r^2$. Therefore the transformed equation has the same form as the given equation.

19. The easiest way to see that we have an ellipse is to note that the discriminant is $B^2 - 4AC = -467 < 0$. The transformed equation (with approximate coefficients) is

$$(41.16376790)u^2 + (2.836232100)v^2 = 1,$$

the angle of rotation is $\arctan(0.765690976)$ (we are still using approximate values, of course); that is, about 0.6534 radians -- about $37.438°$. Because the values D' and E' are zero, the ellipse has its center at the origin (in both the xy-system and the uv-system). If we write the equation of the ellipse in the standard form

$$\left(\frac{u}{0.155862788}\right)^2 + \left(\frac{v}{0.593784855}\right)^2 = 1,$$

it follows that -- because the end points of the major axis are farthest from the origin and the end points of the minor axis are closest to the origin -- we can find the coordinates of these four points in the xy-system, and thereby obtain the answer in the text.

Section 10.8

4. Ellipse, foci at $(0,0)$ and $(8/15, 0)$, directrix $x = -4$, eccentricity $e = 1/4$ (so that $p = 4$), and vertices at the points $(-4/5, 0)$ and $(4/3, 0)$. Its graph appears at the top of the next page, on the left.

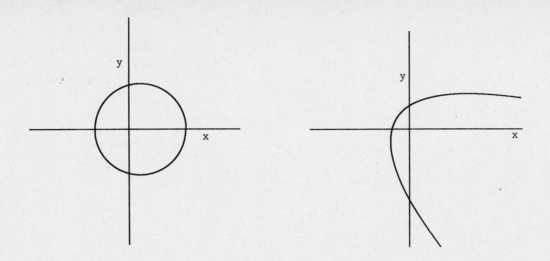

10. To begin with,

$$-\sqrt{3} \cos \xi + \sin \xi = A \cos(\xi - \alpha)$$

for some angle α and some number A. Equivalently,

$$A(\cos \xi \cos \alpha + \sin \xi \sin \alpha) = -\sqrt{3} \cos \xi + \sin \xi.$$

Set $\xi = 0$, then $\xi = \pi/2$ to discover that $A = -2$ and $\alpha = -\pi/6$. Therefore the equation given may be written in the form

$$r = \frac{2}{1 - \cos(\xi + \{\pi/6\})}.$$

The "unrotated" equation is

$$r = \frac{2}{1 + \cos \xi},$$

the equation of a parabola, opening to the right, with directrix $x = -2$, focus at $(0,0)$, and vertex at $(-1,0)$. Rotate that parabola $30°$ clockwise, with pivot at the origin, to obtain the graph shown above on the right.

13. The directrix equation may be put in the form $r \sin \xi = 2$, so $y = 2$ is a directrix. The eccentricity is $1/3$, so the equation is

$$r = \frac{2/3}{1 + (1/3) \sin \xi} = \frac{2}{3 + \sin \xi}.$$

223

16. Reference: Problem 11. We are given $r = 3 \sec \xi$. It follows that $r \cos \xi = 3$; that is, a directrix is $x = 3$. Also $p = 3$ and $e = 1$. The standard polar equation is therefore

$$r = \frac{3}{1 + \cos \xi}.$$

This is equivalent to $r + r \cos \xi = 3$; that is,

$$x^2 + y^2 = (3 - x)^2 = 9 - 6x + x^2.$$

Hence one answer is $y^2 + 6x = 9$.

19. Reference: Problem 14. From the polar equation

$$r = \frac{2}{1 - (2/3) \sin \xi}$$

we obtain $9(x^2 + y^2) = 36 + 24y + 4y^2$, which can be written in the form

$$9x^2 + 5y^2 = 24y + 36.$$

22. Given: Focus $(0,0)$, eccentricity e, and directrix $x = +p$. The equation $|OP| = e|PQ|$ yields

$$r = e(p - x) = e(p - r \cos \xi);$$

thus $r + er \cos \xi = pe$, and so

$$r = \frac{pe}{1 + e \cos \xi}.$$

25. From the figure at the right we may read the information

$$\frac{pe}{1 + e} = 4500$$

and

$$\frac{pe}{1 - e} = 9000.$$

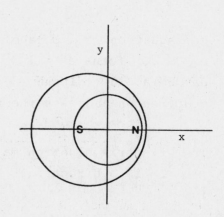

Therefore $pe = 4500(1 + e) = 9000(1 - e)$, and it follows that $e = 1/3$ and $p = 18,000$. The polar equation of the orbit is

224

$$r = \frac{6000}{1 + (1/3)\cos\xi}.$$

The satellite crosses the equatorial plane when $\xi = \pi/2$, which yields $r = 6000$. So the height of the satellite above the surface of the earth then is $h = 6000 - 4000 = 2000$ (miles).

28. See the figure below for the meaning of the various symbols. Because $T/A_2 = 15/A_1$, we find that $T = 15(A_2/A_1)$.

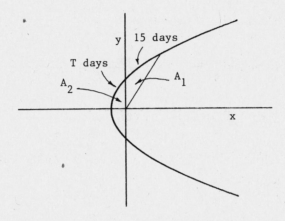

Now

$$A_1 = \frac{1}{2} \int_{\pi/3}^{\pi/2} \frac{1}{(1 - \cos\xi)^2}\, d\xi.$$

The substitution $u = \tan(\xi/2)$ transforms this integral into

$$A_1 = \frac{1}{2} \int_{1/\sqrt{3}}^{1} \frac{1 + u^2}{4u^4}\, du = \frac{1}{6}(3\sqrt{3} - 2).$$

The same substitution yields

$$A_2 = \frac{1}{2} \int_{\pi/2}^{\pi} \frac{1}{(1 - \cos\xi)^2}\, d\xi = \frac{1}{3}.$$

It follows that $T = \frac{30}{23}(3\sqrt{3} + 2) \sim 9.3863$ days.

4.   Given: $y^2 = 4(x + y)$.   Thus

$$y^2 - 4y + 4 = 4x + 4 = 4(x + 1);$$

it follows that $(y - 2)^2 = 4(x + 1)$.   So the graph is a parabola; it has directrix $x = -2$, axis $y = 2$, vertex at $(-1,2)$, focus at $(0,2)$, and it opens to the right.

10.   The given equation can be written in the form

$$\frac{(y - 1)^2}{4} - \frac{(x + 1)^2}{9} = 1.$$

So the graph is a hyperbola with center $(-1,1)$.   Because $c = \sqrt{13}$, the foci are at the points $(-1, 1 + \sqrt{13})$ and $(-1, 1 - \sqrt{13})$.   The vertices are at $(-1,3)$ and $(-1,-1)$. The transverse axis is vertical, of length 4, and the conjugate axis is horizontal, of length 6. The eccentricity is $\frac{1}{2}\sqrt{13}$, the directrices are

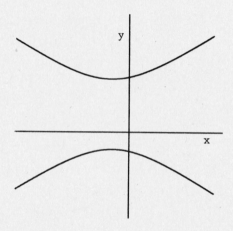

$$y = -1 + \frac{2}{13}\sqrt{13}$$

and

$$y = -1 - \frac{2}{13}\sqrt{13},$$

and the asymptotes have the equations

$$3y = 2x + 5 \quad \text{and} \quad 3y = -2x + 1.$$

16.   In a uv-coordinate system rotated 45° from the xy-system, the given equation takes the form

$$v^2 - \frac{1}{2}u^2 = 1.$$

226

This is the equation of a
hyperbola with center $(0,0)$,
vertices $(0,1)$ and $(0,-1)$;
the foci are at $(0,\sqrt{3})$ and
$(0,-\sqrt{3})$. The transverse
axis is parallel to the v-axis
and has length 2, the conjugate
axis has length $2\sqrt{2}$. The
eccentricity is $e = \sqrt{3}$, the
directrices satisfy

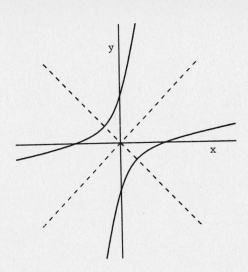

$$|v| = \frac{1}{3}\sqrt{3},$$

and the asymptotes satisfy

$$|v| = \frac{1}{2}|u|\sqrt{2}.$$

22. Multiply each side by r to obtain $y^2 = x$. This is the
equation of a parabola with axis the x-axis, opening to the right,
with vertex $(0,0)$, directrix $x = -1/4$, and focus $(0,1/4)$.

28. Given:

$$r = \frac{1}{1 + \cos\xi}.$$

This is a conic section having eccentricity $e = 1$, so it is a
parabola with focus at $(0,0)$. Also $p = 1$, so the directrix is
$x = 1$ and the vertex is at $(0,1/2)$. It opens to the left and
its axis is the x-axis.

31. The region whose area is sought is shown below on the left.

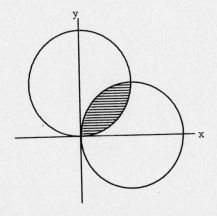
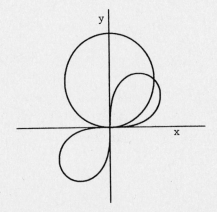

34. The two regions are shown on the right at the bottom of the previous page. The curves cross at the points where $\sin \xi = 0$ and where $\cos \xi = \sin \xi$. We obtain the two solutions $r = 0$ and $r = \sqrt{2}$, $\xi = \pi/4$. The area of the small region is

$$A_S = \frac{1}{2} \int_0^{\pi/4} \{(2 \sin 2\xi) - (2 \sin \xi)^2\} \, d\xi,$$

which turns out to be $\frac{1}{2}(4 - \pi) \sim 0.214602$. The area of the large region is

$$A_L = \int_0^{\pi/2} \sin 2\xi \, d\xi = 1.$$

Therefore the total area outside the circle but within the lemniscate is $\frac{1}{4}(8 - \pi) \sim 1.214602$.

37. The circle and the cardioid are shown on the left, below. They intersect only at the pole.

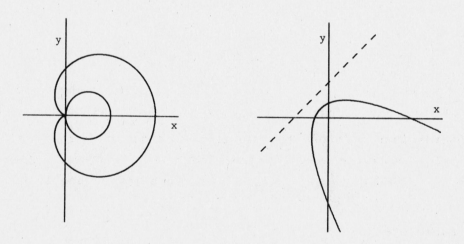

40. From the figure at the right, above, we see that matters would be greatly simplified if we were to rotate 45° counterclockwise to obtain the situation shown in the figure at the top of the next page. The parabola in the latter figure has equation

$$r = \frac{2^{3/2}}{1 - \cos \xi}.$$

Therefore the parabola in the first figure has equation

$$r = \frac{2^{3/2}}{1 - \cos(\xi + \{\pi/4\})}.$$

After a considerable amount of algebra we find we can write the Cartesian equation of the first parabola in the form

$$x^2 + 2xy + y^2 - 8x + 8y - 16 = 0.$$

46. We use the figure below. Note that we introduce a uv-coordinate system; in the rest of this discussion, all coordinates will be

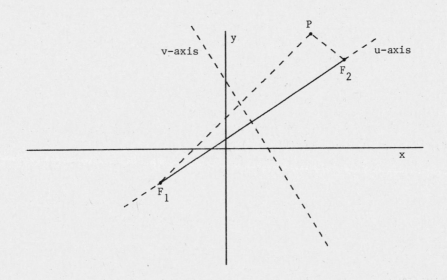

uv-coordinates. Choose the new axes so that $F_1 = F_1(c, 0)$ and $F_2 = F_2(-c, 0)$, $c > 0$. Suppose that $P = P(u, v)$. Then

$$|PF_2| = 2a + |PF_1|,$$

and therefore

$$\{(u + c)^2 + v^2\}^{1/2} = 2a + \{(u - c)^2 + v^2\}^{1/2}.$$

Consequently

$$(u + c)^2 + v^2 = 4a^2 + 4a\{(u - c)^2 + v^2\}^{1/2} + (u - c)^2 + v^2.$$

Successive simplifications produce

$$4uc - 4a^2 = 4a\{(u - c)^2 + v^2\}^{1/2};$$

$$uc - a^2 = a\{(u - c)^2 + v^2\}^{1/2};$$

$$u^2c^2 - 2a^2uc + a^4 = a^2u^2 - 2a^2uc + a^2c^2 + a^2v^2;$$

$$u^2c^2 - a^2u^2 - a^2v^2 = a^2c^2 - a^4;$$

$$u^2(c^2 - a^2) - a^2v^2 = a^2(c^2 - a^2).$$

Now $|F_1F_2| > 2a$, so $c > a$. Thus $c^2 - a^2 = b^2$ for some $b > 0$. Hence

$$b^2u^2 - a^2v^2 = a^2b^2;$$

that is,

$$\frac{u^2}{a^2} - \frac{v^2}{b^2} = 1.$$

Therefore the locus of $P(u,v)$ is a hyperbola with vertices $(a,0)$ and $(-a,0)$ and foci $(c,0)$ and $(-c,0)$ (because $c^2 = a^2 + b^2$), and therefore the hyperbola has foci F_1 and F_2.

Finally, if a circle with radius r_2 is centered at F_2 and another with radius r_1 is centered at F_1, with r_2 and r_1 satisfying the equation $r_2 = 2a + r_1$, then the two circles will intersect at a point on the hyperbola. You may thereby construct by straightedge-and-compass methods as many points lying on the hyperbola as you please.

49. Given: $3x^2 - y^2 + 12x + 9 = 0$. Then

$$4x^2 + 12x + 9 = x^2 + y^2;$$

$$(2x + 3)^2 = r^2;$$

$$r = 3 + 2r \cos \xi.$$

It follows that

$$r = \frac{3}{1 + 2 \cos \xi}.$$

Therefore the graph is a hyperbola with eccentricity $e = 2$.

230

52. Here, the loop has polar equation

$$r = \frac{5 \cos^2 \xi \sin^2 \xi}{\cos^5 \xi + \sin^5 \xi}$$

for $0 \le \xi \le \pi/2$. Therefore the area it bounds is

$$A = 25 \int_0^{\pi/4} \frac{\cos^4 \xi \sin^4 \xi}{(\cos^5 \xi + \sin^5 \xi)^2} \, d\xi.$$

The substitution $u = \tan \xi$ transforms this integral into

$$A = 25 \int_0^1 \frac{u^4}{(1 + u^5)^2} \, du = \frac{5}{2}.$$

Section 11.1

1. $\displaystyle \lim_{x \to 1} \frac{x - 1}{x^2 - 1} = \lim_{x \to 1} \frac{1}{2x} = \frac{1}{2}.$

Of course, l'Hôpital's rule is not necessary here, but it may be applied.

4. $\displaystyle \lim_{x \to 0} \frac{e^{3x} - 1}{x} = \lim_{x \to 0} \frac{3e^{3x}}{1} = 3.$

7. $\displaystyle \lim_{x \to 1} \frac{x - 1}{\sin x} = \frac{0}{\sin 1} = 0.$

Note that l'Hôpital's rule does not apply.

10. $\displaystyle \lim_{x \to \pi/2} \frac{1 + \cos 2z}{1 - \sin 2z} = \frac{1 + \cos \pi}{1 - \sin \pi} = \frac{0}{1} = 0.$

13. $\displaystyle \lim_{x \to \infty} \frac{\ln x}{x^{0.1}} = \lim_{x \to \infty} \frac{1/x}{(0.1)x^{-0.9}} = \lim_{x \to \infty} \frac{10}{x^{0.1}} = 0.$

16. $\displaystyle \lim_{t \to \infty} \frac{t^2 + 1}{t \ln t} = \lim_{t \to \infty} \frac{2t}{1 + \ln t} = \lim_{t \to \infty} \frac{2}{1/t} = +\infty.$

It is also correct to say that this limit does not exist.

231

22. 3/8

28. $1/\sqrt{2}$

34. 3

40. 1

46. -1/2

Section 11.2

1. $\displaystyle\lim_{x \to 0} x \cot x = \lim_{x \to 0} \frac{x \cos x}{\sin x} = (1)(\cos 0) = 1.$

4.   Let $u = \sin x.$ Then the given limit becomes

$$\lim_{u \to 0^+} u \ln u = \lim_{u \to 0^+} \frac{\ln u}{1/u} = \lim_{u \to 0^+} \frac{1/u}{-(1/u^2)}$$

$$= \lim_{u \to 0^+} (-u) = 0.$$

7.   Let $u = 1/x.$ Then the given limit becomes

$$\lim_{u \to \infty} \frac{e^u - 1}{u}, \text{ which does not exist.}$$

10. Replace $\cos 3x$ by $\cos^3 x - 3 \sin^2 x \cos x$; replace $\tan x$
     by $(\sin x)/(\cos x).$ The limit is -3.

16. $(x + 1)^{1/2} - x^{1/2} = \dfrac{x + 1 - x}{(x + 1)^{1/2} + x^{1/2}}$

$$= \frac{1}{(x + 1)^{1/2} + x^{1/2}} \to 0 \text{ as } x \to \infty.$$

22. Let $y = (x + \dfrac{1}{x})^x.$ Then

$$\ln y = x \ln(1 + \frac{1}{x})$$

232

$$= x \ln\left(\frac{x + 1}{x}\right)$$

$$= x\{\ln(x + 1) - \ln x\}$$

$$= \frac{\ln(x + 1) - \ln x}{1/x}.$$

Now apply l'Hôpital's rule to find that

$$\lim_{x \to \infty} \ln y = \lim_{x \to \infty} \frac{\ln(x + 1) - \ln x}{1/x}$$

$$= \lim_{x \to \infty} \frac{x - (x + 1)}{-(x + 1)/x}$$

$$= \lim_{x \to \infty} \frac{x}{x + 1} = 1.$$

Therefore $y \to e$ as $x \to +\infty$.

25. The limit of the natural logarithm of the expression in question is $-1/6$. A calculator estimate of this limit is particularly misleading.

28. 1

34. Let $Q = x^5 - 3x^4 + 17$. Then

$$Q^{1/5} - x = \frac{Q - x^5}{Q^{4/5} + Q^{3/5}x + Q^{2/5}x^2 + Q^{1/5}x^3 + x^4}.$$

The numerator is just $-3x^4 + 17$. Now <u>carefully</u> divide each term in numerator and denominator by x^4; put this divisor within each radical in the denominator. Then let x increase without bound to see that the limit is $-3/5$.

Section 11.3

4. $\frac{1}{1 - x} = 1 + x + x^2 + x^3 + x^4 + \frac{x^5}{(1 - z)^6}$

for some z between 0 and x.

10. $f(x) = -7 + 5x - 3x^2 + x^3.$

16. $\tan x = 1 + \dfrac{2}{1!}\left(x - \dfrac{\pi}{4}\right) + \dfrac{4}{2!}\left(x - \dfrac{\pi}{4}\right)^2 + \dfrac{16}{3!}\left(x - \dfrac{\pi}{4}\right)^3$

$$+ \dfrac{80}{4!}\left(x - \dfrac{\pi}{4}\right)^4 + \dfrac{Q(z)}{5!}\left(x - \dfrac{\pi}{4}\right)^5$$

for some z between $\pi/4$ and x, where

$$Q(z) = 16\sec^6 z + 88\sec^4 z \tan^2 z + 16\sec^2 z \tan^4 z.$$

22. First,

$$\sin x = x - \dfrac{1}{6}x^3 + \dfrac{1}{120}(\cos z)x^5$$

for some z between 0 and x. We require

$$\left|\dfrac{x^5}{5!}\cos z\right| < 10^{-6};$$

$$|x^5| < (120)(10^{-6}).$$

Answer: $|x| < 0.16438$. (The actual error for x in this range is never as great as 0.000001.)

25. Note that $35°$ corresponds to $7\pi/36$ radians, close to $\pi/6$.

28. Take $x = 105$, $a = 100$, and $f(x) = \sqrt{x}$. With $n = 3$ we find the error to be less than

$$\dfrac{(15)(105 - 100)^4}{(16)(24)(10^7)} \sim 0.00000244.$$

Therefore

$$\sqrt{105} \sim 10 + \dfrac{5}{1!(2)(10)} - \dfrac{25}{2!(4)(1000)} + \dfrac{(3)(125)}{3!(8)(100000)}$$

$$\sim 10.24695$$

(the same as the true value to five places).

1. $\displaystyle\int_4^\infty x^{-3/2}\,dx = \lim_{t\to\infty}\left[\frac{2}{x^{1/2}}\right]_t^4 = 1.$

4. $\displaystyle\lim_{t\to 0}\left[3x^{1/3}\right]_t^8 = 6.$

7. $\displaystyle\left[\frac{2}{(x-1)^{1/2}}\right]_\infty^5 = 1.$

10. $\displaystyle\int_0^3\frac{1}{(x-3)^2}\,dx = \lim_{t\to 3^-}\left[-\frac{1}{x-3}\right]_0^t$ -- diverges.

13. Integrate from -1 to 0, from 0 to 8, and if both integrals converge then add the results.

16. $\displaystyle\left[-\frac{1}{(x^2-4)^{1/2}}\right]_{-\infty}^\infty = 0.$

22. Diverges because $\displaystyle\int_0^\pi \sin^2 x\,dx = \frac{\pi}{2}.$

28. $\displaystyle\int_0^\infty\frac{1+x}{1+x^2}\,dx$ dominates $\displaystyle\int_0^\infty\frac{x}{1+x^2}\,dx$, which diverges.

34. The force exerted on m by dy is $\dfrac{Gm\rho}{a^2+y^2}\,dy$. The horizontal component of that force is

$$dF = \frac{Gm\rho}{r^2}(\cos\xi)\,dy.$$

So the total horizontal force is

$$F = \int_{-\infty}^\infty\frac{Gm\rho}{r^2}(\cos\xi)\,dy.$$

Now $r^2 = a^2 + y^2$ and $\cos \xi = \dfrac{a}{r}$.   So

$$\cos \xi = \frac{a}{(a^2 + y^2)^{1/2}} ;$$

$$F = 2 \int_0^\infty \frac{Gm\rho a}{(a^2 + y^2)^{3/2}} \, dy.$$

With the aid of Formula 52 of the endpapers of the text, we find that

$$F = 2Gm\rho a \left[\frac{y}{a^2(a^2 + y^2)^{1/2}} \right]_0^\infty$$

$$= \frac{2Gm\rho}{a} \left(\lim_{y \to \infty} \frac{y}{(a^2 + y^2)^{1/2}} \right) = \frac{2GM\rho}{a} .$$

Section 11.5

4. $I = \displaystyle\int_1^2 \ln x \, dx = T_{10} + \dfrac{1}{1200z^2} , \quad 1 < z < 2.$

$$T_{10} + \frac{1}{4800} < I < T_{10} + \frac{1}{1200} .$$

Now $T_{10} \sim 0.385877937$,   so

$$0.386086 < I < 0.386712.$$

(The true value is $-1 + 2 \ln 2 \sim 0.386294$.)

10.   Result: $1.999854 < \displaystyle\int_0^\pi \sin x \, dx < 2.000270$

(true value: 2).

13.   The key condition is $1/(12n^2) \leq 0.005$,   and it follows that we must choose $n > 4.08$ -- therefore we take $n = 5$.

16. The fourth derivative of the integrand is

$$f^{(4)}(x) = \frac{105}{16(1 + x)^{9/2}}.$$

Because $0 \leq x \leq 1$, $|f^{(4)}(x)| \leq 105/16$. We require

$$\frac{1^5}{180n^4} \frac{105}{16} < 0.005,$$

which implies that $n > 1.6433$; we take $n = 2$. The value of the integral is $2(\sqrt{2} - 1) \sim 0.828427125$, $S_2 \sim 0.828848851$, and the difference between them is less than 0.000422.

19. Volume: $V = \frac{h}{6}(0 + 4\pi(\frac{r}{2})^2 + \pi r^2) = \frac{1}{3}\pi r^2 h$.

22. Take $r_0 = 0$, $r_m = b$, $r_1 = 0$, and $H = 2a$. Then

$$V = (\frac{2a}{6})(4\pi b^2) = \frac{4}{3}\pi a b^2.$$

25. For $4/(12n^2) \leq 0.005$, we need $n > 8.16$; use $n = 10$. Then $T_{10} \sim 1.112332$ (true value: approximately 1.11144797).

28. The volume is

$$V = \int_{-5}^{5} \pi(25 - x^2)^2 \, dx$$

$$= \pi \int_{-5}^{5} (x^4 - 50x^2 + 625) \, dx$$

$$= \pi \left(\frac{10}{6}(0 + (4)(625) + 0) - \frac{10^5}{120}(1) \right)$$

(a consequence of the solution of Problem 26). The value of the last expression is the exact value of the volume: $10000\pi/3$.

4. $\displaystyle \lim_{x \to 0} \frac{x - \sin x}{x^3} = \lim_{x \to 0} \frac{1 - \cos x}{3x^2} = \lim_{x \to 0} \frac{\sin x}{6x} = \frac{1}{6}$.

10. Combine the two terms into a single fraction. Then l'Hôpital's rule is not required (but may be applied). The limit is -2.

13. Let $\displaystyle y = \ln(\{e^{2x} - 2x\}^{1/x}) = \frac{1}{x} \ln(e^{2x} - 2x)$. Evaluate

$$\lim_{x \to \infty} \frac{\ln(e^{2x} - 2x)}{x}.$$

16. $\displaystyle \int_{-4}^{0} (x + 4)^{-1/2} \, dx = \lim_{t \to -4^+} \left[2\sqrt{x + 4} \right]_{t}^{0} = 4$.

22. Some people evaluate improper integrals without using the limit notation, although they are certain to get the correct answer only if they remain aware that limits are involved. Here's how they'd write a solution to this problem:

$$\int_{0}^{2} (x - 1)^{-2/3} \, dx = \left[3(x - 1)^{1/3} \right]_{0}^{1} + \left[3(x - 1)^{1/3} \right]_{1}^{2}$$

$$= \left[3(x - 1)^{1/3} \right]_{0}^{2} = 3 - (-3) = 6.$$

25. The first four derivatives are $-2x \exp(-x^2)$, $(4x^2 - 2)\exp(-x^2)$, $(12x - 8x^3)\exp(-x^2)$, and $(16x^4 - 48x^2 + 12)\exp(-x^2)$.

28. $\displaystyle \tan^{-1} x = \frac{\pi}{4} + \frac{x - 1}{2} - \frac{(x - 1)^2}{4} + \frac{(x - 1)^3}{12}$

$$+ \frac{z(1 - z^2)}{(1 + z^2)^4} (x - 1)^4$$

for some number z between 1 and x.

34. $\cos x = 1 - \dfrac{x^2}{2!} + \dfrac{x^4}{4!} - \dfrac{x^6}{6!} \cos z$

where z is between 0 and x. Because $|\cos z| \leq 1$, we have

$$\left| \cos x - \left(1 - \dfrac{x^2}{2} + \dfrac{x^4}{24} \right) \right| \leq \dfrac{1}{6!} \leq 0.000139.$$

Result: Two-place accuracy.

43. See the figure below. The formula for the curve $y = f(x)$ is $f(x) = R - Kx^2$. Now

$$f(H/2) = r = R - \dfrac{1}{4} KH^2,$$

so $\dfrac{1}{4} KH^2 = R - r = \delta;$ therefore $K = 4\delta/H^2$, and thus

$$f(x) = R - \dfrac{4\delta}{H^2} x^2.$$

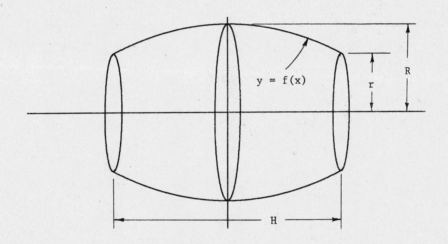

Now

$$V = \int_{-H/2}^{H/2} \pi \{f(x)\}^2 \, dx.$$

Let $g(x) = \pi \{f(x)\}^2$. Then

$$g(x) = \pi \left(R^2 - \dfrac{8R\delta x^2}{H^2} + \dfrac{16\delta^2 x^4}{H^4} \right).$$

Consequently

$$g^{(4)}(z) = \frac{(24\pi)(16\delta^2)}{H^4} .$$

Now it's easy to verify that $g(-H/2) = \pi r^2 = g(H/2)$; also, $g(0) = \pi R^2$. By Simpson's approximation,

$$V = \frac{H}{6}(\pi r^2 + 4\pi R^2 + \pi r^2) - \frac{(24\pi)(16\delta^2)H^5}{(180)(2^4)H^4}$$

$$= \pi H(\frac{1}{3}r^2 + \frac{2}{3}R^2) - \frac{2\delta^2\pi H}{15}$$

$$= \pi H\left(\frac{2}{3}R^2 - \frac{1}{3}r^2 - \frac{2}{15}\delta^2\right).$$

Section 12.2

4. $\lim\limits_{n \to \infty} \dfrac{n}{10 + (1/n^2)}$ does not exist.

10. $-1 \leq \sin n \leq 1$ for all n,   so by the squeeze law,

$$\lim_{n \to \infty} \frac{\sin n}{3^n} = 0.$$

16. $1/2$, 2, $1/2$, 2, ...   diverges.

22.   Apply l'Hôpital's rule thrice to $\lim\limits_{x \to \infty} \dfrac{x^3}{\exp(x/10)}$ to get the limit 0.

28. $\ln a_n = -\dfrac{1}{n}\ln(0.001) = \dfrac{1}{n}\ln(1000) \to 0$ as $n \to \infty$.

31. $\ln a_n = \dfrac{3}{n}\ln(\dfrac{2}{n}) = \dfrac{3(\ln 2 - \ln n)}{n} \to 0.$

34. $\lim\limits_{n \to \infty} a_n = \lim\limits_{x \to \infty} \dfrac{(2/3)^x}{1 - x^{1/x}} = \lim\limits_{x \to \infty} \dfrac{x^2(2/3)^x \ln(2/3)}{(\ln x) - 1}$

by l'Hôpital's rule.   And

$$\lim_{x \to \infty} x^2(2/3)^x = \lim_{x \to \infty} \frac{x^2}{(3/2)^x}$$

$$= \lim_{x \to \infty} \frac{2x}{(3/2)^x \ln(3/2)} = \lim_{x \to \infty} \frac{2}{(3/2)^x \{\ln(3/2)\}^2}$$

$$= 0. \quad \text{Thus}$$

$$\lim_{x \to \infty} \frac{x^2(2/3)^x \ln(2/3)}{(\ln x) - 1} = 0,$$

and therefore

$$\lim_{n \to \infty} \frac{(2/3)^n}{1 - n^{1/n}} = 0.$$

40. $\tau = \lim_{n \to \infty} (F_{n+1}/F_n) = \lim_{n \to \infty} (F_n + F_{n-1})/F_n$

$$= \lim_{n \to \infty} \{1 + (F_{n-1}/F_n)\}$$

$$= 1 + 1/\{\lim_{n \to \infty} (F_n/F_{n-1})\} = 1 + (1/\tau).$$

Therefore $\tau^2 = \tau + 1$.

Section 12.3

1. Geometric, ratio $\frac{1}{3}$, first term 1: sum $\frac{1}{1 - (1/3)} = \frac{3}{2}$.

4. $\lim_{n \to \infty} 2^{1/n} = 1 \neq 0$: This series diverges by the n-th term test.

7. Geometric, ratio $\frac{1}{3}$.

10. $\lim_{x \to \infty} x^{1/x} = 1 \neq 0$. This series diverges by the n-th term test.

13. Geometric, ratio $r = -\dfrac{3}{e}$. The series diverges because $|r| > 1$.

16. $\displaystyle\sum_{n=0}^{\infty} 1/(2^n) = 1$. So

$$\sum_{n=1}^{k}\left(\frac{2}{n} - \frac{1}{2^n}\right) > \left(\sum_{n=1}^{k} \frac{2}{n}\right) - 1$$

for all positive integers k. Because the harmonic series diverges to $+\infty$, so does

$$\sum_{n=1}^{\infty} \frac{2}{n},$$ and therefore so does the given series.

19. $\dfrac{1/5}{1 - (1/5)} - \dfrac{1/7}{1 - (1/7)} = \dfrac{1}{4} - \dfrac{1}{6} = \dfrac{1}{12}.$

22. The series is geometric with ratio $r = \dfrac{\pi}{e}$, and it diverges because $|r| > 1$.

28. Diverges by the n-th term test ($2^{1/n} \to 1$ as $n \to +\infty$).

34. $\dfrac{307}{909}$

40. The sum of the first k terms is

$$S_k = \frac{1}{4} + \frac{1}{4(2k + 1)(2k + 2)};$$

the sum of the series is therefore $\dfrac{1}{4}$.

46. Total distance traveled:

$$D = a + 2ra + 2r^2a + 2r^3a + 2r^4a + \ldots$$

$$= -a + 2a(1 + r + r^2 + r^3 + r^4 + \ldots)$$

$$= -a + \frac{2a}{1 - r} = \frac{-a + ar + 2a}{1 - r} = a\frac{1 + r}{1 - r}.$$

49. $M_1 = (0.95)M_0$, $M_2 = (0.95)M_1 = (0.95)^2 M_0$, and so on.
Therefore $M_n = (0.95)^n M_0$.

52. Peter's probability of winning is the sum of:

The probability he wins in the first round;

The probability that everyone tosses tails on the first round and Peter wins in the second round;

The probability that everyone tosses tails on the first two rounds and Peters wins in the third round;

. . . .

Thus his probability of winning is

$$\frac{1}{2} + \frac{1}{2^4} + \frac{1}{2^7} + \frac{1}{2^{10}} + \ldots = \frac{4}{7}.$$

Similarly, the probability that Paul wins is $\frac{2}{7}$ and the probability that Mary wins is $\frac{1}{7}$.

Section 12.4

1. $$\int_0^\infty \frac{x}{x^2 + 1}\, dx = \left[\frac{1}{2} \ln(x^2 + 1) \right]_0^\infty = +\infty.$$

Therefore the given series diverges.

4. $$\int_0^\infty (x + 1)^{-4/3}\, dx = \left[-3(x + 1)^{-1/3} \right]_0^\infty = 3 < \infty.$$

Therefore the given series converges.

10. $$\int_0^\infty x e^{-x}\, dx = 1 < \infty, \quad \text{so the given series converges.}$$

16. $$\int_1^\infty \frac{1}{x^3 + x}\, dx = \int_1^\infty \left(\frac{1}{x} - \frac{x}{x^2 + 1} \right) dx$$

$$= \left[(\ln x) - \frac{1}{2} \ln(x^2 + 1) \right]_1^\infty$$

$$= \frac{1}{2} \left[\ln \frac{x^2}{x^2 + 1} \right]_1^\infty = \frac{1}{2} \ln 2 < \infty,$$

and therefore the given series converges.

19. Let $J = \displaystyle\int_1^\infty \ln(1 + \frac{1}{x^2}) \, dx.$ Integrate by parts:

With $u = \ln(1 + x^{-2})$ and $dv = dx,$ we find that

$$J = \left[x \ln(1 + x^{-2}) \right]_1^\infty + 2 \int_1^\infty \frac{dx}{1 + x^2}$$

$$= \lim_{x \to \infty} \left(\frac{\ln(1 + x^{-2})}{1/x} \right) - \ln 2 + \left[2 \tan^{-1} x \right]_1^\infty$$

$$= \left(\lim_{u \to 0^+} \frac{\ln(1 + u^2)}{u} \right) + \pi - \frac{\pi}{2} - \ln 2$$

$$= \frac{\pi}{2} - \ln 2 < \infty, \quad \text{so the series converges.}$$

22. $\displaystyle\int_1^\infty \frac{x}{(4x^2 + 5)^{3/2}} \, dx = \left[- \frac{1}{4(4x^2 + 5)^{1/2}} \right]_1^\infty < \infty.$

Therefore the given series converges.

28. $\displaystyle\int_1^\infty (x + 1)^{-3} \, dx = \left[- \frac{1}{2}(x + 1)^{-2} \right]_1^\infty = \frac{1}{8} < \infty.$

Therefore the given series converges.

34. We require $R_n < (2)(10^{-11})$. This will hold provided that

$$\int_n^\infty \frac{1}{x^6} \, dx \; < \; (2)(10^{-11})$$

because R_n cannot exceed the integral by Theorem 2. So we require

$$\left[-\frac{1}{5x^5} \right]_n^\infty \; < \; (2)(10^{-11}),$$

and it follows that $n^5 > 10^{10}$, and thus that $n > 100$. We therefore choose $n = 101$.

37. Let $S = \displaystyle\sum_{n=1}^\infty \frac{1}{n^5}$. Then

$$S - S_n \; = \; a_{n+1} \; + \; a_{n+2} \; + \; \cdots \; = \; R_n$$

$$= \; \sum_{k=n+1}^\infty \frac{1}{k^5}.$$

$$\int_{n+1}^\infty x^{-5} \, dx \; \leq \; R_n \; \leq \; \int_n^\infty x^{-5} \, dx:$$

$$\left[\frac{1}{4x^4} \right]_\infty^{n+1} \; \leq \; R_n \; \leq \; \left[\frac{1}{4x^4} \right]_\infty^n ;$$

$$\frac{1}{4(n+1)^4} \; \leq \; R_n \; \leq \; \frac{1}{4n^4} .$$

For the accuracy required, we need to have

$$\frac{1}{4n^4} \; - \; \frac{1}{4(n+1)^4} \; < \; 0.0005,$$

and to achieve these ends we choose $n = 6$. Then

$$S_6 + \frac{1}{(4)(7^4)} \leq S \leq S_6 + \frac{1}{(4)(6^4)};$$

$$1.036790390 + 0.000104123 \leq S$$

$$\leq 1.036790390 + 0.000192901,$$

so that

$$1.036894513 \leq S \leq 1.036983291.$$

So we can definitely say that $1.03689 \leq S \leq 1.03699$.

40. Show that $c_n - c_{n+1} = \displaystyle\int_n^{n+1} \frac{1}{x}\, dx - \frac{1}{n+1} > 0.$

Section 12.5

1. Because $n^2 + n + 1 > n^2$ if $n > 0$, this series converges by comparison with the p-series for which $p = 2$.

4. Converges by limit-comparison with the p-series for which $p = \frac{3}{2}$.

7. Diverges by limit-comparison with the harmonic series.

10. Diverges by limit-comparison with the harmonic series.

13. Diverges by <u>careful</u> limit-comparison with the harmonic series.

16. Converges by comparison with the geometric series with ratio $\frac{1}{3}$.

19. Because $n^2 \ln n > n^2$ if $n \geq 3$, this series converges by comparison with the p-series for which $p = 2$.

22. Diverges by limit-comparison with the harmonic series.

25. Converges by comparison with the p-series for which $p = 2$. To show this, show that $\ln n < n$ if $n > 2$ and that $e^n > n^3$ if $n > 4$. To do the latter, sketch the graph of $f(x) = e^x - x^3$. Obtain an estimate of its largest x-intercept (it's approximately 4.5364) and show that the graph of $f(x)$ is decreasing for all larger values of x.

28. Converges by comparison with the geometric series with ratio $\frac{1}{2}$.

34. Show that $\ln n < n$ if $n \geq 1$. Then the given series converges by comparison with the p-series for which $p = 2$.

40. First, $1 + 2 + 3 + \ldots + n = \dfrac{n(n + 1)}{2}$, and so

$$\frac{1}{1 + 2 + 3 + \ldots + n} = \frac{2}{n(n + 1)} = \frac{2}{n} - \frac{2}{n + 1}.$$

So the sum of the first k terms of the given series is

$$S_k = 2\left(1 - \frac{1}{k + 1}\right).$$

Therefore the sum of the series is 2.

Section 12.6

1. Converges by Theorem 1.

4. Diverges by the n-th term test.

7. Converges by Theorem 1.

10. Converges by the ratio test.

13. Converges conditionally -- Theorem 1 for convergence, a careful limit-comparison with the harmonic series to show that the given series is not absolutely convergent.

16. Converges absolutely by the ratio test.

19. Diverges by the n-th term test.

22. Diverges by the n-th term test.

25. Diverges by the n-th term test: $\ln(1/n) = -\ln n$.

28. Claim: $f(x) = \dfrac{1}{x}\arctan x$ is decreasing for $x \geq 2$.   The reason is that

$$f'(x) = \frac{x - (1 + x^2)\arctan x}{x^2(1 + x^2)},$$

so

$$f'(x) < \frac{x - (1 + x^2)}{x^2(1 + x^2)} \qquad \text{if} \qquad x \geq 2;$$

thus for $x \geq 2$,

$$f'(x) < \frac{2x - (1 + x^2)}{x^2(1 + x^2)} = -\frac{(x - 1)^2}{x^2(x^2 + 1)} < 0.$$

Therefore $f(x) = \dfrac{1}{x}\arctan x$ is decreasing for $x \geq 2$,   so the given series converges by Theorem 1.   But the convergence is conditional because

$$\sum_{n=1}^{\infty} \frac{1}{n}\arctan n$$

diverges by limit-comparison with the harmonic series.

34. Because

$$|R_n| = \frac{1}{(n + 1)^2} < 0.0005 \quad \text{when} \quad n > 43.72,$$

we choose $n = 44$.   Numerical notes: $S_{44} \sim 0.8222146356$, $1/(45^2) \sim 0.000493827$,   and the sum of the series itself is about 0.822357033.   (The exact value of the sum is $\pi^2/12$.   You can deduce this from the results of Problem 42 in Section 12.8.)

40. Choose $n \geq 5$; $S_4 \sim 0.971888644$;   the sum of the given series is approximately 0.972119771.   Answer: 0.972.

43. Let $a_n = b_n = \dfrac{(-1)^{n+1}}{\sqrt{n}}$.

Section 12.7

1.

n	$f^{(n)}(x)$	$f^{(n)}(0)$
0	$\ln(1 + x)$	0
1	$(1 + x)^{-1}$	1
2	$-(1 + x)^{-2}$	-1
3	$2(1 + x)^{-3}$	2
4	$-6(1 + x)^{-4}$	-6
5	$24(1 + x)^{-5}$	$4!$
6	$-120(1 + x)^{-6}$	$-(5!)$
7	$720(1 + x)^{-7}$	$6!$
⋮	⋮	⋮

Answer: $x - \dfrac{1}{2}x^2 + \dfrac{1}{3}x^3 - \dfrac{1}{4}x^4 + \dfrac{1}{5}x^5 - \dots$.

4. $1 + \dfrac{x^2}{2!} + \dfrac{x^4}{4!} + \dfrac{x^6}{6!} + \dfrac{x^8}{8!} + \dots$.

10. $1 + 2x + 3x^2 + 4x^3 + 5x^4 + 6x^5 + \dots$.

16. First, $e^{-x} = 1 - x + \dfrac{x^2}{2!} - \dfrac{x^3}{3!}$

$$+ \dfrac{x^4}{4!} - \dots + (-1)^n \dfrac{x^n}{n!} + R_n(x)$$

where

$$R_n(x) = (-1)^{n+1} \dfrac{x^{n+1}}{(n + 1)!} e^{-z}$$

for some number z between 0 and x. So, for $0 \le x \le 1$, z is between 0 and 1, and thus

$$0 \le \dfrac{x^{n+1}}{(n + 1)!} e^{-z} \le \dfrac{1}{(n + 1)!} .$$

249

Therefore

$$e^{-x} = 1 - x + \frac{x^2}{2!} - \frac{x^3}{3!}$$

$$+ \frac{x^4}{4!} - \dots + (-1)^n \frac{x^n}{n!} + (-1)^{n+1} E$$

where $0 \leq E \leq \frac{1}{(n+1)!}$. For $E < 0.001$, we require $(n+1)! > 1000$; choose $n = 6$. Then

$$e^{-x^2} = 1 - x^2 + \frac{x^4}{2!} - \frac{x^6}{3!} + \frac{x^8}{4!}$$

$$- \frac{x^{10}}{5!} + \frac{x^{12}}{6!} - E, \qquad 0 \leq E \leq \frac{1}{(n+1)!}.$$

Therefore, if

$$P(x) = 1 - x^2 + \frac{x^4}{2!} - \frac{x^6}{3!} + \frac{x^8}{4!}$$

$$- \frac{x^{10}}{5!} + \frac{x^{12}}{6!},$$

then

$$P(x) - \frac{1}{5040} \leq e^{-x^2} \leq P(x).$$

Now integrate each member of the above inequality from 0 to 1:

$$\int_0^1 P(x)\, dx - \frac{1}{5040} \leq \int_0^1 e^{-x^2}\, dx \leq \int_0^1 P(x)\, dx.$$

The numerical results are that

$$0.746637622 \leq \int_0^1 e^{-x^2}\, dx \leq 0.746836034.$$

Our estimate: The value of the integral is approximately 0.747. (The true value is approximately 0.746824133.)

22. First,

$$\tan^{-1} x = x - \frac{1}{3} x^3 + \frac{1}{5} x^5 - \dots + (-1)^n \frac{x^{2n+1}}{2n+1} + R_{2n+1}$$

by Eq. (11), where

$$|R_{2n+1}| \leq \frac{|x|^{2n+3}}{2n+3}$$

by Eq. (12).   Also, by Eq. (14),

$$\frac{\pi}{4} = 4 \tan^{-1} \left(\frac{1}{5} \right) - \tan^{-1} \left(\frac{1}{239} \right).$$

Let

$$P(x) = x - \frac{1}{3} x^3 + \frac{1}{5} x^5 - \frac{1}{7} x^7 + \frac{1}{9} x^9.$$

Then

$$P(x) - \frac{x^{11}}{11} \leq \tan^{-1} x \leq P(x)$$

If $x = \frac{1}{5}$;   thus

$$0.19739556 \leq \tan^{-1} \left(\frac{1}{5} \right) \leq 0.19739557.$$

Next,

$$x - \frac{1}{3} x^3 \leq \tan^{-1} x \leq x - \frac{1}{3} x^3 + \frac{1}{5} x^5$$

if $x = \frac{1}{239}$,   and so

$$0.00418407 \leq \tan^{-1} \left(\frac{1}{239} \right) \leq 0.00418408.$$

So

$$0.78539816 \leq \frac{\pi}{4} \leq 0.78539821,$$

and therefore

$$3.14159264 \leq \pi \leq 3.14159284.$$

Consequently $\pi = 3.14159$ to five places.

1.   The ratio test yields the limit $|x|$, so the radius of convergence is 1.   The series has center zero, converges at -1 (by the alternating series test), and diverges when x = 1 (for then it is the harmonic series). Consequently the interval of convergence is $-1 \leqq x < 1$.

4.   The interval of convergence is the single point x = 0.

10. The ratio test leads to the limit

$$|x| \left(\lim_{n \to \infty} (\frac{n}{n+1})^n \right) = \frac{|x|}{e} \, .$$

So the series converges on the interval $(-e, e)$ and diverges if $|x| > e$.   Only if we borrow the result of the final problem of this chapter is it easy to test convergence at the end points $-e$ and e: For large values of n,

$$\frac{n!}{n^n} e^n \sim \frac{(2\pi n)^{1/2} (n/e)^n}{n^n} e^n = \sqrt{2\pi n} \to +\infty,$$

so this series diverges at the end points; the interval of convergence really is $(-e, e)$.

16. $(-\infty, +\infty)$

22. $\dfrac{1}{10} - \dfrac{x}{100} + \dfrac{x^2}{1000} - \dfrac{x^3}{10000} + \ldots$; radius 10.

28. $(9 + x^3)^{-1/2} = \displaystyle\sum_{n=0}^{\infty} \frac{(-1)^n (2n)! x^{3n}}{(n!)^2 2^{2n} 3^{2n+1}}$;

the ratio test gives limit $\dfrac{1}{9} |x|^3$, so the radius of convergence is $9^{1/3}$.

31. Integrate $t^3 - \dfrac{1}{3!} t^9 + \dfrac{1}{5!} t^{15} - \dfrac{1}{7!} t^{21} + \ldots.$

34. $f(x) = x - \dfrac{x^3}{3^2} + \dfrac{x^5}{5^2} - \dfrac{x^7}{7^2} + \dfrac{x^9}{9^2} - \ldots$;

the interval of convergence is $-1 \le x \le 1$.

40. $f(x) = \displaystyle\sum_{n=0}^{\infty} a_n x^n$: $f(0) = a_0 = \dfrac{f^{(0)}(0)}{0!}$.

$f'(x) = \displaystyle\sum_{n=1}^{\infty} n a_n x^{n-1}$: $f'(0) = a_1 = \dfrac{f^{(1)}(0)}{1!}$.

And so on.

Section 12.9

1. Use the binomial series for $4(x + 1)^{1/3}$;   take $x = \dfrac{1}{64}$.

4. We use the series

$$e^{-x} = 1 - \frac{1}{1!} x + \frac{1}{2!} x^2 - \frac{1}{3!} x^3 + \dots .$$

To insure that $|R_n| < 0.0005$,   we impose the condition that

$$\frac{(0.2)^{n+1}}{(n + 1)!} < \frac{1}{2000} ,$$

and it suffices to take $n = 3$.   We find that

$$e^{-0.2} \sim 1 - \frac{0.2}{1!} + \frac{(0.2)^2}{2!} - \frac{(0.2)^3}{3!}$$

$$\sim 0.818666667.$$

Answer: 0.819.   (The true value is approximately 0.818730753.)

10. First,

$$\cos x = 1 - \frac{1}{2!} x^2 + \frac{1}{4!} x^4 - \dots ;$$

the error term in using the Taylor polynomial $P_n(x)$ to approximate $\cos x$ cannot exceed

$$\frac{|x|^{n+1}}{(n + 1)!} ,$$

and here we have $x = \frac{\pi}{36} < 0.0873$. For error less than 0.0005, we need $n \geq 2$; we take $n = 2$, and the error will not exceed 0.000111. Result: $\cos(\pi/36) \sim 0.9961922823$. (The true value is approximately 0.9961946981.)

13. Integration produces the series

$$1 - \frac{1}{3^2 \cdot 2^3} + \frac{1}{5^2 \cdot 2^5} - \frac{1}{7^2 \cdot 2^7} - \cdots .$$

16. For $-1 \leq x \leq 1$, we have

$$(1 + x^4)^{-1/2} = 1 - \frac{1}{2}x^4 + \frac{(1)(3)}{2!2^2}x^8$$

$$- \frac{(1)(3)(5)}{3!2^3}x^{12} + \frac{(1)(3)(5)(7)}{4!2^4}x^{16} - \cdots$$

$$= \sum_{n=0}^{\infty} \frac{(-1)^n (2n)!}{(n!)^2 2^{2n}} .$$

Convergence at the end points -1 and 1 follows from an application of Formula 113 of the endpapers of the text and the alternating series test, but all we need here is absolute convergence for $0 \leq x \leq \frac{1}{2}$. Hence, for such x,

$$1 - \frac{1}{2}x^4 + \frac{(1)(3)}{2!2^2}x^8 - \frac{(1)(3)(5)}{3!2^3}x^{12}$$

$$\leq \frac{1}{(1 + x^4)^{1/2}} \leq 1 - \frac{1}{2}x^4 + \frac{(1)(3)}{2!2^2}x^8 .$$

When we integrate these terms from $x = 0$ to $x = 1/2$, we find that the value of the given integral is trapped between 0.49695344 and 0.496956381; the answer is therefore 0.497 (the true value is approximately 0.496953563).

22. $\dfrac{x - \sin x}{x^3 \cos x} = \dfrac{x^3/3! - x^5/5! + x^7/7! - \cdots}{x^3 - x^5/2! + x^7/4! - \cdots}$

$$= \frac{1/3! - x^2/5! + \cdots}{1 - x^2/2! + \cdots} \rightarrow \frac{1}{6} \quad \text{as } x \rightarrow 0.$$

10. By Problem 8,

$$1 + x + \frac{x^2}{2!} + \frac{x^3}{3!} + \frac{x^4}{4!} < e^x$$

$$< 1 + x + \frac{x^2}{2!} + \frac{x^3}{3!} + \frac{x^4}{4!(1 - x)} .$$

When we take $x = \frac{1}{3}$, we find that

$$1.395576 < e^{1/3} < 1.395834.$$

Therefore $e^{1/3} = 1.396$ to three places. The true value is approximately 1.395612425.

Chapter 12 Miscellaneous Problems

1. $a_n = \dfrac{1 + (1/n^2)}{1 + (4/n^2)}$.

4. $a_n = 0$ for all n, so the limit is zero.

7. $-1 \leq \sin x \leq 1$ for all x, so $\{a_n\} \to 0$ by the squeeze theorem.

10. Apply l'Hôpital's rule thrice to obtain the limit zero.

13. Because e^n/n increases without bound while e^{-n}/n approaches zero, the limit does not exist (it is also correct to say that the given expression approaches $+\infty$).

16. The ratio test involves finding the limit of

$$(\frac{n}{n + 1})^n (n + 1)(n^2 + 2n)(n^2 + 2n - 1) \ldots (n^2 + 1)$$

as n increases without bound. The first factor approaches e, so the limit is $+\infty$. Therefore the series diverges.

22. The given series diverges by the n-th term test:

$$\lim_{n \to \infty} - \frac{2}{n^2} = 0,$$

and therefore

$$\lim_{n \to \infty} 2^{-(2/n^2)} = 1 \neq 0.$$

28. $\lim\limits_{x \to \infty} x \sin \frac{1}{x} = \lim\limits_{u \to 0^+} \frac{\sin u}{u} = 1,$ so the given series diverges by the n-th term test.

31. Is this not the Maclaurin series for $f(x) = e^{2x}$?

34. Limit: $\frac{1}{4} |2x - 3|$. Interval of convergence: $(-1/2, 7/2)$.

40. Limit: $|x - 1|$. Interval of convergence: $(0, 2)$.

43. Use the ratio test.

46. If $\sum a_n$ converges, then $\{a_n\} \to 0$. So $a_n \leq 1$ for all

$n \geq N$ (where N is some sufficiently large integer). So the

series $\sum a_n$ (eventually) dominates $\sum (a_n)^2$; therefore

the latter series also converges.

52. $\ln(1 + x) = x - \frac{1}{2} x^2 + \frac{1}{3} 3 - \frac{1}{4} x^4 + \ldots$

For three-place accuracy, we need the first five terms of this
series, and we find that

$$0.182266666 < \ln(1.2) < 0.182330667.$$

So $\ln(1.2) = 0.182$ to three places.

55. If the Maclaurin series for $(1 - e^{-x})/x$ is integrated from 0
to 1/2, one obtains the numerical series

$$(0.5) - (0.5)^2/(2!2) + (0.5)^3/(3!3) - (0.5)^4/(4!4) + \ldots .$$

Because this series satisfies the hypotheses of the alternating series error estimate, and because its fifth term is less than 0.00006, the sum of its first four terms -- about 0.443793403 -- is within 0.00006 of its sum. Thus the answer is 0.444. The true value of the sum (and the integral) is approximately 0.443842079.

58.
$$\int_0^x \frac{dt}{1 - t^2} = \int_0^x (1 + t^2 + t^4 + t^6 + \ldots) dt$$

$$= \left[t + \frac{1}{3} t^3 + \frac{1}{5} t^5 + \frac{1}{7} t^7 + \ldots \right]_0^x$$

$$= x + \frac{1}{3} x^3 + \frac{1}{5} x^5 + \frac{1}{7} x^7 + \ldots$$

$$= \sum_{n=0}^{\infty} \frac{x^{2n+1}}{2n + 1} .$$

Extra. Here's a nice problem contributed by one of our students. Test for convergence:

$$\sum_{n=1}^{\infty} \frac{1}{(2^1)(2^{1/2})(2^{1/3}) \ldots (2^{1/n})} .$$

Section 13.1

1.   Solve the first equation for $t = x - 1$; substitute in the second: $y = 2(x - 1) - 1 = 2x - 3$.   Answer: $y = 2x - 3$.

4.   First, $x^2 = t$, so $y = 3x^2 - 2$, $x \geq 0$.

7.   From $x = e^t$ we may conclude that $y = 4e^{2t} = 4x^2$.   So the answer is $y = 4x^2$, $x > 0$.

10. Given: $x = 2 \cosh t$, $y = 3 \sinh t$.   Then $(x/2)^2 = 1 + (y/3)^2$,

257

which we may write in the standard form

$$(\tfrac{x}{2})^2 - (\tfrac{y}{3})^2 = 1.$$

But $x \geq 2$, so the graph is the right branch only of the hyperbola with center at $(0,0)$ and with vertices at $(-2,0)$ and $(2,0)$.

13. First, $\dfrac{dy}{dx} = \dfrac{dy/dt}{dx/dt} = \dfrac{9t^2}{4t} = \dfrac{9t}{4}$. So when $t = 1$, the slope is $9/4$ at the point $P(3,5)$ of tangency. Thus an equation of the tangent line is $9x - 4y = 7$.

16. $\dfrac{dy}{dx} = -e^{-2t}$; the point of tangency is $(1,1)$ and the slope there is -1. An equation of the tangent line is $x + y = 2$.

19. Here, $dr/d\xi = \sqrt{3}\exp(\xi\sqrt{3})$. Therefore

$$\cot\psi = \frac{1}{r}\cdot\frac{dr}{d\xi} = \{\exp(-\xi\sqrt{3})\}\{\sqrt{3}\}\{\exp(\xi\sqrt{3})\} = \sqrt{3}.$$

Therefore $\tan\psi = 1/\sqrt{3}$, and therefore $\psi = \pi/6$, a constant, independent of the value of ξ.

22. First,

$$y^2 = t^6 - 6t^4 + 9t^2$$
$$= x^3 - 6x^2 + 9x$$
$$= x(x - 3)^2,$$

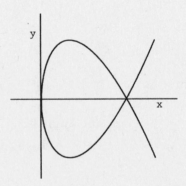

$0 \leq x \leq 4$. Now symmetry about the x-axis is obvious, as are the two intercepts. By implicit differentiation (we find both dy/dx and dx/dy) we may gain even more information about the graph, which is shown at the right.

25. If the slope at $P(x,y)$ is m, then

$$2y \frac{dy}{dx} = 4p, \quad \text{so} \quad y = \frac{2p}{dy/dx} = \frac{2p}{m}.$$

Therefore $4px = y^2 = \frac{4p^2}{m^2}$, and so

$$x = \frac{p}{m^2}, \quad y = \frac{2p}{m}.$$

Section 13.2

1. Note first that $y = 2t^2 + 1$ is always positive, so the curve lies entirely above the x-axis. Moreover, as t goes from -1 to 1, $dx = 3t^2 \, dt$ is also positive, so the area is given by

$$A = \int_{-1}^{1} (2t^2 + 1)(3t^2) \, dt = \frac{22}{5}.$$

4. $$A = \int_{1}^{0} -3e^{2t} \, dt = \frac{3}{2}(e^2 - 1).$$

7. $$V = \int_{-1}^{1} \pi(2t^2 + 1)^2(3t^2) \, dt.$$

10. $$V = \int_{\pi}^{0} -\pi e^{2t} \sin t \, dt = \frac{\pi}{5}(e^{2\pi} + 1).$$

13. $$\left(\frac{dx}{dt}\right)^2 + \left(\frac{dy}{dt}\right)^2 = 2, \quad \text{so}$$

$$L = \int_{\pi/4}^{\pi/2} \sqrt{2} \, dt.$$

16. $$L = \int_{2\pi}^{4\pi} (1 + \xi^2) \, d\xi$$

$$= 2\pi(1 + 16\pi^2)^{1/2} + \frac{1}{2}\ln(4\pi + \{1 + 16\pi^2\}^{1/2})$$

$$- \pi(1 + 4\pi^2)^{1/2} - \frac{1}{2}\ln(2\pi + \{1 + 4\pi^2\}^{1/2}),$$

which is approximately equal to 59.563022.

19. $A = 2\displaystyle\int_0^1 2\pi t^3 (9t^4 + 4)^{1/2}\, dt.$

22. $A = \displaystyle\int_0^{\pi/2} 2\pi (e^\xi \cos \xi)(\sqrt{2}\, e^\xi)\, d\xi = \frac{2}{5}\pi\sqrt{2}\,(e^\pi - 2).$

25. (a) $A = 2\displaystyle\int_0^\pi (b \sin t)(a \sin t)\, dt.$

(b) $V = 2\displaystyle\int_0^\pi (b^2 \sin^2 t)(a \sin t)\, dt.$

28. $A = \displaystyle\int_0^{2\pi} 2\pi a(b + a \cos t)\, dt = 4\pi^2 ab.$

31. Here, $ds = 3a|\sin t \cos t|\, dt,$ so

$$A = (4\pi)(3a)\int_0^{\pi/2} (\sin t \cos t)(a \sin^3 t)\, dt.$$

Section 13.3

4. $2\sqrt{65}$, $12\sqrt{5}$, $20\sqrt{2}$, $<4,-8>$, and $\vec{a}\cdot\vec{b} = -180$,
   so $\vec{a}$ and $\vec{b}$ are not perpendicular to each other.

10. $|\vec{a}| = 13$; choose $\vec{u} = \frac{5}{13}\vec{i} - \frac{12}{13}\vec{j}$, $\vec{v} = -\frac{5}{13}\vec{i} + \frac{12}{13}\vec{j}.$

13. $<3,-2> - <3,2> = <0,04> = -4\vec{j}.$

16. $-5\vec{i}$

19. $\vec{a} \cdot \vec{b} = (2)(8) + (-1)(4) = 12 \neq 0$; not perpendicular.

22. (a) $12\vec{i} - 20\vec{j}$;   (b) $\dfrac{3}{4}\vec{i} - \dfrac{5}{4}\vec{j}$

25. $(2c\vec{i} - 4\vec{j})(3\vec{i} + c\vec{j}) = 0$ when $6c - 4c = 0$,   thus when $c = 0$.

28. $(r + s)<a_1, a_2> = <(r + s)a_1, (r + s)a_2>$

$\qquad\qquad\qquad\quad = <ra_1 + sa_1, ra_2 + sa_2>$

$\qquad\qquad\qquad\quad = <ra_1, ra_2> + <sa_1, sa_2>$

$\qquad\qquad\qquad\quad = r<a_1, a_2> + s<a_1, a_2> = r\vec{a} + s\vec{a}.$

31. $(r\vec{a}) \cdot \vec{b} = <ra_1, ra_2> <b_1, b_2>$

$\qquad\qquad = ra_1 b_1 + ra_2 b_2$

$\qquad\qquad = r(a_1 b_1 + a_2 b_2) = r(\vec{a} \cdot \vec{b}).$

34. Use $\vec{v}_a = \vec{v}_g - \vec{w} = <-500, 0> - 25\sqrt{2}<-1, -1>.$

Section 13.4

1. Note that $\vec{r}$ is a constant vector.

4. $\vec{r}'(t) = <-\sin t, \cos t>$ and $\vec{r}''(t) = <-\cos t, -\sin t>.$
    So $\vec{r}'(\pi/4) = <-\sqrt{2}/2, \sqrt{2}/2>$ and $\vec{r}''(\pi/4) = <-\sqrt{2}/2, -\sqrt{2}/2>.$

7. $\vec{r}'(t) = \vec{i} \sec t \tan t + \vec{j} \sec^2 t;$
    $\vec{r}''(t) = \vec{i}(\sec^3 t + \sec t \tan^2 t) + \vec{j}(2 \sec^2 t \tan t).$
    So $\vec{r}'(0) = \vec{j}$ and $\vec{r}''(0) = \vec{i}.$

10. $\displaystyle\int_1^e <\dfrac{1}{t}, -1> dt = \left[<\ln t, -t> \right]_1^e = <1, 1 - e>.$

13. $(3\vec{i}) \cdot (2\vec{i} - 5t\vec{j}) + (3t\vec{i} - \vec{j}) \cdot (-5\vec{j}) = 11.$

261

16. $\vec{v}(t) = \vec{C}_1 = \langle 0, -2 \rangle$.

$\vec{r}(t) = \langle c, -2t \rangle + \langle C_2, C_3 \rangle$;

$\vec{r}(0) = \langle 2, 3 \rangle = \langle C + C_2, C_3 \rangle$: $\vec{r}(t) = \langle 2, 3 - 2t \rangle$.

22. Write $\vec{u}(t) = \langle u_1(t), u_2(t) \rangle$, $\vec{v}(t) = \langle v_1(t), v_2(t) \rangle$. Then

$$D_t\{\vec{u}(t) + \vec{v}(t)\} = D_t\{\langle u_1(t) + v_1(t)\}, u_2(t) + v_2(t) \rangle$$

$$= \langle u_1'(t) + v_1'(t), u_2'(t) + v_2'(t) \rangle$$

$$= \langle u_1'(t), u_2'(t) \rangle + \langle v_1'(t), v_2'(t) \rangle$$

$$= \vec{u}'(t) + \vec{v}'(t).$$

28. $\vec{r}(t) = \langle a \cos \omega t, b \sin \omega t \rangle$;

$\vec{v}(t) = \langle -a\omega \sin \omega t, b\omega \cos \omega t \rangle$,

$\vec{a}(t) = \langle -a\omega^2 \cos \omega t, -b\omega^2 \sin \omega t \rangle = -\omega^2 \langle a \cos \omega t, b \sin \omega t \rangle$.

Therefore $\vec{a}(t) = c\vec{r}(t)$ where $c = -\omega^2 < 0$. So $\vec{F}(t)$ is a force directed toward the origin and has magnitude proportional to distance from the origin.

Section 13.5

1. Use Equations (3) and (4) and set $y = 0$ to derive the formula

$$(v_0)^2 = \frac{Rg}{\sin 2\alpha}.$$

4. As a consequence of either Problem 2 or Problem 3,

$$R = \frac{1}{g}(v_0)^2 \sin 2\alpha,$$

so

$$\frac{dR}{d\alpha} = \frac{2}{g}(v_0)^2 \cos 2\alpha.$$

Now $dR/d\alpha = 0$ when $\cos 2\alpha = 0$, so that $\alpha = \pi/4$ is the angle that maximizes the range R.

7. We begin with the equations

262

$$x = v_0 t, \qquad y = -16t^2 + 400.$$

We want $y = 0$ when $x = 5280$; it follows that $t = 5$, and thus that $v_0 = 5280/5 = 1056$ (ft/sec).

10. If m is a small mass at the surface of the earth, then -- with R the radius of the earth and M its mass --

$$\frac{GMm}{R^2} = mg.$$

Thus $M = R^2 g/G \sim 5.968 \times 10^{24}$ kg. We used $R = 6,373,002.24$ meters and $g = 9.805416$ meters per second per second.

13. Let m denote the mass of the moon, v its (assumed constant) orbital velocity, r the radius of its orbit, and T its period. Then $27.32 = T = 2\pi r/c$; and if M denotes the mass of the earth, then

$$\frac{GMm}{r^2} = F = \frac{mv^2}{r}.$$

It follows that $r = (GMT^2/4\pi^2)^{1/3} \sim 383,053,726.5$ meters -- that is, approximately $238,018.55$ miles.

16. Here, $mv^2/r = mr\omega^2 = mg/4$. Therefore $v = \frac{1}{2}\sqrt{rg}$. In Example 2, $r = 1320$ (feet), so the maximum velocity is

$$v = 8\sqrt{165} \sim 102.76 \quad (\text{ft/sec})$$

-- about 70 miles per hour.

Section 13.6

4. The curvature is $|(1)(2) - (0)(7)|/(1^2 + 7^2)^{3/2} = \frac{1}{250}\sqrt{2}$.

10. The curvature at x is $f(x) = 2|x|^3/(x^4 + 1)^{3/2}$. It suffices to consider the case in which $x > 0$; if so, then

$$f'(x) = \frac{6x^2(1 - x^4)}{(x^4 + 1)^{5/2}}.$$

It follows that $x = 1$ maximizes $f(x)$, its maximum value is $1/\sqrt{2}$, and the points on the graph of the equation $xy = 1$

263

where the curvature is maximal are $(1,1)$ and $(-1,-1)$.

16. $\vec{a}(t) = \langle -3\pi^2 \sin \pi t, -3\pi^2 \cos \pi t \rangle$. So $a_T = 0$, $a_N = 3\pi^2$.

28. We begin with $\vec{a} = \dfrac{dv}{dt}\vec{T} + \kappa v^2\vec{N}$. Thus

$$\kappa v^2\vec{N} = \vec{a} - \dfrac{dv}{dt}\vec{T};$$

$$\kappa\vec{N} = (\vec{a} - a_T\vec{T})/v^2.$$

Because $|\vec{N}| = 1$ and > 0,

$$\kappa = |\vec{a} - a_T\vec{T}|/v^2 = |a_N|/v^2.$$

Now $a^2 = (a_N)^2 + (a_T)^2$ because $\vec{N}$ is normal to $\vec{T}$. So

$$a_N = \{a^2 - (a_T)^2\}^{1/2}.$$

Therefore

$$\kappa = \dfrac{1}{v^2}\{a^2 - (a_T)^2\}^{1/2}.$$

Now write $\vec{r} = \langle x, y \rangle$ where everything is a function of t and primes denote differentiation with respect to t. It follows that $a_T = v'$ and that

$$a^2 - (a_T)^2 = (x'')^2 + (y'')^2 - (v')^2.$$

The conclusion of Problem 28 now follows.

31. It is immediate that $D = E = F = 0$, and the other equations you obtain should be

$$A + B + C = 1,$$
$$5A + 4B + 3C = 1, \quad \text{and}$$
$$20A + 12B + 6C = 0.$$

Section 13.7

4. $dr/dt = d^2r/dt^2 = e^t$, $d\xi/dt = 2$.

$$D_t \left(r^2 \frac{d\xi}{dt} \right) = D_t (2e^{2t}) = 4e^{2t}.$$

$$\vec{v}(t) = e^t \vec{u}_r + 2e^t \vec{u}_\xi; \quad \vec{a}(t) = -3e^t \vec{u}_r + 4e^t \vec{u}_\xi.$$

10. With the usual meanings of the symbols, we have $b^2 = a^2(1 - e^2)$. With the aid of a calculator and the result of Problem 8, we obtain these results: Its velocity at apogee is approximately 18.2007 miles per second; at perigee, it is approximately 18.8189 miles per second.

Chapter 13 Miscellaneous Problems

4. Note that neither x nor y is ever negative. So first we write

$$\sqrt{x} + \sqrt{y} = 1,$$

then

$$y = (1 - \sqrt{x})^2, \quad 0 \leqq x \leqq 1.$$

The graph is shown below.

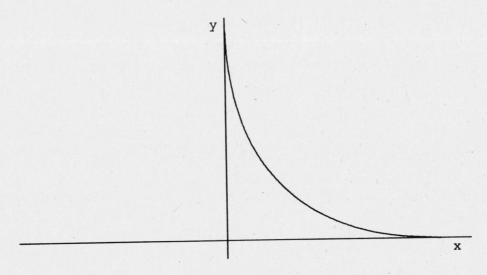

10. $dr/d\xi = \cos \xi$. By the formula in Equation (9) of Section 13.1,

$$\frac{dy}{dx} = \frac{\cos \xi + 2 \sin \xi \cos \xi}{\cos^2 \xi - \sin^2 \xi - \sin \xi}.$$

At $\xi = \pi/3$, $dy/dx = -1$. Also

$$x = r \cos \xi = \frac{1}{4}(2 + \sqrt{3})$$

and

$$y = r \sin \xi = \frac{1}{4}(3 + 2\sqrt{3}).$$

So an equation of the tangent line is

$$x + y = \frac{1}{4}(5 + 3\sqrt{3}).$$

16. $dx/dt = -\tan t,\quad dy/dt = 1.$ So

$$ds = (1 + \tan^2 t)^{1/2} dt = +\sec t\, dt.$$

Therefore

$$L = \int_0^{\pi/4} \sec t\, dt = \ln(1 + \sqrt{2}).$$

22. $dr/d\xi = 4 \sin \xi;\quad y = r \sin \xi.$

$$ds = \{r^2 + (dr/d\xi)^2\}^{1/2} dx\xi = 4\, d\xi.$$

Therefore the surface area is

$$A = \int_0^{\pi/2} (2\pi)(4 \sin \xi \cos \xi)(4)\, d\xi = 16\pi.$$

28. From $r^2 = 2a^2 \cos 2\xi$ we find that

$$2r\frac{dr}{d\xi} = -4a^2 \sin 2\xi,$$

and thus that

$$\frac{dr}{d\xi} = -\frac{1}{r}(2a^2 \sin 2\xi).$$

So

$$r^2 + (dr/d\xi)^2 = r^2 + \frac{4a^4 \sin^2 2\xi}{r^2}$$

$$= \frac{r^4 + 4a^4 \sin^2 2\xi}{r^2}$$

$$= \frac{4a^4 \cos^2 2\xi + 4a^4 \sin^2 2\xi}{r^2} = \frac{4a^4}{r^2}.$$

Therefore

$$ds = \frac{2a^2}{|r|} d\xi.$$

$$A = 2 \int_{\xi=0}^{\pi/4} 2\pi y \, ds = 4\pi \int_0^{\pi/4} \frac{2a^2}{r} y \, d\xi$$

$$= 4\pi \int_0^{\pi/4} \frac{2a^2}{r} r \sin \xi \, d\xi = 4\pi a^2 (2 - \sqrt{2}).$$

34. First show that $a = -\omega^2 r$; conclude that

$$-\omega^2 x = x'' \quad \text{and} \quad -\omega^2 y = y'',$$

so that $x(t) = A \cos \omega t + B \sin \omega t$ and $y(t) = C \cos \omega t + D \sin \omega t$. Then use the given initial data to find A, B, C, and D.

40. Show that the curvature is $ab/(a^2 \sin^2 \xi + b^2 \cos^2 \xi)^{3/2}$. The maximum of the denominator minimizes the curvature, and vice versa. It turns out that the extrema of the denominator occur at integral multiples of $\pi/2$. At integral multiples of π, the curvature is a/b^2; at odd integral multiples of $\pi/2$, the curvature is b/a^2. We are given $a > b$, so $b/a^2 < a/b^2$ (show this). So the minimal curvature is b/a^2, and occurs at the points $(0,-b)$ and $(0,b)$. The maximal curvature is a/b^2, and occurs at $(a,0)$ and at $(-a,0)$.

Section 14.1

4. $9\vec{i} - 3\vec{j} + 3\vec{k}$; $-14\vec{i} - 21\vec{j} + 43\vec{k}$; -34; $3\sqrt{21}$; $(2\vec{i} - 3\vec{j} + 5\vec{k})/\sqrt{38}$

7. $(\vec{a} \cdot \vec{b})/|\vec{a}||\vec{b}| = -13/\sqrt{250}$; $\xi = \cos^{-1}(-\frac{13}{50}\sqrt{10})$

-- approximately 2.536 radians; that is, about 145.3°.

10. $\cos \xi = -\frac{1}{10}\sqrt{2}$, so $\xi \sim 1.71269$; that is, 98° 7' 48".

16. $(x - 3)^2 + (y - 1)^2 + (z - 2)^2 = 5^2$; that is,

$$x^2 + 6x + y^2 - 2y + z^2 - 4z - 11 = 0.$$

19. If r is the radius, then $r^2 = 9 + 25 + 4 = 38$. So the equation of the sphere can be written in the form

$$(x - 4)^2 + (y - 5)^2 + (z + 2)^2 = 38.$$

22. $(x - 4)^2 + (y - \frac{9}{2})^2 + (z + 5)^2 = \frac{85}{4}$;

Center: $(4, 9/2, -5)$. Radius: $\frac{1}{2}\sqrt{85}$.

28. $x^2 + y^2 + z^2 + 7 = 0$: No points satisfy this equation.

34. $\overrightarrow{PQ} = <3,1,0>$, $\vec{F} = <1,0,-1>$: $W = \vec{F} \cdot \overrightarrow{PQ} = 3$.

37. Begin with the observation that $|\vec{a} + \vec{b}|^2 = (\vec{a} + \vec{b}) \cdot (\vec{a} + \vec{b})$.

40. $\overrightarrow{AB} = <2,-3,2>$, $\overrightarrow{AC} = <2,3,5>$, and $\overrightarrow{BC} = <0,6,3>$. Let A denote the angle at the vertex A. Then

$$\cos A = (\overrightarrow{AB} \cdot \overrightarrow{AC})/(|\overrightarrow{AB}||\overrightarrow{AC}|) = 5/\sqrt{646}.$$

Thus the angle at A is about 1.37278 (radians). Similarly, B is about 1.12202 and C is about 0.64679.

46. See the figure at the top of the next page. Given: d is the perpendicular distance from P_1 to L. Then

$$d = |comp_{\vec{n}}(\overrightarrow{P_0P_1})| = (n \ \overrightarrow{P_0P_1})/|\vec{n}|$$

$$= |ax_1 - ax_0 + by_1 - by_0|/(a^2 + b^2)^{1/2}.$$

Because P_0 is on L, $ax_0 + by_0 + c = 0$. Then the result of Problem 46 follows.

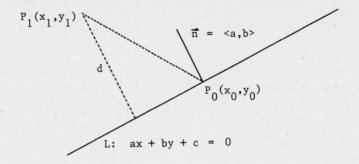

$P_1(x_1, y_1)$

$\vec{n} = <a, b>$

d

$P_0(x_0, y_0)$

L: $ax + by + c = 0$

Section 14.2

1. $\vec{a} \times \vec{b} = \begin{vmatrix} \vec{i} & \vec{j} & \vec{k} \\ 5 & -1 & -2 \\ -3 & 2 & 4 \end{vmatrix} = (-4 + 4)\vec{i} - (20 - 6)\vec{j} + (10 - 3)\vec{k}$

$$= -14\vec{j} + 7\vec{k}.$$

4. $-24\vec{j} - 24\vec{k}$

7. You should find that

$$(\vec{a} \times \vec{b}) \times \vec{c} = -\vec{i} + \vec{j} \quad \text{while} \quad \vec{a} \times (\vec{b} \times \vec{c}) = -\vec{k}.$$

10. $\vec{PQ} = <0, -1, 1>$ and $\vec{PR} = <-1, 0, 1>$. So the area A of the triangle PQR is given by

$$A = \frac{1}{2} |\vec{PQ} \times \vec{PR}| = \frac{1}{2} \text{ABS} \begin{vmatrix} \vec{i} & \vec{j} & \vec{k} \\ 0 & -1 & 1 \\ -1 & 0 & 1 \end{vmatrix}$$

$$= \frac{1}{2} |<-1, -1, -1>| = \frac{1}{2} \sqrt{3}.$$

(Because of the standard notation for determinants, we're using the programming language function ABS(x) = $|x|$ for clarity here.)

269

13. $V = |\overrightarrow{OP} \cdot \overrightarrow{OQ} \times \overrightarrow{OR}|$ where $\overrightarrow{OP} = \langle 1,3,-2 \rangle$, $\overrightarrow{OQ} = \langle 2,4,5 \rangle$, and $\overrightarrow{OR} = \langle -3,-2,2 \rangle$.

22. First, $(\vec{a} \times \vec{b}) \times (\vec{c} \times \vec{d})$ is perpendicular to $\vec{a} \times \vec{b}$ and $\vec{a} \times \vec{b}$ is perpendicular to $\vec{a}$ and to $\vec{b}$. So $(\vec{a} \times \vec{b}) \times (\vec{c} \times \vec{d})$ lies in the plane determined by $\vec{a}$ and $\vec{b}$; that is,

$$(\vec{a} \times \vec{b}) \times (\vec{c} \times \vec{d}) = r_1\vec{a} + r_2\vec{b}.$$

(If $\vec{a}$ is parallel to $\vec{b}$, then $\vec{a} \times \vec{b} = \vec{0}$; in this case, take $r_1 = 0 = r_2$.) The other case follows by symmetry (or by interchanging $\vec{a}$ with $\vec{c}$ and $\vec{b}$ with $\vec{d}$ in the above proof).

Section 14.3

4. A vector parallel to the line is $\overrightarrow{P_1P_2} = \langle -6,3,5 \rangle$. If $\langle x,y,z \rangle$ is on the line through P_1 and P_2 then

$$\langle x,y,z \rangle = \overrightarrow{OP_1} + t\overrightarrow{P_1P_2}$$

where $O = (0,0,0)$ is the origin. That is,

$$\langle x,y,z \rangle - \langle 0,0,0 \rangle = t\langle -6,3,5 \rangle;$$

it follows that parametric equations of the line in question are

$$x = -6t, \quad y = 3t, \quad z = 5t.$$

7. The equation of the plane has the form $x + 2y + 3z = D$ for some constant D. Because $(0,0,0)$ is in the plane, $D = 0$.

10. $y = 12$

13. A line perpendicular to the xy-plane is parallel to the unit vector k. The x- and y-coordinates of all points on such a line are the same (in this case, $x = y = 1$) and the z-coordinates of such points are arbitrary. Parametric equations: $x = 1$, $y = 1$, $z = t$. Symmetric equations: $x - 1 = 0 = y - 1$.

16. The line contains $Q(3,3,1)$ (set $t = 1$) and $R(0,2,2)$ (set $t = 2$). Now $\overrightarrow{RQ} = \langle 3,1,-1 \rangle$ and $\overrightarrow{OP} = \langle 2,-1,5 \rangle$;

$$\overrightarrow{OP} + t\overrightarrow{RQ} = \langle 2,-1,5 \rangle + t\langle 3,1,-1 \rangle.$$

Answers: $x = 2 + 3t, \quad y = -1 + t, \quad z = 5 - t;$

$$\frac{x - 2}{3} = \frac{y + 1}{1} = \frac{z - 5}{-1}.$$

22. $x + y - 2z = -2$

25. A normal to the first plane is $\vec{i}$ and a normal to the second is $\vec{i} + \vec{j} + \vec{k}$. If ξ is the angle between these two normals (by definition, this is the angle between the planes) then

$$\cos \xi = \frac{\langle 1,0,0 \rangle \cdot \langle 1,1,1 \rangle}{\sqrt{3}},$$

Therefore $\xi = \arccos(1/\sqrt{3})$ (about $54° \, 44' \, 8''$).

28. When $x = 0$, $y = 1/2$ and $z = 7/2$. Similarly, $(1,1,1)$ lies on the line. So one of the many correct answers is

$$x = 1 + t, \quad y = 1 + \frac{t}{2}, \quad z = 1 - \frac{5t}{2}.$$

31. The xy-plane has equation $z = 0$, so the plane with equation $3x + 2y - z = 6$ meets it in the line with equation $3x + 2y = 6$. Two points on this line are $P(2,0,0)$ and $Q(0,3,0)$. In order to contain the third point $R(1,1,1)$, the plane in question must have normal vector $\overrightarrow{PQ} \times \overrightarrow{PR} = \langle 3,2,1 \rangle$. Hence it has an equation of the form $3x + 2y + z = D$ for some constant D. Because the point $(1,1,1)$ is in the plane, $D = 6$.

34. Suppose that the lines meet at (x,y,z). Then the simultaneous equations that result have solution $P(1,-1,2)$. The first line also contains $Q(2,1,3)$ and the second also contains $R(3,5,6)$. A normal to the plane is $\overrightarrow{PQ} \times \overrightarrow{PR} = \langle 2,-2,2 \rangle$; use $\langle 1,-1,1 \rangle$ instead. Answer: $x - y + z = 4$.

40. You may assume without loss of generality that $a \neq 0$. Then the

271

point $(-d_1/a, 0, 0)$ lies on the first plane. The desired result now follows.

Section 14.4

4. $\vec{v}(t) = 2t<3,4,-12>;$ $\vec{a}(t) = 2<3,4,-12>;$ $v(t) = |26t|$

10. $\vec{v}(t) = <t, 7-t, 3t>,$ $\vec{r}(t) = <5 + \frac{1}{2}t^2, 7t - \frac{1}{2}t^2, \frac{3}{2}t^2>$

16. $\vec{r}(t) = <3 - t + \sin 3t, 3 + \cos 3t, 2t^2 - 7t>$

22. Let $\vec{v}(t)$ denote the velocity vector of the moving particle. If the speed $|\vec{v}(t)|$ of the particle is constant, then

$$\vec{v}(t) \cdot \vec{v}(t) = C$$

where C is a constant. Now differentiate each side of this identity with respect to time t.

25. Because $\vec{F} = k\vec{r}$, $\vec{r}$ and $\vec{a}$ are parallel. So

$$D_t(\vec{r} \times \vec{v}) = (\vec{r} \times \vec{a}) + (\vec{v} \times \vec{v}) = \vec{0} + \vec{0} = \vec{0}.$$

Therefore $\vec{r} \times \vec{v} = \vec{C}$, a constant vector. Consequently the vector $\vec{r}$ is always perpendicular to the constant vector $\vec{C}$. This holds for every point on the trajectory of the particle, and thus every point on the trajectory lies in the plane through the origin with normal vector $\vec{C}$.

Section 14.5

1. $\displaystyle\int_0^\pi \{(6 \cos 2t)^2 + (6 \sin 2t)^2 + 64\}^{1/2} \, dt = 10\pi.$

4. $(ds/dt)^2 = t^2 + (1/t)^2 + 2 = (t + t^{-1})^2;$ integrate ds from $t = 1$ to $t = 2$ to get $s = (3/2) + \ln 2.$

7. $\vec{v} = \vec{i} + \vec{j}\cos t - \vec{k}\sin t$; $\vec{a} = -\vec{j}\sin t - \vec{k}\cos t$.
   So $\vec{v} \times \vec{a} = -\vec{i} + \vec{j}\cos t - \vec{k}\sin t$. Therefore

$$|\vec{v} \times \vec{a}| = \sqrt{2} \quad \text{and} \quad |\vec{v}| = \sqrt{2}.$$

Therefore the curvature is $1/2$.

10. The curvature is $(t^4 + 5t^2 + 8)^{1/2}/(t^2 + 2)^{3/2}$.

13. $\vec{v} = <1, 2t, 3t^2>$ and $\vec{a} = <0, 6, 2t>$.

$$v = (1 + 4t^2 + 9t^4)^{1/2}; \quad \frac{dv}{dt} = \frac{4t + 18t^3}{(1 + 4t^2 + 9t^4)^{1/2}}.$$

$\vec{v} \times \vec{a} = <6t^2, -6t, 2>$; $|\vec{v}| = (9t^4 + 4t^2 + 1)^{1/2}$.

So $a_T = \dfrac{4t + 18t^3}{(1 + 4t^2 + 9t^4)^{1/2}}$

and $a_N = \kappa v^2 = 2\{(9t^4 + 9t^2 + 1)/(9t^4 + 4t^2 + 1)\}^{1/2}$.

16. $\vec{T}(1,1,1) = <1, 2, 3>/\sqrt{14}$ and $\vec{N}(1,1,1) = <-11, -8, 9>/\sqrt{266}$.

19. $v(t) = \sqrt{3}\,e^t$ and the curvature is $\frac{1}{3}\sqrt{2}\,e^{-t}$.

22. Because $s = 2t$, $t = s/2$. Answer:

$$x = 2\cos(s/2), \quad y = 2\sin(s/2), \quad z = 0.$$

Section 14.6

1. A plane with intercepts $x = 20/3$, $y = 10$, $z = 2$.

4. A cylinder with rulings lines parallel to the z-axis. It meets
   the xy-plane in the hyperbola $x^2 - y^2 = 9$.

7. An elliptic cone; see the text for a general discussion.

10. A circular cylinder with axis the x-axis.

16. Parabolic cylinder, parallel to the y-axis; its trace in the xz-plane is the parabola with vertex $x = 9$ and $z = 0$ and opening in the negative x-direction.

22. A cylinder having the graph $x = \sin y$ as its trace in the xy-plane.

28. A hyperboloid of one sheet, resembling the general example shown in the text.

34. Replace x by $(x^2 + y^2)^{1/2}$. Answer: A paraboloid opening along the negative z-axis and with equation $z = 4 - x^2 - y^2$.

40. $4x^2 = y^2 + z^2$

46. Hyperbolas (both branches), except that the trace in the xy-plane itself consists of the coordinate axes.

52. Projection of the intersection: $2x^2 + 3z^2 = 5 - 3x^2 - 2z^2$. That is, $x^2 + z^2 = 1$: a circle.

Section 14.7

1. Cylindrical first, spherical second: $(0, \pi/2, 5)$; $(5, 0, \pi/2)$

4. $(2\sqrt{2}, -\pi/4, 0)$; $(2\sqrt{2}, \pi/2, -\pi/4)$

10. $(2\sqrt{5}, \tan^{-1}(-2), -12)$; $(2\sqrt{41}, \cos^{-1}(-\sqrt{41}/6), \tan^{-1}(-2))$

16. The lower nappe of the cone $z^2 = 3r^2$, vertex at the origin, axis the z-axis, opening downward.

22. From its Cartesian equation $z = 10 - 3x^2 - 3y^2$ we see that the surface is a circular paraboloid opening downward, with highest point $(0,0,10)$.

28. $r(\cos \xi + \sin \xi) = 4$; $\rho \sin \phi \cos \xi + \rho \sin \phi \sin \xi = 4$.

34. Take $\rho = 3960$ (miles).

Atlanta: $\phi = 56.25°,$ $\xi = -84.40°.$

San Francisco: $\phi = 52.22°,$ $\xi = -122.42°.$

Therefore Atlanta is at $P_1(x_1, y_1, z_1)$ where

$x_1 \sim 321.3,$ $y_1 \sim -3276.9,$ and $z_1 \sim 2200.1;$

San Francisco is at $P_2(x_2, y_2, z_2)$ where

$x_2 \sim -1670.8,$ $y_2 \sim -2642.0,$ and $z_2 \sim 2426.0.$

The cosine of the central angle between the two cities is then

$$(\overrightarrow{OP_1} \cdot \overrightarrow{OP_2})/(|\overrightarrow{OP_1}||\overrightarrow{OP_2}|) \sim 0.858073636.$$

This means that the angle itself is about $30.89902595°;$ that is, about 0.5392897386 radians. The arc length between the two cities is the product of the radius of the earth and this angle (in radians), and that's approximately $2135.587365.$ Answer: The great circle distance between San Francisco and Atlanta is about 2136 miles.

37. We found the rectangular coordinates of the point of the journey nearest the north pole to be approximately

(x, y, z) = $(15.99750973, 26.41463504, 3959.879587).$

The central angle between this point and the North Pole has cosine z/R where $R = 3960;$ that angle turns out to be about 0.00779839 radians. Multiply by R to get the closest approach to the North Pole in great circle terms, hardly different from the straight-line distance.

Chapter 14 Miscellaneous Problems

10. For $i = 1$ and $i = 2,$ the line L_i passes through the point $P_i(x_i, y_i, z_i)$ and is parallel to $\vec{v}_i = \langle a_i, b_i, c_i \rangle.$ Let L be the line through P_1 parallel to $\vec{v}_2.$ Now, by definition, the lines L_1 and L_2 are skew if and only if they are not coplanar. But L_1 and L_2 are coplanar if and only if the plane determined

by L_1 and L is the same as the plane determined by L_2 and L; that is, if and only if the plane determined by L_1 and L is the same as the plane that contains the segment $\overrightarrow{P_1P_2}$ and the line L. Thus L_1 and L_2 are coplanar if and only if $\overrightarrow{P_1P_2}$, $\vec{v}_1$, and $\vec{v}_2$ are coplanar, and this condition is equivalent (by a theorem from early in Chapter 14) to the condition

$$|\overrightarrow{P_1P_2} \cdot \vec{v}_1 \times \vec{v}_2| = 0.$$

That is, L_1 and L_2 are coplanar if and only if

$$\begin{vmatrix} x_1 - x_2 & y_1 - y_2 & z_1 - z_2 \\ a_1 & b_1 & c_1 \\ a_2 & b_2 & c_2 \end{vmatrix} = 0.$$

This establishes the conclusion given in Problem 10.

16. $x + 2y + 3z = 6$

22. $\dfrac{dx}{dt} = \dfrac{dr}{dt} \cos \xi - (r \sin \xi) \dfrac{d\xi}{dt}$ and

$\dfrac{dy}{dt} = \dfrac{dr}{dt} \sin \xi + (r \cos \xi) \dfrac{d\xi}{dt}.$

Now show that $(dx/dt)^2 + (dy/dt)^2 + (dz/dt)^2$

$$= (dr/dt)^2 + \{r(d\xi/dt)\}^2 + (dz/dt)^2.$$

28. Replace y by r to obtain $(r - 1)^2 + z^2 = 1$. Simplify this to $r^2 - 2r + z^2 = 0$, then convert to the rectangular equation $x^2 + y^2 + z^2 = 2(x^2 + y^2)^{1/2}$.

34. Because $z = ax^2 + by^2$ is a paraboloid (not a hyperboloid), we know that $ab > 0$. The projection into the xy-plane of the intersection K has the equation $ax^2 - Ax + by^2 - By = 0$. We may also assume that $a > 0$ and $b > 0$ (multiply through by -1 if necessary). It follows by completing squares that this projection is either empty, a single point, or an ellipse. In the latter case, it follows from Problem 32 that K is an ellipse.

Section 15.2

1. The domain is the coordinate plane.

4. The points in the plane on or within the circle with equation
    $x^2 + y^2 = 4$; that is, the points of the disk of radius 2 and
    centered at the origin.

7. All points in the plane except for those on either of the two lines
    $y = x$ and $y = -x$.

10. All points in space for which $xyz > 0$.   This consists of the
    interior of the first octant (the points where x, y, and z are
    all positive) together with three other octants (one where x is
    positive and y and z are both negative, etc.).

13. The plane that meets the xz-plane in the line $z = x$ and the
    yz-plane in the line $z = y$.

16. The paraboloid $z = 4 - r^2$ with highest point $(0,0,4)$,
    symmetric about the z-axis and opening downward.

19. The lower nappe of a 45° cone with vertex at $(0,0,10)$, symmetric
    about the z-axis, and with cylindrical equation $z = 10 - r$.

22. Some typical level curves of $f(x,y) = x^2 - y^2$ are shown below.

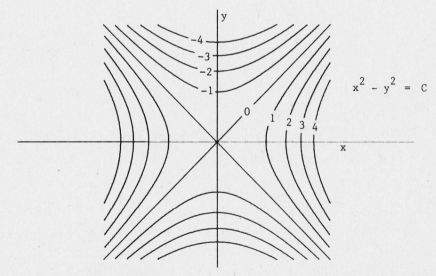

25. The level curves are vertical translates of the graph of $y = x^3$.

28. The level curves are circles centered at $(3,-2)$.

277

31. The level surfaces are circular paraboloids $z = C + r^2$ symmetric about the z-axis and opening upward. They are vertical translates of the "standard" parabolic surface with equation $z = r^2$.

34. The level surfaces are circular hyperboloids of two sheets symmetric about the z-axis, both nappes of the 45° cone $z = r$ with vertex at $(0,0,0)$ and symmetric about the z-axis, and circular hyperboloids of one sheet symmetric about the z-axis.

40. The traces of the surface in planes parallel to the yz-plane are vertical translates of the graph of the cubic equation $z = 2y^3 - 3y^2 - 12y$, which has one local maximum, one local minimum, and one inflection point. The traces of the surface in planes parallel to the xz-plane are vertical translates of the parabola $z = x^2$.

Section 15.3

4. 0   10. 0   16. 1, 1

28. On the line $x = 1$, $f(x,y)$ has limit 1. On the line $y = 1$, $f(x,y)$ has limit 1/3. Therefore f has no limit at $(1,1)$ and consequently cannot be defined there to be continuous there.

Section 15.4

4. $(2x + x^2y)e^{xy}$, $x^3 e^{xy}$

10. $y/(1 + x^2y^2)$, $x/(1 + x^2y^2)$

16. $\partial f/\partial u = (4u - 4u^3 - 6uv^2)\exp(-u^2 - v^2)$,
     $\partial f/\partial v = (6v - 4u^2v - 6v^3)\exp(-u^2 - v^2)$

22. Both are $10x + 4y^3$

31. A normal to the plane at (x,y,z) is $<2x, 2y, -1>$. So a normal to the plane at $(3,4,25)$ is $<6,8,-1>$. Therefore an equation of the tangent plane is $6x + 8y - z = 15$.

34. $2x + 2y - \pi z = 4 - \pi$

40. $3x - 4y - 5z = 0$

46. You should find that

$$u_{xx} = -m^2 \exp(-\{m^2 + n^2\}kt) \sin mx \cos ny.$$

49. $P_V = -nRT/V^2, \quad V_T = nR/P, \quad$ and $\quad T_p = V/nR.$

52. Let $P(a,b,c)$ be a point on the paraboloid $z = x^2 + y^2.$ Note that $c = a^2 + b^2, \quad z_x(P) = 2a,$ and $z_y(P) = 2b.$ Thus the tangent plane at P has equation

$$2a(x - a) + 2b(y - b) - (z - c) = 0;$$

substitution of $a^2 + b^2$ for c yields the equation

$$2(ax + by) = z + a^2 + b^2.$$

In the xy-plane, we have $z = 0,$ so the tangent plane meets the xy-plane in the line with equation

$$2ax + 2by = a^2 + b^2.$$

Now $(x,y) = (a/2, b/2)$ satisfies this equation, so the point $Q(a/2, b/2)$ is on the line. The line has slope $-a/b,$ so the normal to the line has slope $b/a.$ The segment OQ has this slope, so OQ is a perpendicular from the origin O to this line. Its length is $(a^2 + b^2)^{1/2},$ so the line is tangent to the circle with center O and that same radius. The equation of that circle is therefore $x^2 + y^2 = (a^2 + b^2)/2,$ and the result in the problem now follows.

Section 15.5

4. $(-1, 0, -1)$)   10. $(1, -1, -1)$

13. The only possible extremum is $f(1,1) = 1.$ Put $x = 1 + h,$ $y = 1 + k.$ Then $f(x,y) = h^2 + k^2 + 1,$ so that $(1,1)$ yields 1 as the global minimum value of $f.$

16. Here, $f(x,y) \sim 3x^4 + 6y^4$ when either $|x|$ or $|y|$ is large, and therefore f has a global minimum but no global maximum. The critical points yield the values $f(0,0) = 7$, $f(1,0) = 14$, $f(0,1) = 9$, and $f(1,1) = 16$. Therefore $f(0,0) = 7$ is the global minimum value of $z = f(x,y)$.

19. The only critical point of $f(x,y)$ occurs at $(1,-2)$. Because $f(x,y) \sim \exp(-x^2 - y^2)$ when either $|x|$ or $|y|$ is large and because $f(x,y) > 0$ for all x and y, f has no global minimum value, so in this case it has the global maximum value e^5.

22. Global maximum: $f(0,1) = 1 = f(1,1)$. Global minimum: $f(1/2,0) = -1/4$.

28. We shall minimize $x^2 + y^2 + z^2$ given the side condition $xyz = 1$. Let $f(x,y) = x^2 + y^2 + 1/(xy)^2$. The four critical points of f are $(-1,-1)$, $(-1,1)$, $(1,-1)$, and $(1,1)$. It's clear that all four yield minima. So there are four points on the surface $xyz = 1$ nearest the origin; they are $(1,-1,-1)$, $(-1,1,-1)$, $(1,1,1)$, and $(-1,-1,1)$.

31. Maximize $V = xyz$ given $x + 2y + 3z = 6$.

34. Let (x,y,z) be an arbitrary point of the plane $2x - 3y + z = 1$. We shall minimize

$$f(x,y,z) = (x - 3)^2 + (y + 2)^2 + (z - 1)^2$$

given $2x - 3y + z = 1$. We minimize

$$g(x,y) = (x - 3)^2 + (y + 2)^2 + (3y - 2x)^2;$$

both partial derivatives of g are zero when (simultaneously)

$$10x - 12y = 6 \quad \text{and} \quad -12x + 20y = -4.$$

It turns out that $x = 9/7$, that $y = 4/7$, and (thereby) that $z = 1/7$. This is the nearest point by a geometric argument, or by an argument similar to those in Section 15.5.

37. Maximize $V = V(x,y) = 4xy(1 - x^2 - y^2)$ with domain the circular disk $x^2 + y^2 \le 1$.

40. Suppose that the cubes have edges x, y, and z, respectively. We are to maximize and minimize

$$A = 6x^2 + 6y^2 + 6z^2$$

given $x^3 + y^3 + z^3 = V$ (a constant). Note that x, y, and z are also nonnegative. Write

$$A = A(x,y) = 6x^2 + 6y^2 + 6(V - x^3 - y^3)^{2/3}.$$

Then $A_x(x,y) = 0 = A_y(x,y)$ at the following points:

$x = 0$, $y = 0$, $z = V^{1/3}$: $A = 6V^{2/3}$.

$x = 0$, $y = (V/2)^{1/3} = z$: $A = 12(V/2)^{2/3}$.

$y = 0$, $x = (V/2)^{1/3} = z$: $A = 12(V/2)^{2/3}$.

$x = y = z = (V/3)^{1/3}$: $A = 18(V/3)^{2/3}$.

The coefficients of $V^{2/3}$ in the above expressions for A are, in the same order, 6, 7.56, 7.56, and 8.65 (the last three are approximations). Therefore, to obtain the maximum surface area, make three equal cubes, each of edge length $(V/3)^{1/3}$. To obtain minimal surface area, make one cube of edge length $V^{1/3}$.

Section 15.6

4. $dw = (ye^{x+y} + xye^{x+y})\,dx + (xe^{x+y} + xye^{x+y})\,dy$.

10. $dw = ye^{uv}\,dx + xe^{uv}\,dy + xyve^{uv}\,du + xyue^{uv}\,dv$.

16. $dw = (1 - 2p^2)qr\exp(-\{p^2 + q^2 + r^2\})\,dp$

$\qquad + (1 - 2q^2)pr\exp(-\{p^2 + q^2 + r^2\})\,dq$

$\qquad + (1 - 2r^2)pq\exp(-\{p^2 + q^2 + r^2\})\,dr$.

19. $df = -\dfrac{dx + dy}{(1 + x + y)^2}$. Therefore

$\Delta f \sim -\dfrac{0.02 + 0.05}{(1 + 3 + 6)^2} = -0.0007$

281

(the true value is approximately -0.000695).

22. $df = \dfrac{(x + y + q)yz - xyz}{(x + y + z)^2} dx$

$+ \dfrac{(x + y + z)xz - xyz}{(x + y + z)^2} dy$

$+ \dfrac{(x + y + z)xy - xyz}{(x + y + z)^2} dz.$

Take $x = 2$, $y = 3$, $z = 5$, $dx = -0.02$, $dy = 0.03$, and $dz = -0.03$.   Then

$$\Delta f \sim \frac{1}{10}(-0.24 + 0.21 - 0.09) = -0.012.$$

(The true value is approximately -0.012323.)

28. Think of y as implicitly defined as a function of x by means of the equation $2x^3 + 2y^3 = 9xy$.   It follows that

$$\frac{dy}{dx} = \frac{3y - 2x^2}{2y^2 - 3x}$$

and therefore that the slope of the tangent line to the graph of $2x^3 + 2y^2 = 9xy$ at the point $(1,2)$ is $4/5$.   The straight line through $(1,2)$ with that slope has equation

$$y = 2 + \frac{4}{5}(x - 1);$$

when $x = 1.1$, we have

$$y_{curve} \sim y_{line} = 2 + \frac{4}{5}(0.1) = 2.08.$$

The true value of y is approximately 2.0757625.

34. -229.768 (cm^3)

Section 15.7

1. $\dfrac{dw}{dt} = \dfrac{dw}{dx}\,\dfrac{dx}{dt} + \dfrac{dw}{dy}\,\dfrac{dy}{dt}$

$\qquad = -2x\exp(-x^2 - y^2) - yt^{-1/2}\exp(-x^2 - y^2)$

$\qquad = -(2t + 1)e^{-t^2 - t}.$

4. $\dfrac{dw}{dt} = \dfrac{2t}{1 + t^2}.$

10. $r_x = y^2 + z^2 + 2(xy + yz + xz) - 4x - 2y - 2z;$

$\quad r_y = x^2 + z^2 + 2(xy + yz + xz) - 2x - 4y - 2z;$

$\quad r_z = x^2 + y^2 + 2(xy + yz + xz) - 2x - 2y - 4z.$

16. $w_x = 6x$ and $w_y = 6y.$

22. $x - y - z = 0$

40. Show that

$$w_x = \frac{4xy^2}{(x^2 + y^2)^2}\,f'(u)$$

and that

$$w_y = -\frac{4x^2 y}{(x^2 + y^2)^2}\,f'(u).$$

Section 15.8

1. $\langle 3, -7 \rangle$

4. $\left\langle \dfrac{1}{8}\pi\sqrt{2}, -\dfrac{3}{8}\pi\sqrt{2} \right\rangle$

10. $\langle 160, -240, 400 \rangle$

16. $\dfrac{4}{3}\sqrt{3}$

22. The maximum value is $1/\sqrt{5}$; it occurs in the direction $<2,1>$.

28. $6x + 18y + 15z = 73$

40. We continue the notation of the solution of Problem 39. First,

$$\vec{\nabla F} \times \vec{\nabla G} = <-8y - 6z, 4z + 8x, -6x + 4y>.$$

For the tangent line to be horizontal, we require $-6x + 4y = 0$
-- that is, $3x = 2y$.   So we have the three equations

$$3x = 2y,$$

$$z^2 = x^2 + y^2, \qquad \text{and}$$

$$2x + 3y + 4z = -2.$$

Their simultaneous solution yields the answers:

Low point: $x = (52 + 16\sqrt{13})/39 \sim 2.812534,$

$y = (26 + 8\sqrt{13})/13 \sim 4.218801,$

$z = (-8 - 2\sqrt{13})/3 \sim -5.070368.$

High point: $x = (52 - 16\sqrt{13})/39 \sim -0.145867,$

$y = (26 - 8\sqrt{13})/13 \sim -0.218801,$

$z = (-8 + 2\sqrt{13})/3 \sim -0.262966.$

Section 15.9

1. The method leads to the simultaneous equations

$$2x = 2\lambda x,$$

$$2y + 2\lambda y = 0.$$

Their solutions: $x = 0$ or $\lambda = 1$.

284

4. The method yields $<8x, 18y> = \lambda<2x, 2y>$. It follows that one of x and y is zero. So the minimum occurs at $(-1, 0)$ and at $(1, 0)$, where the value of f is 4. The maximum value is 9, and occurs at $(0, 1)$ and at $(0, -1)$.

7. You should find that $2\lambda x = 8\lambda y = 18\lambda z = 1$. This leads to $z^2 = 16/49$ while $x = 9z$ and $y = 9z/4$.

10. We let $g(x, y, z) = x^2 + y^2 - 1$ and $h(x, y, z) = 2x + 2y + z - 5$. The equation $\vec{\nabla f} = \lambda \vec{\nabla g} + \mu \vec{\nabla h}$ then takes the form

$$<0, 0, 1> = \lambda<2x, 2y, 0> + \mu<2, 2, 1>.$$

It follows that $\lambda x = -1 = \lambda y$; because $\lambda \neq 0$, $x = y$. So $x = y = \sqrt{2}/2$ or $x = y = -\sqrt{2}/2$. In the first case we see that $z = 5 - 2\sqrt{2}$; in the second, $z = 5 + 2\sqrt{2}$. It follows that the maximum is $5 + 2\sqrt{2}$ and that the minimum is $5 - 2\sqrt{2}$.

16. (Problem 32 of Section 15.5) Frontage: x. Depth: y. Height: z. Given $xyz = 8000$, minimize the cost

$$C(x, y, z) = 2xy + 4xz + 8yz.$$

The method yields

$$<2y + 4z, 2x + 8z, 4x + 8y> = \lambda<yz, xz, xy>.$$

Because x, y, and z are positive, we find that

$$\lambda xyz = 2xy + 4xz = 2xy + 8yz = 4xz + 8yz$$

and thus that $x = 2y = 4z$. Thus $8z^3 = 8000$, and so we find that $z = 10$, $y = 20$, and $x = 40$. Answer: The building should have a frontage of 40 feet, depth 20 feet, and height 10 feet. (This is a minimum by the usual argument -- if any of the variables is near zero, then one of the others is very large, and this produces a large value for the cost C.)

19. (Problem 38 of Section 15.5) We are to minimize volume $V = 4xyz$ given $g(x, y, z) = x^2 + y^2 + z^2 - R^2 = 0$:

$$<4yz, 4xz, 4xy> = \lambda<2x, 2y, 2z>.$$

Because x, y, and z are positive at the maximum, we quickly find that $x = y = z$. Then we use the condition $g(x,y,z) = 0$ to find the answer: V_{max} occurs when $x = y = z = R/\sqrt{3}$ and $V_{max} = 4R^3\sqrt{3}/9$.

22. Maximize A by maximizing

$$f(x,y,z) = A^2 = s(s - x)(s - y)(s - z)$$

given the constraint $g(x,y,z) = 2s - x - y - z = 0$ (where s is constant). The method yields

$$\langle s(x - y)(x - z), s(s - x)(s - z), s(s - x)(s - y)\rangle = \lambda\langle 1, 1, 1\rangle.$$

Therefore

$$s(s - x)(s - y) = s(s - x)(s - z) = s(s - y)(s - z).$$

Now $s \neq 0$, so

$$s^2 - sx - sy + xy = s^2 - sy - sz + yz = s^2 - sx - sz + xz;$$

it follows that

$$x(s - z) = y(s - z) \quad \text{and} \quad y(s - x) = z(s - x).$$

If $s = x$ (say), the triangle degenerates to a line segment:

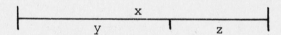

This yields minimum area zero. So at maximum, all three of $s - x$, $s - y$, and $s - z$ are positive. It follows that $x = y = z$, and therefore that the triangle with fixed perimeter and maximum area is an equilateral triangle.

Section 15.10

1. $f(x,y) = 2(x + 1)^2 + (y - 2)^2 - 1.$

4. $y + 3 = 0 = x - 2$ at $(2,-3)$. $AC - B^2 = -1 < 0$, so f has no extrema.

7. $x^2 + y = 0 = x + y^2$ at $(0,0)$ and at $(-1,-1)$. At the first critical point, $AC - B^2 = -9 < 0$; no extremum there.

At $(-1,-1)$, $AC - B^2 = 27$ and $A = -6$. Therefore f has the local maximum value 4 at $(-1,-1)$.

10. No extremum at $(0,0)$; local maximum at $(1,1)$.

16. The equations $6x + 12y - 6 = 0 = 12x + 6y^2 + 6$ lead to $x = 1 - 2y$ and $y^2 - 4y + 3 = 0$, and thus $(-1,1)$ and $(-5,3)$ are the only two critical points. But $\Delta = 72y - 144$, so the first is not an extremum and the second yields a local minimum for f.

28.

(x,y)	A	B	C	Δ	Classification	z
$(0,0)$	2e	0	4e	$8e^2$	Local minimum	0
$(0,1)$	-2	0	-8	16	Local maximum	2
$(0,-1)$	-2	0	-8	16	Local maximum	2
$(1,0)$	-4	0	2	-8	Saddle point	1
$(-1,0)$	-4	0	2	-8	Saddle point	1

See the figure below for a geometric summary of the critical points of the function.

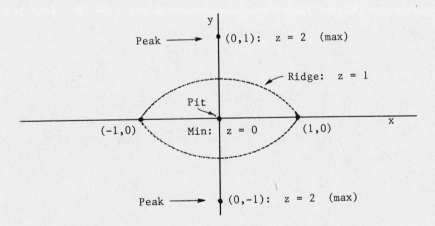

34. Both partials are zero when $4x^3 + 8x - 16 = 0 = -2y$. We solve the first of these equations by Newton's method, obtaining the solution $x \sim 1.1795$. (There is no other solution because $h(x) = 4x^3 + 8x - 16$ has a positive first derivative.) Thus the only critical point is close to $(1,1895,0)$. But $\Delta < 0$ for all (x,y) because $\Delta = -24x^2 - 16$. Hence the critical point we found does not yield an extremum; f has no extrema.

4.   121.7

7.   107, because $p \sim (19.38)(\ln w) + 17.95$.

10.   Profit in A: $x(1000 - 10x) - 30000 - 20x$.
     Profit in B: $y(2000 - 15y) - 30000 - 20y$.
     Total profit:

$$P = P(x,y) = -10x^2 - 15y^2 + 980x + 1980y - 30000.$$

Both partial derivatives of P vanish at $(x,y) = (49,66)$;
note that $P(49,66) = 59416$.   Next, $P(0,66) = 35340$ and
$P(49,0) = -5990$.   For large x and for large y, $P(x,y) < 0$.
So P is maximized within a large rectangle in the first quadrant
with two sides on the coordinate axes.   Therefore (49,66) yields
the global maximum value of the profit: $59,416.00.

13.   Let x be the number of sheep, y the number of hogs, and z the
     number of head of cattle. Suppose that 60 cattle use 1 unit of
     land.   Then each head of cattle uses 1/60 units of land.   And by
     similar reasoning, each hog uses 1/120 units of land and each
     sheep uses 1/80 units of land.   This leads to the side condition

$$\frac{x}{80} + \frac{y}{120} + \frac{z}{60} = 1$$

for each unit of land available.   We write this in the simpler form
$3x + 2y + 4z = 240$.   An additional condition in the problem
is that $y \geq x + z$.   We are now to maximize the profit P per
unit of land, given by

$$P(x,y,z) = 10x + 8y + 20z.$$

The domain of P is the triangular region shown in the figure at
the top of the next page.   It is obtained as follows: Draw the
part of the plane with equation $3x + 2y + 4z = 240$ that
lies in the first octant (because none of x, y, or z can be
negative).   The lines of intersection of that plane with the
nonnegative coordinate planes is shown as a pair of dashed lines.
The condition that $y \geq x + z$ implies that only the part of
the first plane to the <u>right</u> of the second may be used as the
domain of P.   Thus we arrive at the shaded triangle as the domain

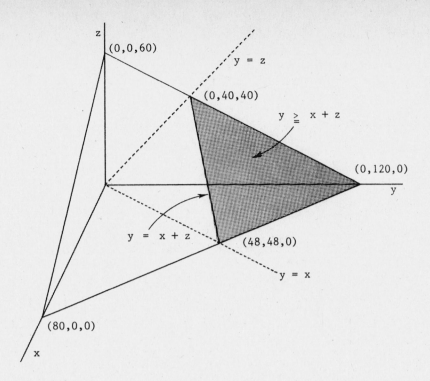

of the profit function. Finally, because P is a linear function
of x, y, and z, its maximum and minimum values occur at the
vertices of the shaded triangle. Here, then, are the results:

Vertex	Profit
(48,48,0)	$864 per unit of land
(0,120,0)	$960 per unit of land
(0,40,40)	$1120 per unit of land

Were it not for the restriction of the state law mentioned in the
problem, the farmer could maximize her profit per unit of land by
raising only cattle: P(0,0,60) = 1200. Answer: Raise 40 hogs
and 40 head of cattle per unit of land, and no sheep.

16. You should find that

$$A = 2\{(x_1)^2 + (x_2)^2 + (x_3)^2 + \ldots + (x_n)^2\},$$

$$B = 2(x_1 + x_2 + x_3 + \ldots + x_n), \quad \text{and}$$

$$C = 2n.$$

4. $\quad g_x(0,0) \;=\; \lim_{h \to 0} \dfrac{g(h,0) - g(0,0)}{h}$

$\qquad\qquad\;\; = \;\lim_{h \to 0} \dfrac{1}{h}\left(\dfrac{h \cdot 0}{h^2 + 0^2} - 0\right) \;=\; 0.$

10. You should obtain

$$u_{xx} \;=\; \frac{4\pi^2}{(4\pi kt)^{5/2}}\,(x^2 - 2kt)\exp(-x^2/4kt).$$

16. First find the equation of the tangent plane. Let (a,b,c) be the
point of tangency; note that $abc = 1$. Let $F(x,y,z) = xyz - 1$;
then $\overrightarrow{\nabla F} = \langle yz, xz, xy\rangle$, so that a normal to the plane is

$$\{\overrightarrow{\nabla F}\}(a,b,c) \;=\; \langle bc,\, ac,\, ab\rangle,$$

and the plane therefore has equation

$$bc(x - a) + ac(y - b) = ab(z - c) \;=\; 0;$$

that is, $bcx + acy + abz = 3$. Its intercepts are $x_0 = 3/bc$,
$y_0 = 3/ac$, and $z_0 = 3/ab$. By the formula $V = hB/3$, its
volume is $9/2$.

22. Write

$$w \;=\; w(u,v) \;=\; \int_u^v f(t)\,dt$$

where $u = g(x)$, $v = h(x)$. Then $F(x) = w(u(x), v(x))$.
Consequently

$$F'(x) \;=\; w_u u_x + w_v v_x$$

$$= \; -f(u)g'(x) + f(v)h'(x)$$

$$= \; f(h(x))h'(x) - f(g(x))g'(x).$$

28. $(0,b)$, $(0,-b)$, $(a,0)$, and $(-a,0)$.

34. Let $x = I_1$ and $y = I_2$. Minimize $f(x,y) = R_1x^2 + R_2y^2$ given the constraint $g(x,y) = x + y - I = 0$ (I, R_1, and R_2 are all constants). The Lagrange multiplier method gives the vector equation $\langle 2R_1x, 2R_2y \rangle = \lambda \langle 1,1 \rangle$. It follows without any difficulty that

$$I_1 = x = \frac{R_2 I}{R_1 + R_2} \quad \text{and} \quad I_2 = y = \frac{R_1 I}{R_1 + R_2}.$$

40. We seek the extrema of $f(x,y) = x^2y^2$ given the constraint $g(x,y) = x^2 + 4y^2 - 24 = 0$. The Lagrange multiplier method gives the following results: The maximum value 36 of f occurs at the four points $(2\sqrt{3}, \sqrt{3})$, $(-2\sqrt{3}, \sqrt{3})$, $(2\sqrt{3}, -\sqrt{3})$, and $(-2\sqrt{3}, -\sqrt{3})$. The minimum value 0 of f occurs at the four points $(2\sqrt{6}, 0)$, $(-2\sqrt{6}, 0)$, $(0, \sqrt{6})$, and $(0, -\sqrt{6})$.

46. Global minimum -2 at $(1,-2)$ and at $(-1,-2)$; saddle point at $(0,-2)$.

Section 16.1

1. $\displaystyle\int_0^2 \int_0^4 (3x + 4y)\, dx\, dy = \int_0^2 (24 + 16y)\, dy = 80.$

4. $\displaystyle\int_{-2}^1 \int_2^4 x^2y^3\, dy\, dx = \int_{-2}^1 (64x^2 - 4x^2)\, dx = 180.$

10. $\displaystyle\int_0^{\pi/2} \cos x\, dx = 1.$

16. $\displaystyle\int_0^{\pi/2} (y - 1)\, dy = \frac{\pi}{8}(\pi - 4).$

22. $\displaystyle\int_0^\pi \int_{-\pi/2}^{\pi/2} (\sin x \cos y)\, dy\, dx$

$$= \int_0^\pi 2 \sin x\, dx\ =\ 4.$$

25. $\displaystyle\int_0^1 \int_0^1 x^n y^n\, dx\, dy\ =\ \int_0^1 \frac{1}{n+1} y^n\, dy.$

$$=\ \frac{1}{(n+1)^2}\ \to\ 0\quad \text{as}\quad n\ \to\ +\infty.$$

Section 16.2

1. $\displaystyle\int_0^1 \Big[y + xy \Big]_0^x dx\ =\ \int_0^1 (x + x^2)\, dx\ =\ \frac{5}{6}.$

4. $\displaystyle\int_0^2 \Big[\frac{1}{2} x^2 + xy \Big]_{y/2}^1 dy\ =\ \int_0^2 (\frac{1}{2} + y - \frac{5}{8} y^2)\, dy$

$$=\ \frac{4}{3}.$$

7. $\displaystyle\int_0^1 \int_x^{\sqrt{x}} (2x - y)\, dy\, dx\ =\ \int_0^1 \Big[2xy - \frac{1}{2} y^2 \Big]_x^{x^{1/2}} dx$

$$=\ \int_0^1 (2x^{3/2} - \frac{1}{2} x - 2x^2 + \frac{1}{2} x^2)\, dx$$

$$=\ \Big[\frac{4}{5} x^{5/2} - \frac{1}{4} x^2 - \frac{1}{2} x^3 \Big]_0^1\ =\ \frac{1}{20}.$$

10. 36

16. $\displaystyle\int_0^1 \int_y^{y^{1/4}} (x - 1)\, dx\, dy \;=\; -\frac{2}{15}$.

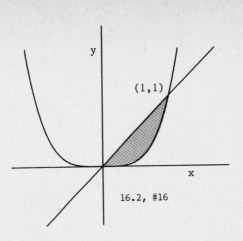

16.2, #16

22. $\displaystyle\int_0^{\sqrt{\pi}} \int_0^x (\sin x^2)\, dy\, dx \;=\; 1$

Section 16.3

1. The area is

$$A \;=\; \int_0^1 \int_{y^2}^y 1\, dx\, dy \;=\; \frac{1}{6}$$.

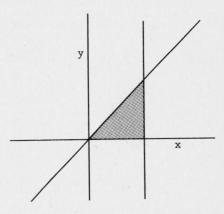

16.2, #22

4. $\displaystyle A \;=\; \int_1^3 \int_{2x + 3}^{6x - x^2} 1\, dy\, dx \;=\; \frac{4}{3}$.

7. $\displaystyle A \;=\; \int_{-2}^2 \int_{2x^2 - 3}^{x^2 + 1} 1\, dy\, dx \;=\; \frac{32}{3}$.

10. $\pi - \dfrac{2}{3}$

13. The volume is

$$V \;=\; \int_0^1 \int_0^2 (y + e^x)\, dy\, dx$$

$$=\; \int_0^1 \left[\frac{1}{2} y^2 + y e^x \right]_0^2 dx \;=\; \int_0^1 (2 + 2e^x)\, dx$$

$$= \left[2x + 2e^x \right]_0^1 = 2 + 2e - 2 = 2e.$$

16. The volume is

$$V = \int_0^2 \int_0^{4-2y} (3x + 2y) \, dx \, dy$$

$$= \int_0^2 \left[\frac{3}{2} x^2 + 2xy \right]_0^{4-2y} dy$$

$$= \int_0^2 (24 - 16y + 2y^2) \, dy = \frac{64}{3}.$$

22. $\frac{837}{70}$

34. Region of integration: $x^2 + y^2 \leq 4$. Volume: 24π.

Section 16.4

1. $A = \int_0^{2\pi} \int_0^1 r \, dr \, d\xi.$

4. $A = \int_{-\pi/4}^{\pi/4} \int_0^{2\cos 2\xi} r \, dr \, d\xi = \frac{\pi}{2}.$

7. $A = 2 \int_{\pi/6}^{\pi/6} \int_0^{1-2\sin\xi} r \, dr \, d\xi.$

10. $\frac{3\pi}{2}$

13. $\displaystyle\int_0^{\pi/2}\int_0^1 \frac{r}{1+r^2}\,dr\,d\xi$

16. $\displaystyle\int_{\pi/4}^{\pi/2}\int_0^{\csc\xi} r^3\cos^2\xi\,dr\,d\xi \;=\; \frac{1}{12}.$

19. The volume is

$$V \;=\; \int_0^{2\pi}\int_0^1 (2 + r\cos\xi + r\sin\xi)r\,dr\,d\xi$$

$$=\; \int_0^{2\pi}\left[r^2 + \frac{1}{3}r^3\cos\xi + \frac{1}{3}r^3\sin\xi \right]_0^1 d\xi$$

$$=\; \int_0^{2\pi}\left(1 + \frac{1}{3}\cos\xi + \frac{1}{3}\sin\xi\right) d\xi$$

$$=\; \left[\xi + \frac{1}{3}\sin\xi - \frac{1}{3}\cos\xi \right]_0^{2\pi} \;=\; 2\pi.$$

22. $\displaystyle V \;=\; \int_0^{2\pi}\int_0^{1+\cos\xi} (1 + r\cos\xi)r\,dr\,d\xi$

$$=\; \frac{1}{6}\int_0^{2\pi}(3 + 9\cos^2\xi + 2\cos^4\xi)\,d\xi \;=\; \frac{11\pi}{4}.$$

28. Domain of integration: the disk $x^2 + y^2 \leqq 1$.

$$V \;=\; \int_0^{2\pi}\int_0^1 r(1 - r^2)\,dr\,d\xi \;=\; \frac{\pi}{2}.$$

31. $V = \int_0^{\pi/2} \int_0^{\sqrt{2\sin 2\xi}} r^3 \, dr \, d\xi.$

34. The polar form of the integral is

$$\int_0^{\pi/2} \int_0^{\infty} \frac{r}{(1 + r^2)^2} \, dr \, d\xi.$$

Section 16.5

1. $M = \int_0^1 \int_0^{1-x} xy \, dy \, dx = \frac{1}{24}.$

   $M_y = \int_0^1 \int_0^{1-x} x^2 y \, dy \, dx = \frac{1}{60}.$

   Therefore $\bar{x} = \frac{2}{5}$; $\bar{y} = \frac{2}{5}$ by symmetry.

4. $M = \int_{-3}^3 \int_0^{9-y^2} x^2 \, dx \, dy = 23328/35.$

   $M_y = \int_{-3}^3 \int_0^{9-y^2} x^3 \, dx \, dy = 139968/35.$

   So $\bar{x} = 6$; $\bar{y} = 0$ by symmetry.

10. $M = 2 \int_0^1 \int_0^{\exp(-x^2)} xy \, dy \, dx = \frac{e^2 - 1}{4e^2}.$

    $M_x = 2 \int_0^1 \int_0^{\exp(-x^2)} xy^2 \, dy \, dx = \frac{e^3 - 1}{9e^3}.$

Hence $\bar{y} = \dfrac{4(e^2 + e + 1)}{9e(e + 1)}$. By symmetry, $\bar{x} = 0$.

16. $M = \dfrac{2}{3} a^3$, $M_x = \dfrac{1}{8} \pi a^4$, $M_y = 0$; $\bar{x} = 0$, $\bar{y} = \dfrac{3}{16} \pi a$.

22. $I_0 = \dfrac{2}{5} a^5$.

28. We found $M = 96/5$ in Problem 14. $I_x = 84256/135 \sim 624.12$ and $I_y = 8032/105 \sim 76.495$. Therefore $\hat{x} = \sqrt{251/63} \sim 1.996$ and $\hat{y} = \sqrt{2633/81} \sim 5.701$.

34. Let k denote the density of the lamina. We find that

$$I_0 = \frac{1}{4} k\pi ab(a^2 + b^2).$$

Because its area is πab, its mass is $M = k\pi ab$. Hence the answer may also be written in the form

$$I_0 = \frac{1}{4} M(a^2 + b^2).$$

Section 16.6

1. $\displaystyle\iiint_T f(x,y,z)\, dV = \int_0^1 \int_0^3 \int_0^2 (x + y + z)\, dx\, dy\, dz$

$\displaystyle = \int_0^1 \int_0^3 \left[\frac{1}{2} x^2 + xy + xz \right]_0^2 dy\, dz$

$\displaystyle = \int_0^1 \int_0^3 (2 + 2x + 2y)\, dy\, dz$

$\displaystyle = \int_0^1 \left[2y + y^2 + xyz \right]_0^3 dz$

$$= \int_0^1 (15 + 6z) \, dz = \left[15z + 3z^2 \right]_0^1 = 18.$$

4. $$\int_{-2}^6 \int_0^2 (4 + 4y + 4z) \, dy \, dz$$

$$= \int_{-2}^6 (8 + 8z) \, dz = \left[8z + 4z^2 \right]_{-2}^6 = 192.$$

10. $$\int_{-1}^1 \int_{-2}^2 \int_{y^2}^{8-y^2} z \, dz \, dy \, dx$$

$$= \int_{-1}^1 \int_{-2}^2 (32 - 8y^2) \, dy \, dx$$

$$= \int_{-1}^1 (128 - \frac{128}{3}) \, dx = \frac{512}{3}.$$

16. $128/3$

22. $M_{yz} = 0 = M_{xz};\quad M_{xy} = \frac{\pi}{4} R^4.$

28. $\frac{1}{2} \pi R^4 H$

34. $M = k/2,\quad M_{yz} = k/4 = M_{xz}$ (by symmetry), $\quad M_{xy} = k/3.$

37. $$V = 2 \int_0^1 \int_0^x \int_0^{(1-x^2)^{1/2}} 1 \, dz \, dy \, dx = \frac{2}{3}.$$

$$M_{xy} = \frac{1}{4}, \quad M_{yz} = M_{xz} = \frac{3}{32} \pi.$$

40. 4π

Section 16.7

1. $V = \displaystyle\int_0^{2\pi} \int_0^2 \int_{r^2}^4 r \, dz \, dr \, d\xi$

$= 2\pi \displaystyle\int_0^2 (4r - r^3) \, dr = 2\pi \left[2r^2 - \frac{1}{4} r^4 \right]_0^2 = 8\pi.$

4. Use the sphere $r^2 + z^2 \leq a^2$, $0 \leq \xi \leq 2\pi$. We find its moment of inertia about the x-axis:

$I_z = \displaystyle\int_0^{2\pi} \int_0^a \int_{-(a^2 - r^2)^{1/2}}^{(a^2 - r^2)^{1/2}} r^3 \, dz \, dr \, d\xi$

$= 2\pi \displaystyle\int_0^a 2r^3 (a^2 - r^2)^{1/2} \, dr.$

Let $r = a \sin u$. This substitution yields

$I_z = 4\pi a^5 \displaystyle\int_0^{\pi/2} (\cos^2 u - \cos^4 u)(\sin u) \, du$

$= 4\pi a^5 \left[\frac{1}{5} \cos^5 u - \frac{1}{3} \cos^3 u \right]_0^{\pi/2} = \frac{8}{15} \pi a^5.$

The answer may also be written in the form $I_z = \frac{2}{5} Ma^5$ where M is the mass of the sphere.

7. Mass:

$M = \displaystyle\int_0^{2\pi} \int_0^a \int_0^h rz \, dz \, dr \, d\xi$

299

$$= \pi \int_0^a rh^2 \, dr = \left[\frac{\pi}{2} r^2 h^2\right]_0^a = \frac{1}{2}\pi a^2 h^2.$$

10. The diagram at the right shows the intersection of the xy-plane with the sphere and the cylinder. The plane and the sphere intersect in the curve $r = 2$ and the cylindrical equation of the sphere is $r^2 + z^2 = 4$. The plane intersects the cylinder in the curve $r = 2 \cos \xi$. Thus the volume V of their intersection is given by

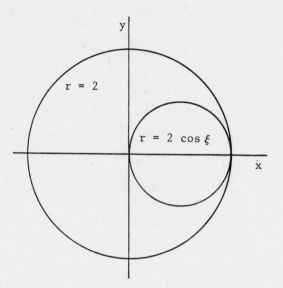

$$V = 4 \int_0^{\pi/2} \int_0^{2 \cos \xi} \int_0^{(4 - r^2)^{1/2}} r \, dz \, dr \, d\xi$$

$$= 4 \int_0^{\pi/2} \int_0^{2 \cos \xi} r(4 - r^2)^{1/2} \, dr \, d\xi$$

$$= 4 \int_0^{\pi/2} \left[-\frac{1}{3}(4 - r^2)^{3/2}\right]_0^{2 \cos \xi} d\xi$$

$$= \frac{32}{3} \int_0^{\pi/2} (1 - \sin^3 \xi) \, d\xi = \frac{16}{9}(3\pi - 4).$$

16. Let k denote the density of the cylinder and h its height. Then $M = \pi a^2 hk$. We choose coordinates so that the z-axis is the axis of symmetry of the cylinder and its base rests on the xy-plane. Then

$$I_z = \int_0^{2\pi} \int_0^a \int_0^h kr^3 \, dz \, dr \, d\xi = \frac{1}{2}\pi a^4 hk$$

$$= (\pi a^2 hk)(\tfrac{1}{2} a^2) = \tfrac{1}{2} Ma^2.$$

22. Locate the hemisphere with its base in the xy-plane and symmetric about the z-axis. Then

$$M = \tfrac{1}{4} k\pi a^4 \quad \text{and} \quad M_{xy} = \tfrac{2}{15} \pi k a^5.$$

It follows that its centroid is at $(0, 0, \tfrac{8}{15} a)$.

25. $M_{xy} = \tfrac{1}{8} \pi a^4$

28. $I_z = \tfrac{1016}{21} \pi a^7$

Section 16.8

1. $\{1 + (z_x)^2 + (z_y)^2\}^{1/2} = \sqrt{11}$. The area of the ellipse is 6π, so the answer is $6\pi\sqrt{11}$.

4. $\{1 + (z_x)^2 + (z_y)^2\}^{1/2} = (1 + x^2)^{1/2}$. So the answer is

$$\int_0^1 \int_0^x (1 + x^2)^{1/2} \, dy \, dx$$

$$= \int_0^1 x(1 + x^2)^{1/2} \, dx = \left[\tfrac{1}{3} (1 + x^2)^{3/2} \right]_0^1$$

$$= \tfrac{1}{3} (2\sqrt{2} - 1) \sim 0.609476.$$

10. $A = \tfrac{\pi}{6} (17\sqrt{17} - 1) \sim 36.1769.$

16. $A = 2a^2(\pi - 2)$, about 18% of the total surface area.

22. (b) The area in question is given by

$$A = \int_0^{2\pi} \int_0^{\pi/6} a^2 \sin \phi \, d\phi \, d\xi$$

$$= 2\pi \left[-a^2 \cos \phi \right]_0^{\pi/6} = 2\pi a^2 (1 - \frac{1}{3}\sqrt{3}),$$

about 21.13% of the total surface area.

Section 16.9

4. $x = \frac{1}{2}(u + v)^{1/2}$, $y = \frac{1}{2}(u - v)^{1/2}$, and

$$J = -\frac{1}{8(u^2 - v^2)^{1/2}}.$$

7. $J = -\frac{1}{5}$

10. First, $x = (u^2 v)^{-1/3}$, $y = (uv^2)^{-1/3}$, and $J = 1/(3u^2 v^2)$. It follows that the area of the region is 1/8.

13. The Jacobian is 6r.

16. $r = z^{1/2}$, $t = \{z/(x^2 + y^2)\}^{1/2}$, and $\xi = \arctan(y/x)$. The Jacobian of the transformation is $2(r/t)^3$. The volume of R turns out to be $45\pi/8$.

19. The spherical integral is

$$\lim_{a \to \infty} \int_0^{2\pi} \int_0^{\pi} \int_0^a \rho^3 \exp(-k\rho^2) \sin \phi \, d\rho \, d\phi \, d\xi.$$

Chapter 16 Miscellaneous Problems

1. $\int_0^1 \int_0^{x^3} (1 + x^2)^{-1/2} \, dy \, dx$

4. $\displaystyle\int_0^4 \int_0^{y^{3/2}} x \cos y^4 \, dx \, dy$

7. $V = \displaystyle\int_0^1 \int_y^{2-y} (x^2 + y^2) \, dx \, dy.$

10. The domain of the integral will be the elliptical region bounded by the ellipse with equation $(x/2)^2 + y^2 = 1$. Let us use the transformation $x = 2r \cos \xi$, $y = r \sin \xi$. The Jacobian of this transformation is $2r$. The difference in the z-values of the two paraboloids turns out to be $8(1 - r^2)$, and the volume of the region between them is 8π.

13. Use the same transformation as in the solution of Problem 10.

16. $M = 6/35$; $M_y = 55/504 = M_x$; the centroid is at the point $(275/432, 275/432) \sim (0.636574, 0.636574)$.

22. $V = 1/12$

25. Suggestion: Place the cone with its vertex at the origin and with the z-axis its natural axis of symmetry. Then use cylindrical coordinates.

28. $V = \dfrac{1}{12} \pi a^3$.

31. $V = \displaystyle\int_0^\pi \int_0^{1 + \cos \xi} 2\pi r^2 \sin \xi \, dr \, d\xi.$

34. $\dfrac{2}{3} a$

40. The average distance of points of the cone from its vertex is

$$\frac{(H^2 + R^2)^{3/2} - H^3}{2R^2} = \frac{L^3 - H^3}{2R^2}$$

where L is the slant height of the cone.

46. The surface area can be written in the form

$$A = 4 \int_0^1 \int_0^{(1-x^2)^{1/2}} (1 + x^2)^{1/2} \, dy \, dx$$

$$= 4 \int_0^1 (1 - x^4)^{1/2} \, dx;$$

this is the integral we choose to approximate. We use Simpson's approximation and obtain the estimate 3.49608, though very many subintervals are needed.

49. Use the transformation $u = xy$, $v = x^2 - y^2$; its Jacobian is $-2(4u^2 + v^2)^{1/2}$.

Section 17.1

13. $\operatorname{div} \vec{F}(x,y,z) = 0$;

$$\operatorname{curl} \vec{F}(x,y,z) = \begin{vmatrix} \vec{i} & \vec{j} & \vec{k} \\ \partial/\partial x & \partial/\partial y & \partial/\partial z \\ yz & xz & xy \end{vmatrix}$$

$$= \langle x - x, \, y - y, \, z - z \rangle = 0.$$

16. $\operatorname{div} \vec{F}(x,y,z) = 12$; $\operatorname{curl} \vec{F}(x,y,z) = \langle 2,3,1 \rangle$.

22. Write $\vec{F} = \langle P,Q,R \rangle$ and $\vec{G} = \langle S,T,U \rangle$. Then

$$\operatorname{div}(a\vec{F} + b\vec{G}) = \operatorname{div}\langle aP + bS, \, aQ + bT, \, aR + bU \rangle$$

$$= aP_x + bS_x + aQ_y + bT_y + aR_z + bU_z$$

$$= a(P_x + Q_y + R_z) + b(S_x + T_y + U_z)$$

$$= (a \operatorname{div} \vec{F}) + (b \operatorname{div} \vec{G}).$$

28. Write $\vec{F} = \langle P,Q,R \rangle$. Then

$$\text{div}(\text{curl } \vec{F}) = \text{div} < R_y - Q_z, \ P_z - R_x, \ Q_x - P_y >$$

$$= R_{yx} - Q_{zx} + P_{zy} - R_{xy} + Q_{xz} - P_{yz} = 0$$

provided $R_{yx} = R_{xy}$, $Q_{zx} = Q_{xz}$, and $P_{zy} = P_{yz}$; these equations hold in any region where (say) all second-order partial derivatives are continuous, a condition that normally holds in applications.

34. $\vec{\nabla} \times \dfrac{1}{r^3}\vec{r} = \dfrac{1}{r^3} \begin{vmatrix} \vec{i} & \vec{j} & \vec{k} \\ \partial/\partial x & \partial/\partial y & \partial/\partial z \\ x & y & z \end{vmatrix}$

$$= \dfrac{1}{r^3} < 0, 0, 0 > = \vec{0}.$$

37. $\text{div}(r\vec{r}) = \text{div}\{(x^2 + y^2 + z^2)^{1/2} < x, y, z >\}$

$$= \dfrac{\partial}{\partial x}\{x(x^2 + y^2 + z^2)^{1/2}\} + \dfrac{\partial}{\partial y}\{y(x^2 + y^2 + z^2)^{1/2}\}$$

$$+ \dfrac{\partial}{\partial z}\{z(x^2 + y^2 + z^2)^{1/2}\}$$

$$= 3(x^2 + y^2\, z^2)^{1/2} + \dfrac{x^2}{(x^2 + y^2 + z^2)^{1/2}}$$

$$+ \dfrac{y^2}{(x^2 + y^2 + z^2)^{1/2}} + \dfrac{z^2}{(x^2 + y^2 + z^2)^{1/2}}$$

$$= 3r + r = 4r.$$

40. $\text{grad}(r^{10}) = \text{grad}\{(x^2 + y^2 + z^2)^5\}$

$$= < 5(x^2 + y^2 + z^2)^4(2x), \ 5(x^2 + y^2 + z^2)^4(2y), \ 5(x^2 + y^2 + z^2)^4(2z) >$$

$$= 10(x^2 + y^2 + z^2)^4 < x, y, z > = 10r^8\vec{r}.$$

Section 17.2

1. $dx = 4\,dt$, $dy = 3\,dt$, and $ds = 5\,dt$. Also

$$f(t) = (4t - 1)^2 + (3t + 1)^2 = 25t^2 - 2t + 2.$$

Therefore

$$\int_C f(x,y) \, ds = \int_{-1}^{1} (25t^2 - 2t + 2)(5 \, dt) = \frac{310}{3} \, ;$$

$$\int_C f(x,y) \, dx = \frac{248}{3} \quad \text{and} \quad \int_C f(x,y) \, dy = 62 .$$

4. Note that $ds = dt$. So

$$\int_C (2x - y) \, ds = \int_0^{\pi/2} (2 \sin t - \cos t) \, dt = 1 \, ;$$

$$\int_C (2x - y) \, dx = \int_0^{\pi/2} (2 \sin t \cos t - \frac{1 + \cos 2t}{2}) \, dt$$

$$= \frac{4 - \pi}{4} \, ;$$

$$\int_C (2x - y) \, dy = \int_0^{\pi/2} (-2 \sin^2 t + \sin t \cos t) \, dt$$

$$= \frac{1 - \pi}{2} \, .$$

7. Use y as the parameter.

10. If $f(x,y) = \frac{1}{2} x^2 + 2xy - \frac{1}{2} y^2$, then

$$\vec{\nabla f} = \langle x + 2y, \, 2x - y \rangle .$$

Therefore the given integral is independent of the path. Hence

$$\int_C (x + 2y) \, dx + (2x - y) \, dy = f(-2,-1) - f(3,2) = -9 .$$

13. $$\int_C \vec{F} \cdot \vec{T} \, ds = \int_{t=0}^{\pi} (y \, dx - x \, dy + z \, dz)$$

$$= \int_0^{\pi} (\cos^2 t + \sin^2 t + 4t) \, dt = \pi + 2\pi^2.$$

16. C is parallel to $<2,3,3>$, so C may be parametrized by

$$\vec{r}(t) = <1,-1,2> + <2t, 3t, 3t> = <2t+1, 3t-1, 3t+2>;$$

that is, we let $x = 2t + 1$, $y = 3t - 1$, and $z = 3t + 2$ for $0 \le x \le 1$. Then $ds = \sqrt{22} \, dt$, so

$$\int_C xyz \, ds = \int_0^1 (2t+1)(3t-1)(3t+2)\sqrt{22} \, dt = 7\sqrt{22}.$$

19. If the wire has constant density k, then the total mass of the wire is $M = \pi a k$ and the mass of a segment of length ds is $dm = k \, ds$. Parametrize the wire as follows:

$$x = a \cos \xi, \quad y = a \sin \xi, \quad 0 \le \xi \le \pi.$$

Then compute

$$M_x = \int_C y \, dm.$$

22. $$I_z = \int_C (x^2 + y^2) \, dm = 90k\pi^2 = 9M.$$

25. (a) $$W = \int_0^1 \frac{ky}{1+y^2} \, dy;$$ (b) $$W = \int_1^0 \frac{kx}{1+x^2} \, dx.$$

28. We assume that the particle moves uniformly, so that its path may be parametrized as follows:

$$\vec{r}(t) = <\cos t, \sin t>, \quad 0 \le t \le 2\pi.$$

Then

307

$$W = \int_0^{2\pi} \langle -\sin t, \cos t \rangle \cdot \langle -\sin t, \cos t \rangle \; dt$$

$$= \int_0^{2\pi} (\sin^2 t + \cos^2 t) \; dt = 2\pi.$$

Section 17.3

1. If $\vec{\nabla f} = \vec{F} = \langle 2x + 3y, 3x + 2y \rangle$ then $f_x(x,y) = 2x + 3y$, so $f(x,y) = x^2 + 3xy + g(y)$. Then $3x + g'(y) = f_y(x,y) = 3x + 2y$, so we may choose $g(y) = y^2$. Answer: One potential function for $\vec{F}$ is $f(x,y) = x^2 + 3xy + y^2$.

4. $f(x,y) = x^2 y^2 + x^3 + y^4$

10. $f(x,y) = e^x \sin y + x \tan y$

22. $\left[xe^y + ye^x \right]_{(0,0)}^{(1,-1)} = \dfrac{1}{e} - e.$

28. Choose g such that $\vec{F} = \vec{\nabla g}$. Then $P = g_x$, $Q = g_y$, and so on. Assume as usual that the second-order partial derivatives of g are continuous to obtain the desired conclusion.

Section 17.4

1. $\displaystyle\int_{-1}^{1} \int_{-1}^{1} (2x - 2y) \; dy \; dx = \int_{-1}^{1} 4x \; dx = 0.$

4. $\displaystyle\int_{0}^{1} \int_{x^2}^{x} (y + 2y) \; dy \; dx = \dfrac{1}{5}.$

308

7. $$\int_0^\pi \int_0^{\sin x} 1 \; dy \; dx$$

10. $Q_x - P_y = 0$, so the value of the integral is zero.

13. Let C denote the circle with the parametrization given in the problem. The area of the circular disk it bounds is given by

$$A = \oint_C x \; dy = \oint_C (a \cos t)(a \cos t) \; dt$$

$$= a^2 \int_0^{2\pi} \frac{1}{2}(1 + \cos 2t) \; dt = \pi a^2.$$

16. The area is $5/12$.

22. (a) $(0, \frac{4a}{3\pi})$; (b) $(\frac{4a}{3\pi}, \frac{4a}{3\pi})$

Section 17.5

1. Parametrization: $u = x$, $v = y$. Use

$$\vec{r}(u,v) = \langle u, v, 1 - u - v \rangle.$$

Then $|\vec{r}_u \times \vec{r}_v| = \sqrt{3}$. Let D denote the first-quadrant region bounded by the x-axis, the y-axis, and the line $x + y = 1$. Then

$$\iint_S f(x,y,z) \; dS = \iint_D xy(1 - x - y)\sqrt{3} \; dx \; dy$$

$$= \sqrt{3} \int_0^1 \int_0^{1-x} (xy - x^2 y - xy^2) \; dy \; dx = \frac{1}{120}\sqrt{3}.$$

4.   In spherical form the function f has the formula

$$f(\rho, \phi, \xi) = \rho^3 \sin^2 \phi \cos \phi.$$

A suitable parametrization for S is

$$\vec{r}(\phi, \xi) = \langle \sin \phi \cos \xi, \sin \phi \sin \xi, \cos \phi \rangle,$$

$0 \le \xi \le 2\pi$, $0 \le \phi \le \pi/2$.   Next you should find that

$$\vec{r}_\phi \times \vec{r}_\xi = \langle \sin^2 \phi \cos \xi, \sin^2 \phi \sin \xi, \cos \phi \sin \phi \rangle;$$

it follows that $dS = |\sin \phi| \, d\phi \, d\xi = \sin \phi \, d\phi \, d\xi$.   Thus the surface integral becomes

$$\int_0^{2\pi} \int_0^{\pi/2} \rho^3 \sin^3 \phi \cos \phi \, d\phi \, d\xi.$$

With the aid of the fact that $\rho = 1$, we find the value of this integral to be $\pi/2$.

Alternative solution: Describe S as follows:

$$z = h(x,y) = (1 - x^2 - y^2)^{1/2}$$

for $x^2 + y^2 \le 1$.   Show that $dS = \dfrac{1}{z} \, dx \, dy$.   Then show that the integral takes the form

$$\iint_D (x^2 + y^2) \, dx \, dy$$

where D is the disk $x^2 + y^2 \le 1$.   Use polar coordinates.

7.   Parametrize S by $\vec{r}(u,v) = \langle u, v, 3u + 2 \rangle$ on the disk D: $u^2 + v^2 \le 4$.   Then

$$\frac{\partial(y,z)}{\partial(u,v)} = -3, \qquad \frac{\partial(z,x)}{\partial(u,v)} = 0, \qquad \text{and} \qquad \frac{\partial(x,y)}{\partial(u,v)} = 1.$$

Therefore

$$\iint_S \vec{F} \cdot \vec{n} \, dS = \iint_D (-6y + 3z) \, du \, dv$$

$$= \iint_D (-6v + 9u + 6) \, du \, dv$$

$$= \int_0^{2\pi} \int_0^2 (6 - 6r \sin \xi + 9r \cos \xi) r \, dr \, d\xi$$

$$= \int_0^{2\pi} (12 - 16 \sin \xi + 24 \cos \xi) \, d\xi = 24\pi.$$

10. 44π

13. Checkpoints: $M = \dfrac{\pi\delta}{6}\{(4a^2 + 1)^{3/2} - 1\};$

$$M_{xy} = \frac{\pi\delta}{60}\{1 + (24a^4 + 2a^2 - 1)(4a^2 + 1)^{1/2}\}.$$

16. We write ω in place of the Greek psi (and, as usual, ξ in place of theta) to obtain

$$I_z = a\delta \int_0^{2\pi} \int_0^{2\pi} (b + a \cos \omega)^3 \, d\omega \, d\xi.$$

19. Checkpoints: The flux across the lower surface is -243π and the flux across the upper surface is 1701π.

Section 17.6

1. First, $\operatorname{div} \vec{F} = 3$. So

$$\iiint_B \operatorname{div} \vec{F} \, dV = \iiint_B 3 \, dV = (3)(\tfrac{4}{3})(\pi)(1)^3 = 4\pi.$$

A unit normal is $\vec{n} = \langle x, y, z \rangle$, and $\vec{F} \cdot \vec{n} = 1$. So

$$\iint_S \vec{F} \cdot \vec{n} \, dS = (1)(4\pi)(1)^2 = 4\pi.$$

311

Both values are 4π; this verifies the divergence theorem in this special case.

4. Here, $\mathrm{div}\,\vec{F} = y + z + x$; on the face where $z = 0$, $0 \leq x \leq 2$, and $0 \leq y \leq 2$, we have $\vec{F} \cdot \vec{n} = 0$. On the opposite face we find that $\vec{F} \cdot \vec{n} = 2x$. The surface integral of $\vec{F} \cdot \vec{n}$ on that face is equal to 8. Similar results hold on the other four faces, and both integrals in the divergence theorem are equal to 24.

7. Let C denote the solid cylinder. Then

$$\iint_S \vec{F} \cdot \vec{n}\, dS \;=\; \iiint_C (3x^2 + 3y^2 + 3z^2)\, dV$$

$$= 3 \int_0^{2\pi} \int_0^3 \int_{-1}^4 (r^2 + z^2)\, r\, dz\, dr\, d\xi.$$

10. Let B denote the solid bounded by S; note that

$$\mathrm{div}\,\vec{F} \;=\; x^2 + y^2.$$

So

$$\iint_S \vec{F} \cdot \vec{n}\, dS \;=\; \iiint_B \mathrm{div}\,\vec{F}\, dV$$

$$= \int_0^{2\pi} \int_0^3 \int_{r^2}^9 r^3\, dz\, dr\, d\xi \;=\; \frac{243}{2}\,\pi.$$

25. Let B denote the region bounded by the paraboloid and the plane. In cylindrical coordinates, $\mathrm{div}\,\vec{F} = 4(r^2 + z^2)^{1/2}$. And

$$\iint_S \vec{F} \cdot \vec{n}\, dS \;=\; \iiint_B \mathrm{div}\,\vec{F}\, dV$$

$$= \int_0^{2\pi} \int_0^{25} \int_0^{\sqrt{25 - z}} 4r(r^2 + z^2)^{1/2}\, dr\, dz\, d\xi$$

$$= \frac{8}{3} \pi \int_0^{25} \{(25 - z + z^2)^{3/2} - z^3\} \, dz.$$

Let

$$J = \int_0^C \{(z - a)^2 + b^2\}^{3/2} \, dz.$$

Later we will use the following values:

$$b = \frac{3}{2} \sqrt{11}, \quad a = \frac{1}{2}, \quad \text{and} \quad c = 25 = a^2 + b^2.$$

The substitution $z = a + b \tan u$ yields

$$J = b^4 \int_{z=0}^C \sec^5 u \, du.$$

We evaluate J with the aid of Integral Formulas 37 and 28 of the endpapers; after much algebra and arithmetic we find that

$$J = \frac{12982620 + 29403 \ln 11}{128}.$$

It follows that the value of the original integral -- the answer to this problem -- is

$$\frac{\pi(482620 + 29403 \ln 11)}{48} \sim 36201.9672.$$

Section 17.7

1. Because $\vec{n}$ is to be the upper unit normal, we have

    $$\vec{n} = \vec{n}(x,y,z) = \frac{1}{2} \langle x,y,z \rangle.$$

    The boundary curve C of the hemispherical surface S has the parametrization

    $$x = 2 \cos \xi, \quad y = 2 \sin \xi, \quad 0 \leqq \xi \leqq 2\pi.$$

    Therefore

313

$$\iint_S \{\text{curl } \vec{F}\} \cdot \vec{n} \, dS = \int_C 3y \, dx - 2x \, dy + xyz \, dz$$

$$= \int_0^{2\pi} (-12 \sin^2 \xi - 8 \cos^2 \xi) \, d\xi = -20\pi.$$

4.   Parametrize the boundary curves as follows:

C_1: $x = \cos t$, $y = \sin t$, $z = 1$, $0 \leq t \leq 2\pi$;

C_2: $x = \cos t$, $y = -\sin t$, $z = 3$, $0 \leq t \leq 2\pi$.

Then

$$\iint_S \{\text{curl } \vec{F}\} \cdot \vec{n} \, dS = \int_{C_1} \vec{F} \cdot \vec{T} \, ds + \int_{C_2} \vec{F} \cdot \vec{T} \, ds$$

$$= \int_0^{2\pi} (2 \sin^2 t - 2 \cos^2 t) \, dt = 0.$$

7.   Parametrize S (the elliptical region bounded by C) as follows:

$x = z = r \cos t$, $y = r \sin t$, $0 \leq r \leq 2$, $0 \leq t \leq 2\pi$.

Then $\vec{r}_r \times \vec{r}_t = \langle -r, 0, r \rangle$, $dS = r\sqrt{2} \, dr \, dt$;   the upper unit normal for S is

$$\vec{n} = \frac{1}{2} \sqrt{2} \langle -1, 0, 1 \rangle,$$

and $\text{curl } \vec{F} = \langle 3, 2, 1 \rangle$.   So $\{\text{curl } \vec{F}\} \cdot \vec{n} = -\sqrt{2}$.   Hence

$$\int_C \vec{F} \cdot \vec{T} \, ds = \iint_S \{\text{curl } \vec{F}\} \cdot \vec{n} \, dS$$

$$= \int_0^{2\pi} \int_0^2 (-2r) \, dr \, dt = -8\pi.$$

10. Let E be the ellipse bounded by C. Now E lies in the plane with equation $-y + z = 0$, so has upper unit normal

$$\vec{n} = \frac{1}{2}\sqrt{2} <0, -1, 1>.$$

Next, $\text{curl } \vec{F} = <-2z, -2x, -2y>$, so $\{\text{curl } \vec{F}\} \cdot \vec{n} = \sqrt{2}(x - y)$. The projection of E into the xy-plane may be described this way:

$$x^2 + (y - 1)^2 = 1, \quad z = 0;$$

alternatively, by $r = 2 \sin t \ (0 \leq t \leq \pi)$, $z = 0$. Thus

$$\int_C \vec{F} \cdot \vec{T} \, ds = \iint_E \{\text{curl } \vec{F}\} \cdot \vec{n} \, dS = \iint_E \sqrt{2}(x - y) \, dS.$$

A parametrization of E is

$$\vec{w}(r,t) = <r \cos t, \ r \sin t, \ r \sin t>,$$

$$0 \leq t \leq \pi, \quad 0 \leq r \leq 2 \sin t.$$

Next we find that $\vec{n} = \vec{w}_r \times \vec{w}_t = <0, -r, r>$. Therefore $dS = r\sqrt{2} \, dr \, dt$. Consequently

$$\iint_E \sqrt{2}(x - y) \, dS$$

$$= \int_0^\pi \int_0^{2 \sin t} \sqrt{2} \, r(\cos t - \sin t) r\sqrt{2} \, dr \, dt.$$

Answer: -2π.

22. Another of the glories of Western civilization.

$$\vec{L} = \iint_S (\vec{r} - \vec{r}_0) \times (-\rho g z \vec{n}) \, dS$$

$$= \rho g \iiint_V \text{curl}\{z(\vec{r} - \vec{r}_0)\} \, dV \qquad \text{(by Problem 20)}.$$

But $\text{curl}\{z(\vec{r} - \vec{r}_0)\} = (\vec{\nabla z}) \times (\vec{r} - \vec{r}_0) + z\{\text{curl}(\vec{r} - \vec{r}_0)\}$.
It follows immediately that $\vec{\nabla z} = \vec{k}$ and that $\text{curl}(\vec{r} - \vec{r}_0) = \vec{0}$.
Thus

$$\vec{L} = \rho g \iiint_V \cdot \vec{k} \times (\vec{r} - \vec{r}_0) \, dV$$

$$= \rho g \vec{k} \times \left(\iiint_V \vec{r} \, dV - \vec{r}_0 V \right).$$

Consequently $\vec{L} = \vec{0}$ as desired, because

$$\vec{r}_0 = \frac{1}{V} \iiint_V \vec{r} \, dV.$$

Chapter 17 Miscellaneous Problems

1. C is part of the graph of $y = \frac{4}{3} x$ and $ds = \frac{5}{3} dx$. So

$$\int_C (x^2 + y^2) \, ds = \int_0^3 \{x^2 + (\frac{4}{3} x)^2\} \frac{5}{3} \, dx = \frac{125}{3}.$$

4. 115

7. If $\vec{\nabla \phi} = \langle x^2 y, xy^2 \rangle$ then $\phi_x = x^2 y$, so that
$\phi(x,y) = \frac{1}{3} x^3 y + g(y)$. Thus

$$\phi_y = \frac{1}{3} x^3 + g'(y) = xy^2.$$

This is impossible unless x is constant, but x is not constant
on C.

10. Parametrize C: $x = t$, $y = t^2$, $z = t^3$, $1 \leq z \leq 2$.

$$W = \int_C P\,dx + Q\,dy + R\,dz = \int_C z\,dx - x\,dy + y\,dz$$

$$= \int_1^2 (t^3 - 2t^2 + 3t^4)\,dt = \frac{1061}{60}.$$

16. Note that if $P_y < Q_x$ at some point of D, then $Q_x - P_y > 0$ on a small region R surrounding that point, so that

$$\iint_R (Q_x - P_y)\,dA > 0.$$

19. Checkpoints: The flux across the upper surface is 60π and the flux across the lower surface is 12π.

Section 18.1

4. If $y(x) = e^{kx}$ then $y''(x) = k^2 e^{kx}$. So if $|k| = 3$ then $y''(x) = 9e^{kx} = 9y(x)$.

16. $3r^2 e^{rx} + 4re^{rx} - 4e^{rx} = 0$, so $3r^2 + 4r - 4 = 0$. Therefore $r = 2/3$ or $r = -2$.

22. With $y = g(x)$ we have

$$\frac{y - 0}{x - (x/2)} = \frac{dy}{dx}.$$

After simplifications, one answer is therefore

$$\frac{dy}{dx} = \frac{2y}{x}.$$

28. $\dfrac{dv}{dt} = k(250 - v)$

34. $y = \sin x$ or $y = \cos x$ or y identically 1 or -1.

317

40. Try $y = Ax + B$. Substitute to find suitable values of A and B.

Section 18.2

1. $\frac{1}{y^3} dy = x\, dx$:

$$-\frac{1}{2y^2} = \frac{1}{2} x^2 + C_1;$$

$$\frac{1}{y^2} = C - x^2;$$

$$y^2 = \frac{1}{C - x^2}.$$

4. $(1 + \sqrt{y})\, dy = (1 + \sqrt{x})\, dx$:

$$y + \frac{2}{3} y^{3/2} = x + \frac{2}{3} x^{3/2} + C_1;$$

$$3y + 2y^{3/2} = 3x + 2x^{3/2} + C.$$

10. $\arctan y = C + x^3$:

$$\frac{\pi}{4} = \arctan(1) = C;$$

$$y(x) = \tan\left(x^3 + \frac{1}{4}\pi\right).$$

16. $y(x) = \dfrac{1}{1 - x^2 - x^3}$

19. In the notation of Section 18.2 of the text, we have $c = 1$, $g = 32$, $a = \pi/144$, and $A(y) = 9\pi$. So Equation (1) takes the form

$$9\pi\, \frac{dy}{dt} = -\frac{\pi}{144} \sqrt{64y},$$

and hence

318

$$y^{-1/2} \frac{dy}{dt} = -\frac{1}{162}.$$

It follows that $y^{1/2} = C - (t/324)$. Therefore

$$y(t) = (C - \frac{t}{324})^2.$$

Now $9 = y(0) = C^2$, so $C = 3$ (not -3, else y would never be zero). Thus

$$y(t) = (3 - \frac{t}{324})^2$$

where the units are feet and seconds (because those are the units which we used for g and other assorted constants and variables in the problem). The tank will be empty when $y = 0$; that is, when $t = 972$ (sec). Hence the tank will require approximately 16 min 12 sec to empty.

22. Let $h = f^{-1}$ and let a be the area of the hole. We use

$$c = 1, \quad g = 32, \quad \text{and} \quad \frac{dy}{dt} = -\frac{1}{10800}$$

(feet per second). Then

$$-\frac{1}{10800} A(y) = -a\sqrt{64y}$$

where $A(y) = \pi\{h(y)\}^2$. Therefore

$$\{h(y)\}^2 = \frac{86400}{\pi} ay^{1/2},$$

and thus

$$\{h(y)\}^4 = \frac{7464960000}{\pi^2} a^2 y.$$

Finally, because $y = f(x)$ and $x = h(y)$, we have

$$f(x) = \frac{\pi^2}{(86400a)^2} x^4.$$

Now $f(1) = 4$, so $86400a = \pi/2$; it follows that

$$a = \frac{\pi}{172800} = \pi r^2$$

319

where r is the radius of the hole. Therefore

$$r = \frac{1}{240\sqrt{3}}$$

feet; that is, r is approximately 0.02887 inches.

Section 18.3

1. $xy' + y = 3xy$;

$$xy' + (1 - 3x)y = 0;$$

$$y' + (\frac{1}{x} - 3)y = 0.$$

$$\int (\frac{1}{x} - 3)\,dx = C_1 - 3x + \ln x,$$

so an integrating factor is

$$\rho(x) = \exp(-3x + \ln x) = xe^{-3x}.$$

$$(xe^{-3x}y)' = 0;$$

$$xe^{-3x}y = C;$$

$$y(x) = \frac{C}{x}e^{3x}.$$

Now $0 = y(1) = Ce^3$, so $C = 0$. Therefore $y(x)$ is
identically zero.

4. Integrating factor: $\rho(x) = x^{-3}$. Solution:

$$y(x) = x^3(C + \ln x) = x^3(10 + \ln x).$$

7. Given: $(1 + x)y' + y = \cos x$. The left-hand side is already
recognizable as a derivative, so no integrating factor is needed.
Solution:

$$y(x) = \frac{C + \sin x}{1 + x} = \frac{1 + \sin x}{1 + x}.$$

10. $y(x) = -1 + \exp(x + \frac{1}{2}x^2)$

22. (a) $\frac{dx}{dt} = -5x(t)$ and $x_0 = 50$, so $x(t) = 50e^{-5t}$.

Next,

$$\frac{dy}{dt} + \frac{1}{40}y = \frac{1}{20}x = \frac{5}{2}e^{-5t}.$$

An integrating factor is $\rho(t) = \exp(t/40)$, and this leads to the solution

$$y(t) = Ce^{-t/40} - \frac{100}{199}e^{-5t}.$$

The initial condition $y(0) = 50$ determines C, and we find that

$$y(t) = \frac{1}{199}(10050e^{-t/40} - 100e^{-5t}).$$

(c) Use the fact that $\frac{dy}{dt} = 0$ when $y = 2x$.

Section 18.4

4. $\frac{1}{4}(\sqrt{3} - i)$; $\frac{1}{2}\text{cis}(7\pi/6)$

10. $\sqrt{2}\,\text{cis}\,\xi$ for $\xi = \pi/4,\ 13\pi/20,\ 21\pi/20,\ 29\pi/20,\ 37\pi/20$

16. Solution: $(x^2 + a^2 i)(x^2 - a^2 i) = 0$. So

$$x = \pm a\sqrt{\pm i}.$$

But

$$\sqrt{i} = (e^{-\pi/2})^{1/2} = e^{i\pi/4}$$

$$= \cos(\pi/4) + i\sin(\pi/4) = \frac{1 + i}{\sqrt{2}}.$$

Similarly,

$$\sqrt{-i} \;=\; \frac{-1 + i}{\sqrt{2}}\,.$$

Therefore

$$x \;=\; \pm\,\frac{1 \pm i}{\sqrt{2}}\,a\,.$$

Section 18.5

1. Characteristic equation: $r^2 - 4 = 0$, so $r_1 = -2$, $r_2 = 2$.

4. C.E.: $2r^2 - 7r + 3 = 0$. Roots: $r_1 = 3$, $r_2 = 1/2$.
   Solution: $y(x) = Ae^{3x} + Be^{x/2}$.

10. $y(x) = A + Bx + Cx^2 + D\exp(-\frac{3}{5}x)$

16. Roots of the characteristic equation: $-3i$, $-3i$, $3i$, $3i$.
   Solution: $y(x) = (A + Bx)\cos 3x + (C + Dx)\sin 3x$.

22. $y(x) = e^{-x/3}(3\cos\alpha x + 9\alpha\sin\alpha x)$ where $\alpha = \frac{1}{3}\sqrt{3}$.

Section 18.6

4. With $m = 1/4$ (slugs) and $k = 36$ (lb/ft), we find that
   $\omega_0 = 12$ (rad/sec). The solution of $x'' + 144x = 0$ with
   $x(0) = 1$ and $x'(0) + -5$ is

$$x(t) \;=\; \cos 12t - \frac{5}{12}\sin 12t$$

$$=\; \frac{13}{12}\left(\frac{12}{13}\cos 12t - \frac{5}{12}\sin 12t\right)$$

$$=\; \frac{13}{12}\cos(12t + \alpha)$$

where $\alpha = \arctan(5/12) \sim 0.3948$.

(b) $C = \dfrac{13}{12} \sim 1.0833$ (ft)   and $T = \dfrac{2\pi}{12} \sim 0.5236$ (sec).

10.   Underdamped motion: $x(t) = -2e^{-3t} \sin 4t = 2e^{-3t} \cos(4t - \dfrac{\pi}{2})$.

Section 18.7

1. $c_{n+1} = \dfrac{1}{n+1} c_n$;   it follows that $c_n = \dfrac{c_0}{n!}$.

4.   When we substitute $y = \sum c_n x^n$ in the equation $y' + 2xy = 0$, we find that

$$c_1 + \sum \{(b+2)c_{n+2} + 2c_n\}x^{n+1} = 0.$$

Hence $c_1 = 0$ and

$$c_{n+2} = -\dfrac{2}{n+2} c_n.$$

It follows that $c_n = 0$ if n is odd and that

$$c_{2k} = \dfrac{(-1)^k}{k!} c_0.$$

Therefore the solution is

$$y = c_0(1 - x^2 + \dfrac{1}{2!}x^4 - \dfrac{1}{3!}x^6 + \ldots).$$

We easily identify this as $y(x) = c_0 \exp(-x^2)$.

10. $c_{n+1} = -\dfrac{2n-3}{2n+2} c_n$; $\rho = 1$;

$$y(x) = c_0(1 - \dfrac{3}{2}x + \dfrac{3}{8}x^2 + \dfrac{1}{16}x^3 + \ldots)$$

$$= c_0(1-x)^{3/2}.$$

16. $c_{n+2} = \dfrac{4}{(n+1)(n+2)} c_n$; $c_0 = 2$, $c_1 = 0$;

$$y(x) = 2(1 + \dfrac{2^2}{2!}x^2 + \dfrac{2^4}{4!}x^4 + \ldots) = 2\cosh 2x.$$

19. (a) The fact that $y = (1 + x)^\alpha$ satisfies the differential equation $(1 + x)y' = \alpha y$ follows immediately from the fact that $y' = \alpha(1 + x)^{\alpha - 1}$.

(b) When we substitute $y = \sum c_n x^n$ in the differential equation $(1 + x)y' = \alpha y$ we obtain the recurrence formula

$$c_{n+1} = \frac{\alpha - n}{n + 1} c_n.$$

Because $c_0 = 1$ (this is a consequence of the initial condition $y(0) = 1$), the binomial series in (12) follows.

(c) The function $x \to (1 + x)^\alpha$ and the binomial series must agree on $(-1, 1)$ because of the uniqueness of solutions of initial value problems.

Section 18.8

1. Solution: $y(x) = 2e^{-x}$.

x	y	y (true)
0.1	1.8	1.809675
0.2	1.62	1.637462
0.3	1.458	1.481636
0.4	1.3122	1.340640
0.5	1.18098	1.213061
0.6	1.062882	1.097623
0.7	0.956594	0.993171
0.8	0.860934	0.898658
0.9	0.774841	0.813139
1.0	0.697357	0.735759

4. Solution: $y(x) = 2e^{-x} + x - 1$. At $x = 1$, Euler's method yields $y = 0.697357$. The true value is about 0.735759.

10. The solution function $y(x)$ is implicitly defined by means of the equation $y^3 + y = x^2 + 2$.

(continued)

x	y	y (true)
0.1	1.0	1.002495326
0.2	1.005	1.009925863
0.3	1.014925374	1.022129988
0.4	1.029594510	1.038853161
0.5	1.048732375	1.059767509
0.6	1.071990792	1.084496780
0.7	1.098972286	1.112628871
0.8	1.129254209	1.143757585
0.9	1.162410397	1.177478465
1.0	1.198028614	1.213411663

16. $y(1) = 0.738107$

22. Checkpoints: $v(1) = 30.3958$, $v(5) = 77.1221$, $v(30) = 80$, $v(31) = 21.0042$, $v(35) = 20$. The time of impact is about 286.36 seconds after the skydiver leaves the airplane -- about 4 min 40 sec aloft. For accuracy in our computations, we used step size $h = 0.01$ when the skydiver's velocity was changing rapidly, step size 0.1 when the rate of change was moderate, and step size 0.5 when the velocity was constant or nearly so. The time of impact was obtained by linear interpolation.

Chapter 18 Miscellaneous Problems

1. The equation may be written in the form

$$\frac{1}{y^2}\, dy = (2x + \frac{3}{x})\, dx.$$

4. $y(x) = (x + C)\cos x$

10. $y(x) = A + (Bx + C)e^{-x/2}$

16. $y(x) = \exp(\sqrt{2}\, x)\{A \cos(\sqrt{2}\, x) + B \sin(\sqrt{2}\, x)\}$

$$+ \exp(-\sqrt{2}\, x)\{C \cos(\sqrt{2}\, x) + D \sin(\sqrt{2}\, x)\}$$

19. $y(x) = 3e^{2x} - 2e^{-2x}$

22. $y(x) = \frac{2}{3}(1 - e^{-3x})$

28. The transformed equation (using $v = y^{-2}$) has the form

$$\frac{dv}{dx} - \frac{2}{x} v = -2x^2,$$

with solution $v(x) = -2x^3 + Cx^2$. Therefore

$$\{y(x)\}^2 = \frac{1}{Cx^2 - 2x^3}.$$

31. $c_{n+1} = -\frac{1}{n+1} c_n$ for $n \geq 0$. Solution:

$$y(x) = c_0 e^{-x}.$$

34. $c_{n+1} = \frac{3(n-2)}{n+1} c_n$ for $n \geq 0$. Solution:

$$y(x) = c_0(1 - 6x + 9x^2).$$

This manual was written on a TRS-80* Model II microcomputer with Scripsit* 2.1.0 word processing and is stored on two eight-inch SSDD diskettes. It was transferred to paper using a TRS-80 Daisy Wheel II printer equipped with the S-10 (scientific) printwheel. Many of the figures were constructed with use of the TRS-80 plotter-printer driven by a simple program in RSBASIC* (a compiler).

*TRS-80 and Scripsit (C) by Tandy Corporation.

*RSBASIC (C) by Tandy Corporation. Licensed from
   Ryan McFarland Corporation.